# EARLY CHRISTIAN ART

# EARLY
# CHRISTIAN ART

WOLFGANG FRITZ VOLBACH

*Photography by Max Hirmer*

HARRY N. ABRAMS, INC., *Publishers*

NEW YORK

TRANSLATED BY CHRISTOPHER LIGOTA

Library of Congress Catalog Card Number: 61-8333

Illustrations printed in West Germany
Text printed in Holland

# CONTENTS

# FOREWORD

Only in our time has the Late Antique period come fully into its own. There seems to be a many-sided kinship between the two ages. As a result, the study of Late Antique art as well as of its material and spiritual context has been attracting increasing interest. All too long has it been dogmatically held that Late Antiquity, whose lineaments are clearly discernible already in Diocletian's time, brought with it nothing but an atrophy of the antique sense of form, a decline from the heights of classical art. Today its originality is generally recognized: a new artistic intention was, in a hard struggle, finding its own idiom. Medieval art was slowly being born.

The purpose of this book is to give those interested in art pleasure in, and an understanding of, one of the most absorbing periods in human history.

In deciding what to include, the guiding idea has been to bring together what is historically best preserved and artistically most significant. The attempt has also been made to show the interrelations between the different branches of art, since only in its totality can it give a convincing picture of Late Antique proto-medieval artistic creation.

The Western and the Eastern worlds—Rome, Milan, Ravenna, Salonika, and Constantinople—have been given equal attention: the continuity of antique tradition had similar effects in both parts of the Empire, though gradually national differences began to make themselves felt. Although the closest interrelations are to be observed between the southeast provinces—Asia Minor, Syria, Palestine, Egypt, North Africa—and Byzantium, a discussion of their art has not been included, so that the art and culture of the principal cities might stand out the more clearly.

W. F. Volbach

The illustrations in this book, taking full advantage of the photographic techniques of our day, present the main works of Late Antique and Early Christian art, works which have, so far, been known for the most part only in old and often inadequate reproductions. For a long time it had been impossible for anyone to get a clear view of even the most important architectural monuments of that period, either as structural and spatial wholes or in the manifoldness of their component parts in a way commensurate with their historical and artistic significance. To redress the balance, it seemed indicated to offer as many and as complete reproductions as would do justice to buildings like Hagia Sophia and SS. Sergius and Bacchus in Constantinople, Hagios Georgios and Hagios Dimitrios in Salonika, as well as the most significant monuments in Rome, Milan, and Ravenna. Late Antique and Early Christian sculpture has been brought together from Istanbul and Paris, from Rome and the Vatican, from Barletta and Syracuse, from Milan and Ravenna. For the sake of completeness, examples of applied art have been included—silver, gold, and ivories. Pieces like the silver reliquary in San Nazaro Maggiore in Milan, the ivory casket in Brescia, the Chair of Maximian in Ravenna, and a number of others have been photographed in a way that, it is hoped, will bring out their exceptional artistic merits. Painting, especially mosaics, appears as well, mostly in color, including the main works from Italy, and—for the first time—the early mosaics from Salonika. The colorplates have been produced with the greatest care, the guiding principle being fidelity to the original and not spectacular effects. As far as possible, the attempt has been made to give its due not only to the significant detail in a work but to the whole of it and to the color of the surrounding space as well.

I would like to express my gratitude to all those who gave permission to photograph and who facilitated this undertaking.

At the Vatican: Filippo Magi, General Director of the Monumenti, Musei e Gallerie Pontificie; Enrico Josi, Director of the Museo Cristiano Lateranense; Don Anselmo Albareda O.B., Prefect of the Biblioteca Apostolica Vaticana; Antonio Ferrua, General Secretary of the Pontificio Istituto di Archeologia Cristiana; H.E. Mgr. Principi and Signore Vacchini, Fabbrica di S. Pietro. In Rome: Emilio Lavagnino, Soprintendente alle Gallerie ed alle Opere d'Arte Medioevali e Moderne per il Lazio; Pietro Grande and Bianca Maria Felletti-Mai, Directors at the Museo Nazionale; Carlo Pietrangeli, Director of the Collections at the Palazzo dei Conservatori; Enzo Crea, Istituto per la Collaborazione Culturale; the Banco di Santo Spirito. In Milan: Luigi Crema, Soprintendente ai Monumenti della Lombardia; Gian Dell' Acqua, Soprintendente alle Galerie della Lombardia; Gianguido Belloni, Museo d'Arte del Castello Sforzesco; Elia Galli, Preposto Parroco della Basilica di San Nazaro Maggiore; Signora Paola Moroni, Electa Editrice. In Brescia: Gaetano Panazza, Director of the Museo Civico dell'Età Cristiana. In Ravenna: Giuseppe Bovini, Director of the Museo Nazionale d'Antichità and Inspector at the Soprintendenza ai Monumenti della Romagna; Msgr. Mario Mazzotti, Director of the Museo Arcivescovile; Msgr. Mario de Marchi, Battistero Neoniano. In Florence: Filippo Rossi, Soprintendente alle Gallerie per le Province di Firenze, Arezzo e Pistoia. In Rossano: H.E. Msgr. Giovanni Rizzo, Archbishop of Rossano, and Msgr. Salvatore Lovecchio, Curia Arcivescovile and Museo Diocesano. In Salonika: Stylinos Pelekanidis, Ephoros for Byzantine monuments in Northern Greece. In Istanbul: Rüstem Duyuran Effendi, Director, as well as Nazih Firatli and Zeikye Basak, of the Archaeological Museum; Feridun Dirimtekin, Director of the Museum of the Hagia Sophia. In Paris: Jean Charbonneaux, Curator of the Department of Greek and Roman Antiquities, Musée du Louvre; Étienne Coche de la Ferté, Conservateur des Musées Nationaux; Hubert Landais, Curator of the Department of Objets d'Art, Musée du Louvre; Jean Babelon, Director of the Cabinet des Médailles, and Jacques Yvon, also of the Cabinet; P. Verlet, Director, and M. Sallet, Curator, Musée de Cluny; Mme. Cahn, Curator, Musée Dutuit, Petit Palais. In London: Denys Haynes, Head Keeper of the Department of Greek and Roman Antiquities, British Museum; Rupert Bruce-Mitford, Keeper of the Department of British and Mediaeval Antiquities, British Museum; Terence Hodgkinson, and John Beckwith, Victoria and Albert Museum. In New York: Calvin S. Hathaway, Director, Cooper Union Museum for the Arts of Decoration; the staff of the Metropolitan Museum of Art. In Hartford, Conn.:

the staff of the Wadsworth Atheneum. In Washington: the staff of the Dumbarton Oaks Collection. In Berlin: C. Blümel, Director, Antikenabteilung, Staatliche Museen; K. Wessel and Dr. Ristow, Staatliche Museen, Frühchristliche und Byzantinische Abteilung. In Munich: C. Theodor Müller, Director, Bayerisches National-museum.

All new photographs were made in collaboration with Miss Julia Asen who was also in charge of the arrangement of the material. Her technical ability was of the greatest service in what were often difficult photographic undertakings. Her artistic and scholarly understanding was unflagging whether in producing the plates or planning their arrangement. She has the sincere thanks of the undersigned.

MAX HIRMER

AFTER ITS RISE and growth in power during the first two centuries of our era, the Roman Empire found itself engaged, in the third, in a struggle for existence which, between 250 and 270, brought it to the brink of collapse.

The depopulation of the countryside caused by the constant levying of troops, the growth of an urban proletariat, and the wasteful management of latifundia undermined the finances of the state. Extensive imports of all kinds of commodities, with no exports worth mentioning to counterbalance them, bled the Empire of its precious metals, while the soil no longer yielded them in sufficient quantities. The debasement of currency was the natural consequence. And, in addition to all this, there were frequent droughts, turning large tracts of land into desert.

In the North, the Alamanni and the Franks broke through the limes and the Rhine frontier into Gaul. In Britain, the Picts and Scots rose in national rebellion. In the East, the defenses of the lower Danube were in imminent danger from the onset of the Goths, and those of the Euphrates from the Bactrians and Persians. Constant military preparedness on frontiers that could be held only with the greatest difficulty required a financial effort far beyond the means of the imperial treasury, while barbarian princes had to be pacified by costly tributes and yearly subsidies in minted gold. At the same time, the Germanic and Oriental element in the standing army grew steadily.

In the face of impending catastrophe, Diocletian, who became Augustus in 284 and assumed the names Gaius Aurelius Valerius Diocletianus, embarked on a series of thoroughgoing political, economic, and military reforms. Drawing his strength from old Roman tradition, the Emperor put an end to the bane of legionary usurpations and brought relative order and stability to the structure of the state. The political situation required the Emperor's presence above all in the East, so Diocletian moved his residence to Nicomedia in Bithynia. In 305, he abdicated on grounds of ill health, and built himself a sumptuous palace outside his native Salona (Split). But even in his last years, up to his death in 313, he intervened constantly in public affairs.

The political, economic, and social transformation which set in principally under the soldier emperors of the third century, and reached its final stage under the First Tetrarchy at the end of the third and the beginning of the fourth centuries, brought with it a complete change in spiritual climate and therewith in art. Stoic

11

political theory, with Marcus Aurelius as its most important representative, and Hellenistically inspired philosophy declined because of the ever-increasing receptivity on the part of the depressed populace to the otherworldly religions of the East—witness the rapid progress of the cults of Isis and Mithras, as well as the spread of Christianity.

In the early part of his reign, Diocletian had tolerated the various creeds in quest of the hereafter, but in 296 he turned sharply against Manicheanism, which had spread from Persia. Soon after, he began the great persecutions of the Christians. The Emperor ordered a return to the worship of the Roman gods, and, by the edict of 304, required the citizens of the Empire on pain of death to perform the prescribed sacrifices. In the West the persecution ended in 306, but in the East it raged until 313. Refusing to sacrifice to the gods, and, above all, rejecting the emperor cult, the center of official religion, the Christians came to be regarded as the most subversive element in the state. Moreover, since they advocated the equality of all men, the community of goods, and the freeing of slaves, their religion had a distinctly revolutionary flavor.

Only gradually did Christianity loosen its connection with Judaism, and evidence of this connection continued for long, notably in Christian iconography.

8    The dominant Early Christian theme, hope for the hereafter, was visually expressed in many ways: the *orans*, the soul of the deceased entering into eternal glory through prayer; the peacock, favorite symbol of eternal life, or the grape harvest, signifying change in nature and hence the Resurrection. The center of Christian worship, the Eucharist, found symbolic expression in the Multiplication of Loaves and Fishes and the Marriage at Cana, which are also Christian equivalents of the pagan banquet of the dead.

The fish symbol had its Judaic antecedent in fish as food at the Messianic feast. From the second century onward the fish—ICHTHYS—was the symbol of Christ in relation to the sacrament of Baptism. And Baptism and the Eucharist were the two sacraments imparting to the faithful an earnest hope of salvation and eter-
6, 24, 32    nal bliss.

Joy in simple country life had inspired portrayals of grape gathering with *amorini* and of pastoral life as we know them from examples of classical mythology illustrated on the Endymion sarcophagi. Christian art took
6, 7    over these popular motifs of an idyllic art. It may well have been Gentile Christians who allegorized the shepherd theme; the Good Shepherd of the Scriptures, frequently with a lamb on his shoulders, was probably a type
4    taken over from popular bucolic art by the Hellenistic communities of Alexandria and Rome.

The figure of the philosopher, another borrowing from earlier art, appeared on Early Christian sarcophagi together with the *orans* and the rustic motif of the Good Shepherd. Rodenwaldt has shown the derivation of the type from a philosopher's sarcophagus of Plotinus' time, about 270, now in the Lateran Museums, portraying the deceased sitting between two women. Sculptural works like the Lateran sarcophagus show clearly the transition to the Late Antique style. The philosopher as the center of the scene is rendered frontally; the sense of volume is in decline; and the organic structure of the figure is weak. Christian philosopher-sarcophagi are
15    the immediate successors, and from them it is a short step to the reliefs on the Arch of Constantine.
2, 3    The change in artistic intention is particularly evident in the reliefs of the triumphal arch erected by Galerius in Salonika soon after 297 to commemorate his victory over Narses.

There are fundamental stylistic differences as compared with earlier monuments of official art. The angular, sharp folds, produced by deep drilling, create the peculiar interplay of light and shadow that is characteristic of Late Antique art. While some of the scenes, clearly the work of older artists, are still compositionally related to earlier ceremonial representations, the narrative develops in the manner of a frieze in others. Proportions are not uniform and, in certain scenes, numerous overlappings create an effect of confusion.

12

Galerius may possibly have employed artists from the Eastern provinces who brought this style with them.

Unfortunately, so few monuments from this period have survived in the East that the stylistic development cannot be clearly traced. In Rome, on the contrary, an abundance of Christian painting and sculpture from the second half of the third century onward facilitates the reconstruction of the development of Early Christian art up to the fifth century. There is no sudden break with pagan antiquity, and the old models are only gradually discarded. This is shown in a sarcophagus from the Catacomb of Praetextatus (now in the Lateran Museums) with the gathering of grapes, and three representations of the Good Shepherd that differ in no way from pagan bucolic sarcophagi. The oval sarcophagus in Santa Maria Antiqua with Jonah resting after his rescue, an *orans*, a philosopher, a Good Shepherd, the Baptism of Christ, and a fisherman preserves a pre-Diocletian serenity. The drill is not used a great deal, forms are plastically modeled, and space is rendered in perspective. The sarcophagus can thus be dated to about 270.

The development of fresco painting can be followed from the earliest examples in the catacombs of the beginning of the third century to the full flowering of the Late Antique style between 270 and the beginning of the fourth century. Hellenistic elements are in retreat, and, with them, the tendency to project figures into an illusionistic third dimension. They are replaced by a popular art which is already fully articulate in the paintings of the underground funerary chamber, the hypogeum of the Aurelii, on Viale Manzoni, dated to about 235–240. Here, perspective is neglected more and more and the figures appear against a flat ground.

Paintings in Christian catacombs can be studied continuously from the early third century onward. At first, they keep to the type of segmented decoration of wall and ceiling practiced in Roman houses from the Flavian period on. In the Crypt of Lucina, which in the fourth century became part of the Catacomb of Callixtus, the ceiling of the earliest vault, dating from about 220, has a pattern of concentric circles and trapezoidal fields that was common since the Antonines. This division of the ceiling into circles continues, in a simplified form, into the fourth century, for example in the Jewish catacomb of the Villa Torlonia. Where figures appear on the ceilings of these early catacombs, such as the Good Shepherd in the Catacomb of Callixtus, or a little later, the *orans* and Virgin and Child in an *arcosolium* of the Catacomb of Priscilla, they are close to contemporary secular painting in Rome, except that the brush work is lighter and more cursory, and the color more impressionistic. This is perhaps to be explained in part by their locale, the dark funerary chamber, the decoration of which was intended to instruct rather than to afford esthetic enjoyment. Thus, the dating of catacomb frescoes on purely stylistic grounds will always be a problem, and will have to be based, instead, on the dating of the chambers themselves, as Paul Styger attempted in his book on the Roman catacombs. It is an intricate undertaking, for the catacombs were frequently extended in depth subsequent to their original excavation, sometimes on as many as five successive occasions. By and large, however, it can be said that, as with sculpture and coins, the break with older tradition comes about 270. The frescoes in the Vault of Ampliatus and the Catacomb of Domitilla are informed by a new artistic conception. The fine representation in the Catacomb of Priscilla, already mentioned—an *orans*, expressing the hope of salvation, in the center, a philosopher and two other figures on the left and the Virgin and Child on the right—has an almost abstract, linear style. The figures are isolated on a flat surface with no suggestion of volume. The fresco with Christ among the Apostles in the Catacomb of Domitilla, dating from the mid-fourth century, has the same simplified and hard linearism. Christ as teacher and lawgiver is the center of the scene.

Along with these representations of a predominantly symbolic character, there appear, from the beginning of the First Tetrarchy onward with increasing frequency, historical scenes, such as the Baptism of Christ, and

13

His miracles, taken from the New Testament and the Apocrypha, as well as episodes from the Old Testament, such as the Three Hebrews in the Fiery Furnace and Moses Striking the Rock. Eastern antecedents are suggested by the frescoes in Dura-Europos on the Euphrates.

What Diocletian had striven for, Constantine achieved, though by very different methods. He fortified absolute monarchy by making it hereditary. Religious syncretism gave way to Christianity as the state religion. The Divine Being to whom he attributed his victory at the Milvian Bridge (312) inspired the Emperor with awe, and *pietas* became a dominant note of the reign, concomitant with attempts to revive other ancient Roman virtues with Augustus as the exemplar of imperial excellence, and it was no accident that the triumphal arch erected by Constantine to celebrate his victory over Maxentius in 312, and inaugurated in 315, was decorated not only by representations of his own deeds but by reliefs taken from edifices of his venerated predecessors, Trajan, Hadrian, and Marcus Aurelius. For the Emperor, these "spolia" were no mere antiquities but documents of a kindred imperial ideology. From a stylistic point of view, one can hardly imagine a greater contrast than the cosmopolitan imperial manner, with its strong Hellenistic tendency, in the second century reliefs, and the Constantinian reliefs that express local Roman traditions. As such, they also differ widely from the near-contemporary reliefs on the Arch of Galerius, since it shows a strong Eastern influence in the friezes and a more advanced treatment of the relief. But in Rome, there are numerous works stylistically and technically related to the reliefs on the Arch of Constantine: to take two dated examples—a base of a column in the Roman Forum with a sacrificial relief commemorating the decennial of 303, and the scenes from the cult of Attis in Villa Albani dating from about 295. In these, the figures are isolated, set side by side in rigid repetition against a flat surface. The heads, all at one level, produce an effect of solemnity, while the person of the Emperor is given an exalted status by its greater size. Compared with the lively historical or mythological representations of the third century, the Constantinian reliefs seem almost to suggest a lapse in artistic standards, to be accounted for, perhaps, by the political and economic isolation of Rome. After the founding of Constantinople in 324, and the unification of East and West, a more supple style will again be in evidence.

The decline in plastic modeling is to be observed in other branches of official court art as well. In carved portraits, the tendency is toward strict symmetry in composition and in individual features. Sculpture in the round thus comes into line with relief. At the same time, the portrait is markedly spiritualized, partly owing to the heavy drilling of the eyes, a technique still unknown in the third century. Classical traits can still be discerned in the heads of Constantine and Licinius on the triumphal arch, as well as in those on coins. The same applies to the statues of Constantine from the stairs of the Capitol and in the narthex of the Lateran. But the colossal statue of him from the apse of his basilica, now in the Palazzo dei Conservatori, is already much further removed from classical models. Later on in his reign, after 325, under the influence of Oriental art, the Emperor comes to be portrayed as a superhuman hero. Closely related, though more condensed and with a stronger sense of volume, is the bronze head of about 357 in the Palazzo dei Conservatori representing Constantius II. The delightful bust of chalcedony on the scepter from Sainte-Chapelle, now in the Cabinet des Médailles, Paris, is of Constantine, according to tradition, but the softer modeling suggests, perhaps, a later date.

A distinctive feature of Late Antique court art, especially under the Tetrarchy and Constantine, was the use of porphyry as carving material. Its color, close to the imperial purple, made it particularly suitable for the Emperor. The Romans had already quarried the stone near the Red Sea in Egypt under the Early Empire, working it partly on the spot; and, under Diocletian, it became a favorite material. An interesting example is provided by the statues of the Tetrarchs, the Augusti, Diocletian and Maximian, and the Caesars, Constantius

14

Chlorus and Galerius, outside San Marco in Venice. They display the influence of Egyptian and Eastern art, an influence also to be observed in porphyry works of the time of Constantine.

Among the most splendid porphyry pieces of the Constantinian period are the two large sarcophagi of St. Helena and Constantina in Rome. The Mausoleum of Constantina, the daughter of Constantine, today the Church of Santa Costanza, was probably built during her lifetime next to the church of Sant' Agnese fuori le Mura, which she also founded. Her sarcophagus, now in the Vatican, originally was placed in the ambulatory. Its reliefs—*erotes* gathering grapes—continue the theme of the mosaics in the vault of the ambulatory. Antique, almost pagan in their overtones, they lend themselves, nonetheless, to the Christian symbolism of eternal life. The intended reference is to the Eucharist, as in earlier instances in the catacombs. Even more magnificent is the sarcophagus now in the Vatican from the Mausoleum of St. Helena, the Emperor's mother. It may have been made for Constantius Chlorus (died 306), certainly not for Helena if it is true that her remains were removed to Constantinople in 331 while the sarcophagus is known not to have left Rome. It is decorated with battle scenes, conceived entirely in the spirit of Late Antique Alexandrian art, lively and full of movement but offering no indication of space, although the figures are carved almost fully in the round.

Porphyry was to dominate imperial ceremonials in Constantinople. The emperor was born in a porphyry chamber in the palace, made his devotions in Hagia Sophia on porphyry, received foreign emissaries in the Throne Room on porphyry, and was buried in a porphyry sarcophagus in his mausoleum adjoining the Church of the Holy Apostles. After the middle of the fourth century, however, the porphyry quarries were abandoned, and consequently, works in porphyry became rare.

The influence of the Emperor and the new religion was strongest in the field of architecture. Constantine threw himself heart and soul into the task of rebuilding on a vast scale the old Greek colony of Byzantium on the Bosphorus. Now renamed after him, the city was to surpass Rome itself in splendor. Unfortunately, only the barest traces of his magnificent palaces have survived, but contemporary descriptions suggest displays of quite extraordinary sumptuousness. A few fragments of very fine ceiling paintings with portraits have, at least, survived in the palace at Trier. The quality of the mosaics can be inferred from contemporary examples in the basilica at Aquileia, at Antioch, and in the imperial villa at Piazza Armerina in Sicily.

Constantine's basilica near the Forum Romanum, though built to a large extent under Maxentius, also testifies to the Emperor's policy of architectural magnificence. The enormous vaults, still partly extant, attest the technical skill of Roman architects.

The palaces and the new large churches were supplied by court workshops with costly furnishings in gold and silver, as well as precious textiles. The East contributed carpets of great value.

Entirely new tasks confronted the Emperor and his pious mother in the erection of Christian churches. The small places of worship in the private houses of well-to-do Christians had long been insufficient. In the East, where buildings for Christian worship were already in existence, new and larger ones had to be constructed. The Emperor's ecclesiastical foundations sprang up in every part of the Empire—from the imposing double basilica in his early place of residence, Trier, to the sanctuaries in Nicomedia, Antioch, and the Holy Land, and above all, in the two capitals, Rome and Constantinople. For the large baptisteries, such as the one attached to the Lateran, a centralized type of building was usually adopted similar to the mausoleums of St. Helena and Constantina.

After his victory over Maxentius, Constantine presented the bishop of Rome with the Palace of the Laterani in which Maxentius had perhaps resided, and began at once with the construction of what was to be the first

15

large Christian church, the Lateran Basilica, *mater ecclesiarum*. The monumental character of this edifice has been preserved for us in old drawings and paintings; the church itself, severely damaged by fire in 1308 and 1361, was completely rebuilt in the Baroque style by Francesco Borromini between 1646 and 1649. The characteristic features of the Constantinian basilica were the large apse, with the bishop's throne in it, and the altar as the cult center, focusing the eyes of the faithful through the triumphal arch. Arcades borne on columns, with clerestories high above them, separated the nave from the aisles. The roof timbers remained open. The baptistery was erected next to the basilica, and the external wall of the original rotunda is still extant. The present interior octagon, with its eight splendid porphyry columns, was built later, under Sixtus III (432–440), as the inscription
*A*    on the entablature states. A narthex with two chapels was added by Pope Hilarius I (461–468).

The Lateran Basilica was soon followed by the Church of Santi Pietro e Marcellino and the Mausoleum of St. Helena. In 324 the Emperor began the construction of St. Peter's, which was, however, completed only after his death by one of his sons (presumably Constans). The type adopted was that of the Lateran. The basilica subsequently fell into a ruinous condition and was replaced by the present sumptuous edifice begun under
*26, 27*    Pope Julius II.

In the two great achievements, St. John Lateran and St. Peter's, Constantinian architects created the prototype of the Christian basilica. Compared with the pagan temple, the new sacred edifice was revolutionary. The basilical ground plan varied in different parts of the Empire in accordance with varying liturgical requirements,
*B, figs. 1–8*    but the fundamental type remained the same. Thus did the Basilissa, the Church as Queen, as Abercius of Hierapolis had called her, find in the basilica, the royal building, an architectural form worthy of its cult, centered as this was in the sacrifice of the mass, partaken of by the whole congregation. The large hall had its antecedents in the great market basilicas. What was new was the transept, added in the Lateran and in St. Peter's, intended perhaps for holding synods. Also, the growing numbers of the clergy required more space. Where the aisles were doubled, they could be used for processions. The nave was reserved for the congregation, the catechumens being confined to the vestibule and atrium. San Paolo fuori le Mura followed the scheme of these two great basilicas.

Even before the Peace of the Church the veneration of martyrs had transformed the pagan heroum into the martyrium. For these, as Eusebius and other writers attest, the Emperor spared no cost. St. Peter's in Rome, the Church of the Holy Sepulcher in Jerusalem, and the Church of the Nativity in Bethlehem were among his favorite creations. He honored above all those places in Rome where the Apostles had suffered death and lay buried, such as the monument of the Apostle's victory, the tropaeum, for St. Peter near Nero's Circus (326–
*figs. 5, 6*    327) and the tomb of St. Paul on the Via Ostiense. These sites of martyrdom soon began to attract vast crowds of pilgrims. The cult of relics grew. The finding of the True Cross by the Emperor's mother Helena and the veneration of the cross are among the most significant events of this time.

The centralized churches erected by Constantine in the East, especially in Jerusalem, soon became a dominant
*29, 31*    influence in Rome as well. Imperial architecture achieves its fullest articulation in the Mausoleum of Constantina, who died in 354. Formally, Santa Costanza followed earlier imperial mausoleums, such as that of Diocletian in Split or of Galerius in Salonika. But its ground plan is more richly articulated: twelve pairs of coupled columns carry the drum and dome and are surrounded by a vaulted ambulatory with niches. The central space is well lit by large windows in the drum, while the ambulatory, with only narrow rectangular openings in the wall, remains in semidarkness.

The mosaics of the dome were unfortunately destroyed in the time of the Baroque, and can only be reconstructed from old drawings. The lower part consisted of river scenery with birds and boats, cosmic in its

16

A   San Giovanni in Laterano, Rome. The old Basilica. Fresco in San Martino ai Monti, Rome

B   The old Basilica of St. Peter, Rome. Fresco in San Martino ai Monti, Rome

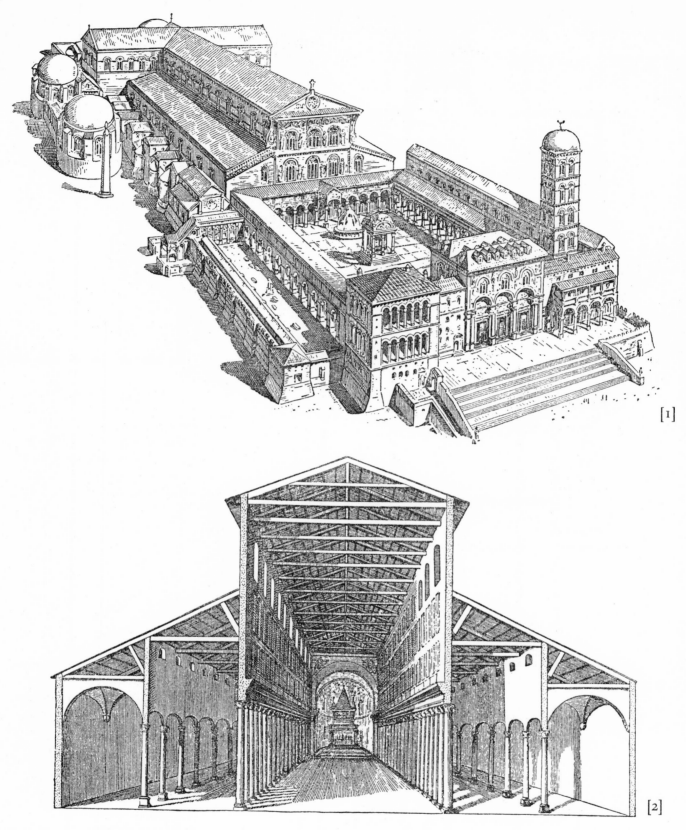

FIGURES I AND 2. The Basilica of St. Peter, Rome. [1] Reconstruction of the building as it appeared during the Middle Ages. [2] Perspective cross section. After: P. Toesca, *Storia dell'arte italiana*, Turin, 1927.

19

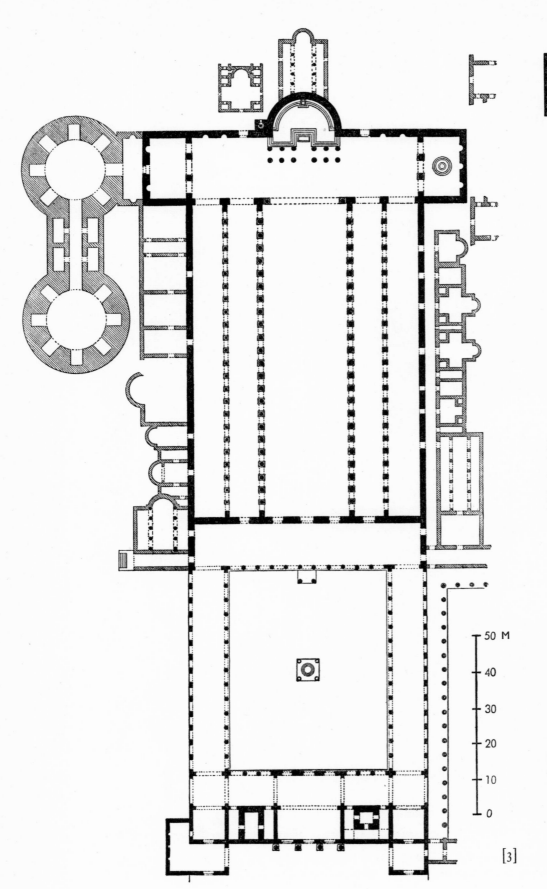

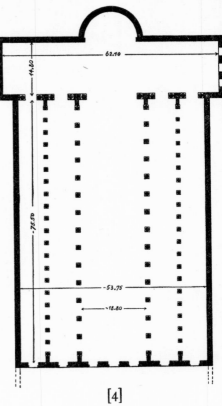

[4]

Length of nave, 75.50 m. (247 ft., 8 in.)
Width of nave, 53.75 m. (176 ft., 4 in.)
Width of center aisle, 18.80 m. (61 ft., 8 in.)
Length of transept, 62.10 m. (203 ft., 9 in.)
Width of transept, 14.80 m. (48 ft., 6 in.)

FIGURE 3. Plan of the Basilica of St. Peter, Rome. Black: 4th- and 5th-century walls. Cross-hatched: Sections added during subsequent centuries. After: G. Dehio and G. von Bezold, *Die Kirchliche Baukunst des Abendlandes*, Stuttgart, 1887-1901.

FIGURE 4. St. John Lateran, Rome. Reconstruction of the plan by P. Marx in F. W. Deichmann, *Frühchristliche Kirchen in Rom*, Basel, 1948.

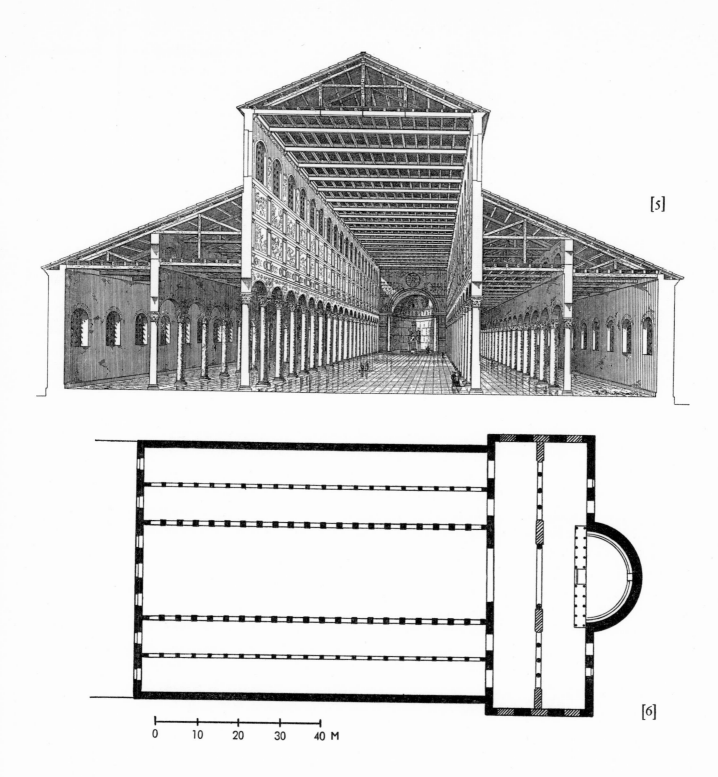

[5]

[6]

FIGURES 5 AND 6. San Paolo fuori le Mura (Basilica ostiensis), Rome. The basilica was built by Constantine the Great to replace the memorial chapel (*cella memoriae*) of St. Paul, was enlarged by Valentinian II in 384 and again by Theodosius the Great, and completed under Honorius. The mosaics, still extant on the triumphal arch, were made for Galla Placidia. Destroyed by fire in 1823 but reconstructed by 1854. [5] Perspective cross section worked out according to the calculations of Hübsch and the views by Piranesi. [6] Plan. Length (including the apse) 120 m. (394 ft.), width 60 m. (197 ft.), width of central aisle 23 m. (75 ft). After: G. Dehio and G. von Bezold, *Die Kirchliche Baukunst des Abendlandes*, Stuttgart, 1887–1901.

21

symbolism. From it rose a candelabra-like pattern of creeping plants, which formed twelve compartments with representations of the superterrestrial world in each. In the central zone there were scenes from the Old en New
*32, 34, 35* Testaments antithetically arranged the Sacrifice of Cain and Abel, the Sacrifice of Elijah, Moses Striking the Rock, and opposed to them miracles of the Lord.

The mosaics in the ambulatory, though much restored, have survived. The spirit of Hellenistic art is here still in evidence. Out of eight fields, two depict the grape harvest with a portrait in each, perhaps of Constantina and her husband. The other fields delight by their simple pattern of scattered foliage punctuated by birds and utensils, Bacchic elements connected with funerary symbolism. The mosaics in the two surviving niches of the transversal axis have a white background. In one, Christ gives the keys to St. Peter, in the other, Christ gives the Scroll of the Law to SS. Peter and Paul. These mosaics may well be somewhat later. They are more or less isolated in Early Christian art, but antecedents and parallels are to be found in floor mosaics, such as the one
*28* with a similar complex of ideas in the nave of the Basilica at Aquileia (312–319) or, more generally, in mosaics from Syria, Palestine, and North Africa.

Santo Stefano Rotondo, built in the second half of the fifth century, probably under Pope Simplicius (468–483), still had the Church of the Holy Sepulcher as its model. Inside, a circular colonnade of twenty columns carried the high drum on a plain architrave. A wide ambulatory with another colonnade described an outer circle.

Once the supremacy of Christianity was assured, new themes appeared in its iconography. Symbolic representations gave way to historical ones which established themselves both in painting and sculpture. In post-Constantinian paintings in catacombs, this change may be seen when Christ is no longer disguised as the teaching philos-
*36* opher but stands forth as the victorious ruler, following the Hellenistic tradition. Judge of the universe in
*41–43* heavenly glory, he delivered the Scroll of Law to St. Peter. The new trend achieved its finest expression in a statuette of Christ, dating from the 350s, now in the Museo Nazionale Romano, Rome. The figure is similar to those appearing in the center of reliefs on contemporary sarcophagi, of which the Sarcophagus of Junius Bassus (died 359) in the Vatican Grottoes is the finest example. The spirit of antiquity finds a last reflection in this youthful Christ, who stands transfigured, unlike the suffering Christ of later centuries. There is a final echo of the unconquerable Sun, of Mithraism, which was a dangerous rival of Christianity as late as the Tetrarchy. Constantine had turned to it for a while, and it is still present in these figures made some twenty years after the Emperor's death.

In addition to miracle scenes, episodes from the Passion, above all Pilate Washing His Hands, became increasingly frequent from the late Constantinian period onward and are the chief themes of Roman sarcophagus sculpture of the fourth century. The death of Christ is alluded to by other scenes, but is never actually portrayed. Old Testament scenes, such as the Sacrifice of Isaac or the representation of the Washing of the Hands, were enough for the believers. The cross of Golgotha served as a symbol of the Crucifixion, as on a sarcophagus in the Lateran Museums.

After his vision on the Milvian Bridge Constantine had XP, the monogram of Christ—Christos—placed on his labarum and on the shields of his soldiers. Even the statue the victorious Emperor wanted erected in the large basilica in the Forum had the labarum in its right hand. Henceforth the Emperor is Christ's standard bearer. He is the earthly deputy of Christ who is now the true king—Christus Rex—enthroned in the firmament, dispenser of the Law. Then, in Theodosian art Christ reveals His divine plenitude of power in the presence of
*41, 46, 36* the Apostles.

A change in style occurs in the latter part of Constantine's reign. The hard, angular relief is replaced by softer,

more elegant modeling, of which the Sarcophagus of Junius Bassus and the statuette of Christ in the Museo    *15*
Nazionale Romano are excellent examples. In the arrangement of figures, especially on frieze sarcophagi, the
crowding so apparent on the Arch of Constantine gives way to a more widely spaced arrangement which en-
hances the narrative element of the representation considerably.

   Genre elements are now introduced, and the personages portrayed become freer and livelier in their movements; at the same time, they are more securely set into the space. Trees or columns often separate individual
scenes. Complex architectural ensembles, frequently recalling the holy places in Palestine, play an ever greater
part in these city-gate sarcophagi, which represent the final stage in this type of sculpture in Rome.    *46, 47*

In the second half of the fourth century, the local Roman style gave way progressively to a return to Hellenistic
traditions. Works like the Sarcophagus of Junius Bassus exemplify this revival, which was partly brought about
by the political situation. Pagan opposition was still powerful, especially among the old senatorial families
who made no secret of their antipathy toward the new state religion. No sooner had Flavius Claudius Julianus
(355–363)—known to history as Julian the Apostate—become Augustus (361), than he reinstated the old Roman    *48, 49, 52*
religion. Himself a disciple of Neoplatonic doctrine, Julian attempted to set up against Christianity an otherworldly idealism. The statues of him that have survived, and his coins, show him in the guise of the bearded
philosopher wearing a priestly diadem. The return to old ways was a political program which initiated a trend
in art. Julian's reign may have been short but the reaction in favor of classical art and the Hellenistic spirit
continued, indeed gained strength under his Christian successors.

The revival can be most clearly observed in products of court art, especially in the East. Sculpture in the round
shows an increasing dependence on ancient models in its more subtle execution, and the artist looks to classical
works for his models. This is combined, however, with strong emphasis on frontality and a more pronouncedly    *50, 51*
spiritualized expression.

   The statue of an emperor from Aphrodisias, now in the Archaeological Museum of Istanbul, probably
Valentinian II as consul, seems the logical next stage after the statue of Julian in Paris; it is lively and has a
genuine sense of volume. The body under the tunic, dalmatic, and toga is clearly discernible, but in the rigid    *56, 57*
position of the head the style of the Theodosian period pierces through. An instance of advanced style is the    *65–67*
excellent portrait of the Emperor Arcadius found in Istanbul, no doubt a piece from a metropolitan workshop.

   Closely related to these imperial portraits is a series of statues of high officials which originated in different
cities, including Ephesus, Athens, and Corinth. Their close stylistic resemblance to a porphyry figure of an    *69–71*
emperor, now in the Museo Arcivescovile in Ravenna, shows that this group of works belongs to court art.
It gives a clear idea of the high quality of Byzantine sculpture about 400. The colossal figure of an emperor in
armor, probably Marcian, that now stands in front of the Church of San Sepolcro in Barletta is somewhat later,    *68*
and possibly also from Constantinople. With this statue the series of monumental official portraits comes to an
end around the middle of the fifth century. The allied portrait of an empress, now in Milan, has the same
high-strung expression and the same over-refined treatment of surfaces as the male portraits. It is probably
Pulcheria, the wife of Marcian, but certainly not the Empress Theodora as has sometimes been suggested.

   Sculpture in the West does not attain the same power of spiritual expression or the same skill of execution.    *64*
The artists, more conservative, remained under the sway of old forms. Drapery is softer, the facial expressions
more human, but the general stylistic development is the same as in the East. The Roman consul, wearing a
toga, now in the Palazzo dei Conservatori in Rome, is indicative of the stage Western art had reached around 400.

The Theodosian style finds an even clearer expression in ornate monuments commemorating victories. Of the two triumphal columns erected in Constantinople by Theodosius and Arcadius respectively, only a few fragments have survived. The Theodosian monument on the Forum Tauri was dedicated in 394, that of Arcadius sometime between 401 and 421. The latter, about 150 feet high, can be reconstructed from old drawings. It followed Roman models, like the columns of Trajan and Marcus Aurelius, showing the Byzantine Emperor triumphant over Gainas and his Goths. But, in contrast to antique models, victory is here attributed to God alone. Flying victories carry the cross inscribed in a wreath, as on the door of Sant' Ambrogio in Milan, thus emphasizing the Christian character of the monument.

54, 55

Of the great obelisk Theodosius brought to Constantinople from Heliopolis in 390 and erected in the Hippodrome, the pedestal alone has survived. One of its reliefs shows the obelisk being raised in the Emperor's presence. On the others Theodosius is seen presiding over chariot races in the circus, and holding a wreath ready for the victor, while musicians and dancers provide entertainment for the thickly packed crowd of spectators. Though parallels with the triumphal scenes on the Arch of Constantine can still be discerned, there is a marked advance in the stylistic elaboration of the solemn, hieratic type. The Emperor is represented in an almost superhuman form. His will is law, and the Church, too, is subordinate to him. Though the court ceremonial might be impregnated with pre-Christian survivals and he himself politically embodied a combination of pagan and Christian elements, Theodosius, in 392, forbade, on pain of the severest penalties, all pagan cult practices.

53

A new artistic intention is discernible in Theodosian art. On the base of the Obelisk of Theodosius, the rigid composition, the symmetrical arrangement of figures in inverted perspective, their strict frontality, and the unrealistic background achieve an abstract effect. Yet the representation on the silver votive platter given away by the Emperor on the occasion of his decennial in 388 is still more ceremonious. Theodosius, wearing the chlamys, is enthroned on the imperial tribunal and flanked by his sons. The idealized rendering conveys the concept of the imperial office, the summit of a hierarchy that is at once worldly and heavenly. The votive platter

109

of about 353 with Constantius II on horseback, now in Leningrad, retains more movement, while the one with Valentinian I (364–375), now in Geneva, marks the transition to the hieratic image. How rapidly this type evolved in the West can be seen from a later example depicting the consul Aspar Ardabur (434), in Florence. In comparison with the Missorium of Theodosius, the composition is much looser; the classicizing tendency is

59

on the wane.

In engraved stones even more than in silver, the fine techniques of Theodosian art come into their own. The large cameo in the Rothschild Collection with the double portrait of Honorius and Maria, perhaps made for their wedding in 398, has the same classicizing tendency as the one of Honorius on the consular diptych of

20

Probus (406), now in Aosta. But the precious stone is executed with greater delicacy than the ivory. Older pieces, such as the cameo depicting Constantine and his family on the cover of the Ada Gospels in Trier, or the chalcedony bust in Paris usually taken to represent Constantine, are not equal to the artistic standards achieved at this time, nor will later periods be able to surpass them.

94

In contrast to the wealth of ivories from the West, frequently securely dated, Byzantium has little to offer; and these few pieces have to be dated on stylistic evidence alone. The unusual pierced panel in the British Museum, with Bellerophon slaying the chimaera, and the diptych in Florence, with scenes from the life of St. Paul

63, 62

on one leaf and Adam in Paradise on the other, show the somewhat dry and stiff style of Byzantine sculpture; however, it is also possible that they were made in the West under strong Byzantine influence.

The diptych in Monza, with Stilicho on one side and his wife Serena and son Eucherius on the other, is

24

undoubtedly of Western origin. Since Stilicho became consul in 400, the piece is almost contemporary with the Honorius cameo to which it is also akin stylistically. The somewhat mannered folds in the dress of Serena recall the elegant female figure in Paris, usually identified, no doubt correctly, as Aelia Flacilla, the wife of Theodosius.

61

And we now come to the style so strikingly embodied in the magnificent gold glass on the large processional cross in Brescia. Painted in enamel, it shows a distinguished lady with her son and daughter. The traditional identification with Galla Placidia (died 460) is chronologically impossible since the glass is a perfect expression of the intellectually refined though decadent society of the beginning of the fifth century, much as the mummy portraits were earlier.

Our knowledge of Theodosian court sculpture provides a framework for classifying a number of other Byzantine reliefs, especially those with religious subjects. Here, too, there is a strong classicizing tendency and conscious imitation of antique works. What differentiates these pieces from their models is the low relief, the lack of any suggestion of depth, and the highly mannered drapery. A comparison of the Nike (or Victory) in the Archaeological Museum in Istanbul, sometimes taken for the Angel of the Annunciation, with older pieces in Rome, such as the Victory from the Baths of St. Helena (317–324) or the Victories on the Arch of Constantine, shows a considerable stylistic development. The Constantinian figures are almost cubical, while the Victory in Istanbul harks back to the flat Hellenistic type in which a subtle and rich treatment of drapery replaces the use of the drill.

72

Another change can be observed in Constantinopolitan monuments about the middle of the fifth century: in the reliefs on the Column of Marcian (ca. 450–452) more plastic rendering is reintroduced. One of the finest examples of the new tendency is the Sarcophagus of a Prince. The angels carrying the monogram of Christ in a wreath, on one of the sides, display the same elegant fall of the drapery as the figures on the base of the Obelisk of Theodosius, while a similar group of angels appears on the base of the Column of Arcadius.

75

73

How heavily Christian artists working in the Eastern capital borrowed from pagan models, particularly the Hellenistic art of Asia Minor, can be seen in the sarcophagus relief with Christ between SS. Peter and Paul, in Berlin. The sarcophagus, perhaps an emperor's, is the last in the long series of Sidamara sarcophagi. The holy personages are still classically beautiful, Christ appearing in celestial majesty, but forms have been simplified and a statuesque calm replaces antique animation. The delightful figures amid foliage on two column drums, worked in high relief, are also animated by ancient Eastern Hellenism.

76, 77

174–179

80

That the new style soon found its way to the West, is indicated by the early sarcophagi from Ravenna, and the vase with religious scenes in the Museo Nazionale Romano in Rome. Similar, though somewhat coarser, are the figures amid foliage on the piers for screens in the Archaeological Museum in Istanbul. The most significant product of this art, the ambo fragments from Salonika, are also in this museum. The ambo now consists of two blocks, the cornices are decorated with luxuriant foliage, and in the niches below appears the Adoration of the Magi with the enthroned Mother of God. Compared with the relief of Christ with SS. Peter and Paul in Berlin, the figures are flatter, the folds more linear and only in the architectural features is there still a close resemblance. Similar conches appear above scenes from the life of Christ on the lintel over the north porch of San Marco in Venice. Furthermore, the three slabs from the Church of St. John Studion are especially remarkable for their iconography. These pieces, depicting respectively the Entry into Jerusalem, *Maiestas Domini*, and a fragment with five Apostles, are also related to Syrian and Palestinian monuments.

78, 79

73

81

82, 83

The dating of the four columns supporting the canopy over the high altar at San Marco in Venice is widely debated and their origin has not been established, though they were probably brought to Venice from the East as booty. The relief decoration is arranged in nine zones, each with scalloped niches separated by colonettes, into which are set scenes from the story of the Virgin, beginning with her birth, and the story of Christ, including the Nativity, miracles, Passion, and Ascension, taken from the New Testament and the Apocrypha. The inscriptions between the zones, partly out of place, were added in the thirteenth century. For this reason alone, the Early Christian dating has been contested and the columns described as medieval copies. The presence of certain iconographic features not known from the earlier period has reinforced this view, and even today the problem of their origin remains unsolved. It is clear, however, that at least two masters worked on the reliefs; those on the two front columns are in a better style, the rendering of the drapery is softer and generally more articulate in execution, while it is harsher on the two back ones. A comparison with East Christian sculpture reveals an affinity with works from Constantinople, particularly with the column drums in the Archaeological Museum in Istanbul. At the same time, the figure types are close to Western products such as the late, arcade-type sarcophagi or the large pyxis with Christ among the Apostles in Berlin.

76, 77
95

These works show that by the beginning of the fifth century the Eastern capital had found a distinctive formal idiom, one that reached maturity in the sixth century. It represented a synthesis of a number of elements bequeathed to Constantinople by Eastern Hellenism, more especially from Asia Minor, Syria, Palestine, and Alexandria, and by the cultures of Pontus and Persia. The basis, however, was the imperial art that had centered in Rome. Indeed, though its various components are still discernible, it was the unifying principle, in a manner analogous to the single body politic, which could assimilate the most varied peoples.

In the West the course of development was different. Difficult political conditions allowed no consistent artistic trend to establish itself. Above all, Rome sank gradually into insignificance, while the old senatorial families, in a vain effort to maintain the city's ancient glory, attempted to stem the advance of the new Christian culture. One step in furthering their political aims was to promote a return to ancient models in the arts. The tendency is at its clearest in commemorative ivories made for them, e.g. the diptych of the vice-prefect of Rome, Rufius Probianus, in Berlin, or the roughly contemporary wedding diptych of the Nicomachi and the Symmachi produced in Rome about 400. A similar inclination to revive classical forms prevailed, but to a lesser extent, at the papal court under Damasus (366–384).

90, 91

103–105

At the same time the political influence of the East Roman emperors was making itself increasingly felt in the old capital, and is reflected in art through obviously Eastern traits, as in the magnificent wooden doors of Santa Sabina.

62, 63

Furthermore, elements of local popular art are still to be observed in many works of the period. But the ever-stronger political influence of Germanic army commanders found no cultural expression. Stilicho in Milan, Odoacer in Rome, and others like them were assimilated into the Mediterranean culture and lived in the Roman environment, as may be seen in the diptych portraying Stilicho and his family, for it completely belongs to the court art of Constantinople. Though the imperial court was profoundly anti-Germanic, the barbarian penetration could not be halted. Thus Alaric reached the outskirts of Rome and only enormous tribute could persuade him to withdraw. But Rome had finished her leading role.

With a brilliant court installed in it, Milan took Rome's place for a while, soon to be supplanted in turn by Ravenna. Honorius moved his capital to Ravenna in 404, induced, no doubt, by the favorable position on the sea and the surrounding marshes which offered some protection against the barbarian menace. Under the Emperor's half sister, Galla Placidia, Ravenna became a great artistic center.

The confused political situation in Italy became increasingly evident in the cultural sphere. While Rome, declining in productivity, showed conservative tendencies and no longer maintained its former pre-eminence, artistic life in Milan was livelier, more progressive, and more open to Eastern influences. St. Ambrose, the leading personality of the city, encouraged artistic production, and his achievements in church singing show a strong inclination for Eastern culture. Buildings so bold in conception as the central-plan Church of San Lorenzo, constructed under his guidance, would have been unthinkable in Rome. The wooden doors of Sant' Ambrogio (376–386), in all likelihood meant for the royal porch, follow Eastern models closely.                           *102*

The fact that St. Ambrose, a militant churchman, and the Alexandrian poet Claudius Claudianus (died 404), · a convinced pagan whose poetry is thoroughly classical, could live at the same court is indication of the strength with which Christian and pagan thinking could still exist side by side around 400.

This coexistence is most pronounced in the applied arts, especially ivory and silver. To isolate the various     *90, 91* schools remains difficult, but at least general lines of development can be discerned. Fortunately, the surviving ivories include pieces whose date and place of origin can be established through the names of those who commissioned them. Thus, the diptych of the Nicomachi and Symmachi was evidently made either in 392 or 402 to celebrate a marriage alliance between these two prominent Roman senatorial families. These panels with pagan representations revert back to the art of the early Empire. Other ivories belong to the same group, such as the diptych in Berlin of Rufius Probianus, vice-prefect of Rome, with its classical border ornament. Another     *92* product of this classicizing tendency, the consular diptych of Probus in Aosta with the image of the Emperor     *93* Honorius, dates a few years later (406). Pieces with Christian subjects were also produced by this school, for example the panel in Milan with the Mary sat the Sepulcher, with figures recalling late fourth-century sarcophagus reliefs stylistically. Another ivory deserving mention in this context is the one in Munich with the Three Marys at the Sepulcher and the Ascension, though here there is a greater sense of volume, as is also the     *95* case in the diptych of the Lampadii in Brescia. Since the Lampadii belonged to the Roman aristocracy, this piece may have been made in Rome, although it has stylistic features pointing to northern Italy. The enthroned Christ among the Apostles on the ivory pyxis in Berlin also has classical elements, but its provenance is difficult     *85–89* to establish and there is even a possibility that it was made by an Eastern artist working at the imperial court in Trier.

The ivory casket in Brescia, dating from the third quarter of the fourth century, belongs to a different school.     *75* Its Old and New Testament scenes recall those on the arcade sarcophagi. The elegant style of the reliefs is influenced by Hellenistic examples from the East. The clear articulation of the scenes, the full modeling of the bodies, and the firm stances of the figures warrant a comparison with the Sarcophagus of a Prince in Istanbul. But the sensitivity characteristic of Theodosian sculpture is lacking, and the author of this piece is to be sought     *98* in the West, most probably in northern Italy.

A change in style is apparent soon after the turn of the century. The figures in the Passion scenes on the Maskell casket, in the British Museum, are both more thickset and less embedded in the background. The narrative element is preserved, as on the sarcophagi. The casket can, with some probability, be dated to the early years of the century on the strength of similarities with the two preserved side panels (in Paris and Berlin)     *100, 101* of a five-part diptych. As for its provenance, an iconographic comparison with the scenes from the life of Christ on the Werden casket in the Victoria and Albert Museum, and with the book cover from the second half of the century in Milan each side of which is made up of five pieces, points to North Italy. On the other hand, the

27

panels in Milan are iconographically so close to the mosaics in Sant' Apollinare Nuovo in Ravenna that they may well have been produced there, for when the court moved from Milan to Ravenna, many artists must have followed.

The fifth century witnessed a rapid evolution in style which can be followed closely in the dated consular diptychs. These writing tablets, bearing the name of the donor, were sent out as gifts by consuls on their assumption of office in Rome. They can thus be securely dated to the year and supply an excellent chronological framework for classifying other works. A conceptual change in the manner of presenting the human figure occurs between the diptych of Probus (406) in Aosta and that of Felix (428) in Paris. They show a progressive loss of volume and space, and a trend away from realism toward abstract forms which is considerably more pronounced in the diptych of Basilius (480) in Florence. The figure of Felix remains imprisoned in the flat surface and the gold embroidered *toga contabulata* over the tunic is barely indicated, while Basilius, in an almost abstract appearance, stands against a background devoid of depth. The connection with classical art has been lost and the foundations of medieval art laid.

In the Eastern part of the Empire the departure from realism never went quite so far, and northern Italy, too, retained at least some continuity with the classical past because of its close artistic links with Byzantium, as is shown by the Ravenna sarcophagi.

The influence of Eastern Hellenism is most apparent in metalwork. Thus the plate in Berlin depicting Artemis, probably made in Ephesus, might easily be the prototype of much embossed silverware in the West. Not only in technique but in iconographic content as well, these pieces of the second half of the fourth century imitate older models. The magnificent vessels and plates of the Mildenhall Treasure in the British Museum, or the vase with Bacchic scenes in Cleveland, at least at first sight almost seem to be classical Alexandrian works. The celebrated dish in Milan from nearby Parabiago was long thought to date from the second century. The purely pagan subject of Cybele and Attis repeats in detail Antonine models, and the technical differences are barely noticeable. Related pieces—for instance, the dish from Corbridge now in the British Museum, with its company of gods, or the one in Cesena depicting a banquet of the gods—show a Hellenistic technique comparable in every way to classical work. Related to them is the votive platter of Theodosius, though the dry rendering of the relief is different from works of Western origin, such as the Parabiago dish. The rich silver treasure from the Esquiline, now for the most part in the British Museum, fits chronologically into this group. It includes the magnificent bridal casket of Secundus and Projecta (died 383), datable by the wedding to about 380, a toilet box, statuettes of four city goddesses, a slim flask with putti, a ewer, an amphora, a spoon, and, finally, an elegant dish depicting the Toilet of Venus which is now in Paris. Although the couple was Christian, and the double portrait and the marriage scene are similar to those on Christian sarcophagi, the other iconographic elements, such as Venus, sea gods with dolphins, the Muses, and the city goddesses, derive from Alexandrian Hellenistic metalwork. The personification of the city of Antioch is a copy of a statue by Eutychides.

The North Italian casket, now in San Nazaro Maggiore in Milan, which St. Ambrose used for the relics of the Apostle Peter sent from Rome by Pope Damasus, is roughly contemporary with the Projecta casket. The technique and arrangement of the five scenes from the Old and the New Testament also bear the stamp of Hellenistic art. It is one of the earliest Christian pieces and the Christ child is still naked, the Magi are represented as philosophers. A comparison with the Parabiago dish shows that this school, working perhaps in Milan, imitated classical silver even more consistently than the Roman master of the Projecta casket.

To the same stage of artistic development also belong such ivories as the pyxis in Bobbio, on which Orpheus is represented, and the diptych in Brescia with a pair of lovers.

28

This artistic revival ends soon after 400 and the sense of volume again grows weaker. Thus on the silver votive platter of the consul Aspar Ardabur, dating from 434, the relief is flat and the figures are isolated.

The new style emerged sooner in goldsmiths' work, as for example in the chiaroscuro background of the pierced ornamental panel in the British Museum, showing a lion hunt.

The progressive lessening of a sense of volume can be traced in various stages in Christian metalwork of the fifth century. The development goes from the vases in London and Rome and the Traprain flask in Edinburgh, which still have the classical spirit, to the silver pyxis from Pola now in Vienna, to the oval silver reliquary from Brivio in Paris and the two reliquaries in the Treasury at Grado, which, however, belong to the second half of the century. These pieces still draw on older subjects but the stylistic change has been considerable, especially in the treatment of folds; the contours are sharp and all plasticity has been lost.

From then on silverwork became rarer, and in Rome seems to have ceased almost completely. Only about 500, with the general revival of the arts in Byzantium, do silversmiths again become active.

Painting too remains conservative in Rome during the Theodosian period. Thus the apsidal mosaic in one of the chapels of the Lateran Baptistery, dating from the end of the century, closely follows earlier works both in its rich acanthus decoration and its general tonality. Similarly, the earliest major apsidal mosaic, the one in Santa Pudenziana, datable soon after 400, is a direct continuation of the classical trend. The figures are still full of life and movement: the bearded Christ, exalted on a throne, is flanked by the Apostles, while personifications of the Church of the Circumcision and the Church of the Gentiles crown two of the Apostles with wreaths, and the cross appears in the heavens above. Particularly antique is the rendering of spatial depth against a background representing the Heavenly Jerusalem. This type of architectural landscape may well have its antecedents in the East. The female figures symbolic of the Church of the Circumcision and the Church of the Gentiles on the entrance wall inside Santa Sabina in Rome (422–433) belong to the same phase of stylistic development.

Among the richest Early Christian mosaic cycles is the one in Santa Maria Maggiore in Rome, put up under Pope Sixtus III (432–440). The original apse is no longer extant but the scenes from the childhood of Christ and symbolic representations on the triumphal arch and some of the Old Testament episodes on the walls of the nave have been preserved. That the latter seem earlier may be because they are based on earlier models, presumably manuscript illuminations, and not because they were actually made first. The movement of the figures is lively, the color pattern still impressionistic.

The scenes from the childhood of Christ, based on the Apocrypha, had to be composed for the occasion, since they reflect the doctrine of the Virgin as the Mother of God promulgated at the Council of Ephesus in 431. The representations on the triumphal arch in Santa Maria Maggiore show less spatial depth than the mosaic in Santa Pudenziana. The figures either move in the foreground plane with all the heads on almost the same level or stand practically one above the other. The over-all impression—partly created by the larger size of the individual tesserae—is less painterly than in the nave, and the calm and solemn bearing of the holy personages indicates a trend toward hieratic representation.

In southern and northern Italy, where stronger Eastern influences were at work, the evolution of painting is more rapid. The frescoes in San Gennaro in Naples as well as mosaic remains in the baptistery adjoining San Gennaro and in Cimitile testify to a considerable degree of orientalization already present at the beginning of the fifth century. Unfortunately, little has survived in Milan. The earliest extant mosaics, perhaps still from the end of the fourth century, are the figures of saints in the atrium of the Cappella di Sant' Aquilino adjoining San Lorenzo, and the Vision of Elijah, of which only the lower, pastoral scene is preserved. Stylistically

*119*

*121*

*120*

*130*

*128, 129*

they are much more progressive than those in Rome. At the same time there is a dependance on classical art comparable to metalwork as in the Parabiago dish and the casket in San Nazaro Maggiore. The apsidal mosaic in Sant' Aquilino with Christ among the Apostles seems more advanced. The individuality of the heads shows a

similar impressionistic tendency. At the same time the arrangement of the scene is strictly symmetrical. The rigid forms and the lack of spatial depth would have been unthinkable without Byzantine influence. Finally, this Ambrosian revival terminates with the figures of saints in the small basilica of San Vittore in Ciel d'Oro, adjoining Sant' Ambrogio. The weakened plastic effect already suggests a knowledge of the manner current in Ravenna.

That so little monumental painting dating from this period has survived in the Eastern part of the Empire is a great loss. But the few extant examples show what high standards prevailed and how strongly it influenced the

Western masters of the Campanian and Milanese schools.

    In Constantinople nothing remains from the Theodosian period. Salonika, on the other hand, can boast a major mosaic cycle in the imposing Hagios Georgios. Theodosius converted this mausoleum into a church by adding an apse, and perhaps dedicated it to Christ, though St. George later became its patron. The mosaics in the dome give us some idea of what has been lost in Constantinople. The upper part is destroyed and only

traces of outlines enable us to recognize a victorious Christ shouldering the cross in the center, and a choir of angels, whose feet are partly still there, looking up toward Him. What has been preserved is the lower zone; it consists of a monumental architectural frieze with saints standing in front of it. Both the elegant structures,

seen in perspective, and the expressive heads of the saints are typical of the Theodosian renaissance. In contrast,

the geometrical patterns in the barrel vaults of the niches recall the antique manner of the designs in Santa

Costanza, and on Hellenistic silk textiles.

    Another work from the middle of the fifth century preserved in Salonika is the apsidal mosaic in the little Church of Hosios David. The youthful Christ is enthroned above the symbols of the Evangelists. The artist has departed from a purely hieratic representation, and by introducing the Vision of Ezekiel, he achieves a more realistic effect that recalls the mosaic in Sant' Aquilino in Milan.

No sooner had the imperial court moved from Milan to Ravenna than artistic production also shifted to Raven-na. Under the patronage of Galla Placidia (died 450), the new capital became the cultural center of the West. After the death of her husband Constantius III, in 421, she was regent on behalf of her son, Valentinius III (died 455). The art of the period bears her imprint.

    A second flowering occurred under Theodoric, king of the Ostrogoths. He entered Ravenna in 493 and built a series of sumptuous edifices, including several new churches which he decorated with costly mosaics; but with his death in 526 the Ostrogothic power declined, and in 540 the Byzantine general, Belisarius, captured the city. Henceforth Ravenna was to be dominated by the power and the culture of Constantinople and soon be-came an outpost of Byzantine court art.

    Political and artistic developments correspond closely. Artistic contacts with Byzantium had already begun un-der Honorius; they were to continue for two hundred years. By and large the same happened in Rome but Ravenna

developed unique stylistic variants that differentiate it from Constantinople, as well as from other centers.

    The palaces of the city were sumptuous but practically nothing of them remains. That they were modeled on

Eastern architecture can be inferred from the representation of Theodoric's palace in Sant' Apollinare Nuovo. The structure is related to the peristyle of Diocletian's palace in Split and perhaps also to the structures erected in Salonika by Galerius, of which only the mausoleum and parts of the triumphal arch have survived.

The early churches of Ravenna follow the basilical type elaborated in Rome. San Giovanni Evangelista, built by Galla Placidia after the death of Honorius (423), was a basilica with a nave and two aisles and a narthex that differed from the Roman churches only in the polygonal exterior of its apse, a trait characteristic of Eastern churches. Furthermore, Byzantine influence is noticeable in such details as the capitals in Sant' Apollinare Nuovo. Other basilicas of this period, Sant' Agata and San Francesco, follow Western patterns.

152

144, 145

More significant for future developments are the edifices with central plans such as the Mausoleum of Galla Placidia, adjoining the narthex of her palace church (Santa Croce), built about 424–425. This cruciform, barrel-vaulted structure with a central dome derives from the martyria in the East. The polygonal Baptistery of the Orthodox, attached to the cathedral, was built under Bishop Neon (ca. 458), and possibly incorporates an earlier structure. The rich interior decoration shows marked Byzantine features. The Baptistery of the Arians was modeled on the former and dates from the reign of Theodoric (after 493). Despite Byzantine influences, there are also Italian antecedents, especially the Lateran Baptistery, which must have exercised a determining influence.

26

154

The Mausoleum of Theodoric still presents a difficult problem. The gigantic monolith crowning it was formerly interpreted as a typically Germanic creation, but the structure should be explained in terms of Mediterranean parallels. Theodoric was an ardent exponent of Mediterranean culture and his dress and court ceremonials were modeled on Constantinople. The most probable antecedents of the tomb are the mausoleums of Galerius in Salonika and of St. Helena in Rome, as well as the rotunda of St. Peter's. In the sixth century, architecture in Ravenna becomes completely Byzantinized.

Sculpture in Ravenna differs markedly from that of Rome. Its characteristic products are sarcophagi, many of which attain a considerable quality. Their stylistic development can be followed almost without a break from the end of the fourth to the end of the fifth century.

Their reliefs are distinct both formally and in content. Simple compositions with few figures contrast sharply with the crowded Roman frieze sarcophagi or those from other parts of Italy, such as the magnificent sarcophagus in Sant' Ambrogio in Milan covered with monumental scenes, placed before the City of God. Biblical scenes are rare. Early works, like the relief with the *traditio legis*, that is, Christ giving the scroll of the law to SS. Peter and Paul, in the Museo Nazionale, or related pieces in the Cathedral and in S. Maria in Porto Fuori, show superficial iconographic similarities to Roman art. Peculiar to Ravenna is that St. Paul rather than St. Peter is often the recipient of the Scroll of the Law.

46, 47

176–178

Connections with Byzantine art, on the contrary, are many and close. As regards iconography, here, as earlier in the fragmentary relief in Berlin, the young, beardless Christ is no longer a philosopher or a worker of miracles, but the King of Heaven. Thus on most sarcophagi, he appears in heavenly glory with a majestic bearing, standing or enthroned between the two most important Apostles. The two palms that sometimes appear at either extremity of the scene symbolize the Heavenly Jerusalem. Stylistically, too, the link with Theodosian sculpture is obvious. The frontality of the figures, their isolation in shallow space, the fine, classicizing folds of the drapery all occur on contemporary Byzantine works like the Sarcophagus of a Prince, the bust of an Evangelist in Istanbul, and the reliefs on the base of the Obelisk of Theodosius. On early Ravenna sarcophagi, dating from about 400, such as the Pignatta sarcophagus and the one in San Francesco, the figures are in a very high relief. About the middle of the fifth century this changes and the figures on the Sarcophagus of Barbatianus in the Cathedral are flatter and more immobile, while on those in the Mausoleum of Galla

73

75

74, 54, 55

174

81

Placidia the relief has become very shallow. In Constantinople this stage is exemplified by reliefs like the one with the Entry into Jerusalem from the church of St. John Studion.

145–147 The same stylistic development is to be observed in mosaics, of which we have an almost complete series for the fifth and sixth centuries in Ravenna.

The decoration, from the first half of the fifth century, in the Mausoleum of Galla Placidia is still classical in style. The scenes are placed against a blue background and are convincingly related to their architectural setting. Represented are the Good Shepherd with his sheep, stags at the spring symbolizing the soul that awaits the Resurrection, St. Lawrence about to meet his martyr's death, and above each of these, solemn figures of the Apostles. The movements of the figures are vividly rendered, the colors naturalistic. The Good Shepherd, in particular, is still close to the spiritual world of the earliest Christian art. As it is not known whether the chapel was intended for a mausoleum, it is uncertain whether the symbolism of the representations was 140–142 meant to be funerary. Hope for the hereafter is, however, a recurrent theme: the Apostles intercede with Christ, the stag is the soul that thirsteth for God (Psalm 42), and the stars in the dome hint that Galla Placidia has been received into eternal bliss. Surely, the artist has placed the cross here as a reference to the Last Judgment.

The mosaics (ca. 430–450) in the Baptistery of the Orthodox are similar in style but have absorbed some of the rigidity prescribed for Byzantine court art. Bishop Neon consecrated the edifice about 458, which is why it is sometimes known by his name. As in Hagios Georgios in Salonika, the mosaic in the dome is divided into three zones. Appropriately, the Baptism of Christ occupies the center; it is surrounded by a procession of Apostles carrying crowns. The lowest zone has a symbolic representation consisting of four altars, each within a stylized basilica and with an open Gospel on it, alternating with four episcopal thrones. The style of the three zones is so 134, 135 homogeneous that they must have been made at the same time. Below the dome between the windows are stucco figures of Old Testament prophets. In spite of an impressionist treatment reminiscent of the mosaics in 149 the Mausoleum of Galla Placidia, they are probably contemporary with the more advanced mosaics in the dome. A comparison with the roughly contemporary mosaics in Hosios David, Salonika, suggests Eastern influences in the rich colors of the Apostles.

How classical the decoration of the Baptistery of the Orthodox is may be seen in contrast with similar but later mosaics in the Baptistery of the Arians attached to the Church of San Giovanni Evangelista and begun under Theodoric (493). The Baptism of Christ again appears in the center of the dome and the Apostles in the second zone. They now converge on the empty throne, the *etimasia*, which now makes clearer the procession in the Baptistery of the Orthodox. Modern critics have tended to explain the mosaic in the dome of the Arian Baptistery as a decadent copy of the mosaics of fifty years before in the other Baptistery; actually, they seem to indicate further iconographic and formal developments. The procession of the Apostles is no longer an 148 organic whole, either in composition or in color; here the figures are isolated and thereby achieve a strict rhythm. A rigid linearism has been introduced into the treatment of drapery. The influence of the antique disappeared almost completely during Theodoric's time and the Byzantine manner dominated. Theodoric's acceptance of the style prevailing in Ravenna is shown by a comparison with the roughly contemporary mosaics, in the archiepiscopal chapel dating from the episcopate of Petrus II (494–519/20). Here the vaulted ceiling of the small, square interior is decorated by a magnificent mosaic depicting a circle with the monogram of Christ in the center supported by four angels who alternate with the symbols of the Evangelists. The mosaic in the vestibule of the chapel is iconographically important, though the lower part is a restoration. Here the

32

youthful Christ as warrior wears a purple chlamys clasped by an imperial fibula. This concept of Christ as the victorious hero, thus equating Him with the emperor, is thoroughly Byzantine.

Theodoric reached the height of his power about 500. Recognized king by the Eastern Roman emperor who lent him the title of Augustus and the right to public statues, he wore the purple and the diadem as insignia of his dignity. He struck coins with his monogram and even medals with the legend *princeps*, but at the same time recognized the supreme sovereignty of the emperor in Constantinople. And just as he cultivated close political relations with the Eastern capital, so he commissioned Byzantine artists to decorate his buildings. Only in the decorative arts do traces of the Germanic style continue.

After the beginning of the sixth century the Hellenistic tradition declines rapidly, and we approach the climax 150–153 of Byzantine artistic creation, the second great revival which begins under the Emperor Anastasius (491–518) and carries the name of Justinian (527–565).

As very little monumental painting has survived in the Eastern Empire, the works in Ravenna from the first half of the sixth century are especially important to the history of Byzantine art, and the mosaics in Sant' Apollinare Nuovo become a valuable source of knowledge. Theodoric built the church, known from the ninth century on as Sant' Apollinare Nuovo, next to his palace as an expression of royal magnificence. It has 152, 153 had a sad history: after the collapse of Gothic rule, Archbishop Agnellus (557–570), bent on stamping out the memory of the Arian king, replaced large parts of the original mosaics in the nave by new ones. In the lowest of the three zones on the north side, he eliminated the scene that had shown Theodoric before Ravenna's port city of Classis and filled the surface between this city and the enthroned Mother of God with a procession of twenty-two female saints headed by the Magi. In the corresponding zone on the south side he removed the figures of the Holy Emperor and his court which had stood in the portico of the palace and inserted the procession of martyrs which approaches Christ, who had been part of the earlier cycle. Despite considerable restoration the differences between the two periods can be clearly distinguished. Unfortunately the sumptuous apse fell victim to an earthquake in the eighth century and it is difficult to reconstruct the character of the original Theodoric decoration in the apse and lower zones of the walls of the nave.

As regards particulars of the lower zones, however, there has survived at the west end of the southern wall the representation of the portico of Theodoric's palace, rendered without perspective, which seems to have resembled the palace of Diocletian at Split. Theodoric stood under the central arch between two high officials; other dignitaries, whose hands can still be seen on the columns of the arcade, stood under the other arches. In 150–151 the pediment of the portico there had probably been a representation of the Emperor on horseback. It is impossible to determine who the martyrs replaced or the identity of the people who had stood before the city of Classis.

On the other hand, in the two upper zones of both sides, the original mosaics from the time of Theodoric have been preserved. Each top zone consists of thirteen scenes from the life of Christ alternating with panels filled with a single conch shell, which are related to the zone below. Below each panel is a figure of a saint who stands between high windows. The choice of the scenes from the life of Christ is unusual: the Nativity and the Crucifixion are absent. Byzantine influence is no doubt at work here, and most particularly in the pronounced isolation of Christ. The purple of his robes derives from imperial usage and he is somewhat larger than the other figures. The lowest zone terminates on the south side in the figure of Christ Enthroned, and on the north, in the Virgin and Child. Both figures are in hieratic frontality, and are surrounded by the angels which replaced the Theodosian mosaics. This courtlike character is enhanced by the processions of saints and martyrs who carry crowns of martyrdom similar to the wreaths high officials might present to the Emperor. This type of scene had already appeared on the base of the Column of Arcadius.

Stylistically the mosaics in the top zone of the nave in Sant' Apollinare Nuovo contrast strikingly to those from the period of Galla Placidia. The few figures, arranged according to a strict rhythmical pattern which appears in each scene, are sparing in gesture and move calmly in a shallow foreground. The rhythmical pattern imposes its rigid requirements even on the color. In the scene of the Multiplication of Loaves and Fishes and the one of the Separation of Goats from Sheep, the main emphasis, falling in the center of the composition, is achieved by the deep purple. The individual components of the scenes are articulated according to the rigid system elaborated by Byzantine art. Soon after, already around 560, this dramatic sense is lost, for the Magi and the martyrs in the two processions are less powerful and their stance less firm.

Under Justinian Byzantine power finds its clearest architectural expression in Ravenna in the Basilica of San Vitale. Archbishop Ecclesius (died 532), who visited Constantinople in 525 and became familiar with its buildings, began the construction, and in this he had financial support from a certain Julianus Argentarius. The church was consecrated in 547 by Archbishop Maximian (546–556) and, as Theodora died in 548, the mosaic in which she appears must have been completed before that date.

Architecturally, San Vitale is typical of churches in Constantinople with central plans such as the Church of SS. Sergius and Bacchus which also has an octagonal plan, deriving, perhaps, from Syrian structures. We know from Procopius and other sources how popular this type of church was in the East. But because it is so remarkably well preserved, San Vitale can give us a particularly fine idea of these magnificent buildings.

The exterior, somewhat marred by the Renaissance portal, is sober in its individual features but achieves great monumentality through the grouping of large, uncluttered masses. The simple, high drum, and the apse projecting to the southeast give the building the variety it needs to avoid a static effect. Eight heavy piers, supporting drum and dome, articulate the interior. Between them are semicircular niches divided into two stories, the upper one forming a gallery reserved for women. Although the mosaics in the dome are lost, the interior decoration is magnificent and the eye is dazzled by the resplendent color of the remaining mosaics, by the stucco ornament, and by the capitals. Architecturally, too, the system of intersecting geometric components and the use of alternating forms, such as piers and columns, creates a powerful sense of movement that culminates in the sanctuary which, lit by large windows high up in the east wall, constitutes the focal point of the structure.

The mosaics decorating the sanctuary and the apse embody a carefully planned theological program that sets forth concisely the essential elements of Christian belief and places the main emphasis on the sacrifice of the mass. The inclusion of the Emperor and Empress in this cycle shows the close connection between the emperor cult and the Church.

The apse is dominated by the representation of Christ as World Ruler seated on the globe above the Four Rivers of Paradise. He tenders a golden wreath to St. Vitalis who is at the left, while Archbishop Ecclesius ap- proaches from the right to present Him with a model of the church. The enclosing arch has the monogram of Christ on its summit, the rest being filled by cornucopias of which the two upper ones are combined with eagles that symbolize imperial power.

Christ also appears in symbolic forms, as *Agnus Dei* (the Lamb of God), in a garland in the center of the vault of the sanctuary. The Lamb of God directly above the altar is a repetition of the reference to the death on the cross symbolized in the sacrifice of the mass.

34

The Old Testament scenes of sacrifice in the lunettes of the sanctuary—the sacrifices of Abel and Melchizedek and the representation of Abraham and the Angel combined with the sacrifice of Isaac—are also a reference to the sacrificial death of Christ and the repetition of the sacrificial death in the sacrifice of the mass at the altar. *164, 166* The remaining space is filled with scenes from the life of Moses, Old Testament prophets, the Four Evangelists, and the Apostles—the hierarchy of the old covenant and the New Testament.

This glorification of the sacrifice of the mass is further enhanced by the presence of the imperial couple. The two founders, surrounded by their court attendants, wait solemnly beside the altar. They stand in full frontality and yet the effect is not one of stiffness, as a slight break in the symmetry endows the scenes with life. In the panel with Justinian the deacon and subdeacon on the right seem to be on the point of stepping out of the frame of the mosaic. One carries a Gospel Book, the other a censer, and Archbishop Maximian, who stands beside them, a cross. The group is approaching the church; once inside, the Emperor will kiss the cross and the Bible while the incense is burned in his honor. It has been suggested that the senator between Justinian and the *165, 167* Archbishop is Julianus Argentarius, but Julianus never achieved senatorial rank. On the Emperor's other side stand two patricians in white chlamydes with a broad purple stripe. Perhaps the one next to the Emperor is Belisarius; the other, between him and the imperial guard, has not been identified. Justinian himself, in full ceremonial robes with the imperial fibula and the purple chlamys, wearing the diadem which custom prescribes he remove when he places on the altar the large paten or a dish with offerings he is holding. Opposite him, the Empress, also in court robes, is holding a precious chalice. She is moving past the fountain of the atrium, to- *168, 169* ward the open church door, the curtain of which is being held by a court official wearing a brown chlamys. *170, 171* The Empress is flanked by a patrician in a white chlamys, perhaps the *praepositus*, and on the other side by ladies- *171–173* in-waiting. The heads in both panels evince such marked individuality that the artist must have used portrait sketches sent from Constantinople.

Sant' Apollinare in Classe was consecrated in 549, two years after San Vitale; construction, begun by Arch- bishop Ursicinus (533–536), was again largely financed by Julianus Argentarius. The exterior shows the same refined use of brick as in the other churches of Ravenna. Inside there is a greater spatial sweep than in the other basilicas. The mosaic decoration of the nave has been lost but that of the apse is among the greatest works of Byzantine Ravenna. The apse is particularly impressive because it is raised above a crypt. In the center of its half-dome stands St. Apollinaris as *orans*. He intercedes for his congregation, symbolized by the six sheep that approach him from each side. The three other sheep that appear in the landscape of Paradise, one on the left and two on the right, represent SS. Peter, James, and John who gaze upward to the cross set in a starry heaven which, with the rest of the decoration, signifies the Transfiguration: against the gold background on either side of the cross Moses and Elijah emerge from clouds, and above all, the hand of God. Below the dome and *186* between the windows, appear the full-length figures of four archbishops of Ravenna—Ursicinus, Ursus, Severus, and Ecclesius. The mosaics on the triumphal arch on the walls between it and the first window on each side are of a later date; the scene on the left side, of inferior artistic quality, was put up in 675; it depicts the granting of privileges to the church of Ravenna by Constantine IV.

The style of the Ravenna mosaics finds an echo in those on the triumphal arch of San Lorenzo fuori le Mura in Rome. Christ, enthroned on a globe, is accompanied by several figures including Pope Pelagius II (died 590), but the restorations are too extensive to permit a stylistic analysis. Pelagius II added a gallery to the church, which, like Sant' Agnese fuori le Mura, follows Eastern models in this respect.

In Constantinople itself only the ruins of one basilica of a similar type have survived from the fifth century—the church of St. John the Baptist, in the former monastery of Studion, known today as Imrahor Camii. Built by John Studion in 463, it is a simple three-aisled structure with an atrium, a narthex, and an apse that is semi-circular internally but three-sided externally. In Salonika not only the Eski Djuma, the former Hagia Pareskevi, originally dedicated to the Virgin, is similar, but also the large basilica of Hosios Dimitrios can be dated to the end of the fifth century by its sculpture. It was burned down in the seventh century, rebuilt according to the same plan, and decorated with new mosaics; it was again destroyed by fire in 1917. In spite of all the restorations, Hosios Dimitrios is the best example of a Byzantine cruciform basilica with five aisles and galleries. The crypt under the apse and transept, discovered some time ago, housed, under a ciborium, the venerated tomb of the saint. It once attracted crowds of pilgrims. This basilica belongs to one of the great periods of Byzantine art and numerous provincial churches, particularly in Greece, Macedonia, and Asia Minor, attest to the popularity of this type of building. Despite their special forms, the two-storied church of Meriamlik, another great center of pilgrimage, and the basilica in Binbirkilisse, were surely influenced by the type of edifice elaborated in the large cities.

The monuments of Ravenna have afforded an excellent introduction to the development of Byzantine art in the sixth century. But to appreciate fully the greatness and significance of this period we must turn to the magnificent buildings of Constantinople. Constantine and Theodosius had provided the basic elements for the capital. As part of their idea of a Christian city, they designed the imperial palace, the cathedral, and the Hippo-drome as one architectural and spatial complex, in which the propinquity of the various buildings to each other *206, 207* symbolically expressed the union of secular and spiritual power. Christ was considered the actual ruler of the world, the emperor His vicar on earth, and protector of the Church. The imperial forums were laid out on a vast scale: from the Forum Tauri to that of Arcadius with its triumphal entrance and triumphal avenue, the *Mese*, which, flanked by sumptuous colonnades, cut straight across the city to the Hippodrome. There were also countless churches, most of them no longer standing, smaller palaces, the large, round building of the Senate, and the Baths, including those of Zeuxippus which Constantine adorned with numerous antique statues. Water was supplied not only from outside but also from a number of cisterns within the city, like the cistern of Yerebatan Seray, or the Binbirdirek cistern. These collected rain water which was drawn through two conduits and distributed throughout the city by the large aqueducts. An imposing spectacle to this day are the vast city walls punctuated by powerful gates and towers which encompassed the city on both the land and the sea sides, built for the most part by Theodosius, which rendered Constantinople impregnable until the Turkish assault in 1453.

What his predecessors had begun, Justinian completed. The Great Palace, between the Hippodrome and the sea wall, was enlarged and made yet more sumptuous. Its vestibule with a bronze door, hence the name *Chalke*, faced Hagia Sophia. A few remains on the sea side have survived but, in spite of descriptions by ancient authors, *186–190* such as Procopius and Constantine Porphyrogenitus, the arrangement of the various parts of the building can no longer be clearly established. Of the magnificent floor mosaics in the palace, only a few fragments in one large hall have so far come to light; these are of hunting scenes and animals, and were made during the Theo-dosian period.

The architectural activity under Justinian and his wife, Theodora, is seen at its most magnificent in two churches: SS. Sergius and Bacchus, today a mosque known as Kücük Aya Sophia (Little Hagia Sophia), and, greatest of all, Hagia Sophia.

The Church of SS. Sergius and Bacchus, situated between the Palace of Hormisdas and the Church of SS.

36

Peter and Paul, has a centralized plan, which may have been the model for San Vitale. A magnificent impression of space has been achieved despite the comparatively small dimensions. Although from the exterior the building appears to be almost a square, with an exedra in each corner, the interior space is rendered octagonal by the eight heavy free-standing piers that support the dome. The large deep niches between the eight piers are cut in two horizontally by a heavy, decorative architrave that supports a gallery which does not, however, extend into the apse, so that the central axis of the building is clearly maintained. The eight-sided structure over the piers flows smoothly into the dome, for the octagonal angles are continued into the eight concave panels of the dome which alternate with the same number of flat panels, a new and striking form of dome construction. The architect—perhaps Anthemius of Tralles—seems to have taken particular interest in the sculptural ornament. The acanthus leaves on the capitals and the architrave are very fine and, like those in Hagia Sophia, have the elegance characteristic of Justinian art. Unfortunately the front of the building was transformed by an addition in Turkish times which concealed the original narthex.

*191–205*

SS. Sergius and Bacchus is but a modest attempt in comparison with the extraordinary architectural feat achieved in the rebuilding of Hagia Sophia. Justinian was now at the zenith of his power, and he seemed to have brought the greatness of Rome to Constantinople through his deeds. He subdued the Alans, the Vandals, and the Moors, and reconquered Africa and Sicily. At home he suppressed the Nike riots of the circus factions, which caused much bloodshed and the destruction by fire of many of the city's buildings, Hagia Sophia among them. To rebuild this church the Emperor summoned to Constantinople the architects Anthemius of Tralles and Isidorus of Miletus. The edifice was to surpass in magnificence the Constantinian original. When Justinian consecrated the church on December 27, 537, he is said to have cried out proudly: "O Solomon, I have excelled thee." Unfortunately, the structure of the comparatively low, flat dome was not stable enough, and the earthquake of 558 brought it down. Isidorus the Younger replaced it by a higher dome which was firmly supported by the arches. The restoration was completed in 562. The genius of the plan lay in the way the dome is supported by the eight piers: the square central space under the dome was closed off on the south and north by colonnades but not on the east and west so that a spatial layout approximating a basilical plan resulted. Anthemius must have brought the idea with him from Asia Minor. The great problem facing the architect was to cover the vast central square with a dome of corresponding dimensions. The solution he adopted was to resist the thrust of the dome, which has no drum, by half-domes of equal radius on the east and west and to rest the complex of dome and semidomes on the octagonally arranged piers. The magnificent dome, pierced by forty windows, is totally visible from every point in the square. Dazzling vistas offer themselves to the visitor through the arcades on the north and south. These are composed of four huge columns which support a gallery of six smaller ones. The arcades run along the whole length of what can be called the nave and even carry across the narthex, and under the western semidome. Only the sanctuary is completely open and displays its full height and beauty. But in spite of the very complicated construction of the building, especially the dome, the niches, the galleries, and the piers, the over-all effect is one of solemn calm, great spaciousness, and rare harmony. Magnificent are the colorful revetments of slabs of verd antique, porphyry, and alabaster, and bewitching is the carved ornament, often cut to look like fine lacework. The capitals are made up of foliage, deeply undercut to achieve an effect of disembodiment of matter. The ornamentation betrays the influence of Eastern art. As for mosaics, they were completely destroyed during the Iconoclastic controversy. The glistening gold and the colorful representations must have been the crowning achievement. The remains of mosaic decoration visible today belong entirely to the Middle Byzantine period.

*194, 195*

*197*

*198, 200, 202 203*

The technique of vaulting and the spatial sweep of the interior recall the architecture of imperial Rome, but as a structural whole Hagia Sophia is entirely new and unique. It is the ultimate achievement of antique art, beyond which no further development was possible.

No doubt the mosaics and paintings in the other churches of the capital were of the same high artistic standard. Nothing remains of them today, and only from descriptions by ancient authors can we estimate the significance of the lost works of art in the Church of the Holy Apostles and Hagia Sophia. How high the quality must have been can be inferred from mosaics in the provinces, especially those in Ravenna and Salonika. In the Monastery of Panagia Kanakaria in Cyprus, an enthroned Madonna between two angels has survived from the seventh century, though in a somewhat damaged condition. Rather different in style is the mosaic of the Transfiguration in the apse of the church of the Monastery of St. Catherine on Mount Sinai. The mosaics in Nicaea are, unfortunately, lost.

Icons from this period are likewise very rare. A few encaustic paintings on panel have survived on Mount Sinai and others from there, now in Kiev, show how far Byzantine art spread in the Eastern world.

238–241 The illuminated manuscripts from this period are closely related to monumental painting. The various schools in which these miniatures were made have not, so far, been definitely determined, but the most important purple codices—the Vienna Genesis, the Sinope Gospels now in Paris, and the Gospel Book at Rossano in Calabria—may well have originated in Constantinople. And even if they were produced in Asia Minor 238, 239 241 or Syria, Byzantine influence predominates in them. They follow older models and show a certain kinship to each other. The Vienna Genesis in particular still adheres to Hellenistic illusionism; the figures illustrating its Old Testament scenes move in space as three-dimensional entities. The treatment is flatter in the illustrations of the codex from Sinope, and also in the Codex Rossanensis in which the isolation of the figures is the most marked. The use of color in the three codices is similar, especially in the heavy paint which again suggests Hellenistic models. To enhance dramatic tension, the artist of the Codex Rossanensis often constructs extremely compact groups which achieve a convincing effect of spatial depth by means of pronounced overlapping; witness the Last Supper, or Christ before Pilate. Architecture and landscape play no part in these representations. Only occasionally, as in the Garden of Paradise where Christ speaks with the wise and the foolish virgins, does one find summary hints of vegetation.

An even clearer example of sixth-century Byzantine style is offered by the illustrated copy of the treatise on plants, etc., by the Greek physician Dioscorides, now in Vienna. It was dedicated about 512 to Juliana Anicia, daughter of the Emperor Anicius Olybrius, who appears in royal apparel, enthroned between two ladies-in-waiting, on the sixth folio. The dating of the manuscript is thus secure. Although the illuminator used an earlier 217 216 model, his style follows that of contemporary monumental painting.

After Justinian there is little of comparable note to be found in painting. Artistic creativeness is visibly at an ebb. The few preserved examples are more abstract, the rendering of bodies lacks all sense of volume. The best illustration of this flat style are the mosaics on the transept piers in Hagios Dimitrios in Salonika, put up after the restoration of the church in 643. On one, St. Demetrius is seen standing between the prefect Leontius, the builder of the original church, and the Bishop John, its restorer. In another, he appears as the protector of two little children. The lack of spatial depth, the frontality of the figures, and their flat rendering show how far art had traveled toward abstraction by the seventh century.

Roman mosaics of the period, especially those in Sant' Agnese and the chapel of San Venanzio attached to the Lateran Baptistery, attest to the West's continued dependence on Eastern models. The frescoes in Santa Maria

Antiqua, and the mosaics from the Oratory of Pope John VII (705–707) in old St. Peter's (now in the Vatican Grottoes) and in Santa Maria in Cosmedin are also close to Eastern painting. But there are already signs here of a new artistic revival.

Entirely classical in spirit are the magnificent frescoes with scenes from the childhood of Christ in the choir of the little Lombard Church of Castelseprio, near Milan. They are the work of an outstanding artist with so personal a style that attempts to date them have ranged from the sixth to the tenth century. The color scheme and the fine treatment of folds also make it difficult to assign this significant painter to a particular school. However, the vivid tones suggest an Eastern master. The transitions in color are so purposeful that at first one is almost tempted to think of a painter from the period of the Palaeologi. The iconography and style recall Byzantine art of the sixth century. A relationship has also been suggested with the frescoes in Santa Maria Antiqua, for instance with the Annunciation by a Greek master, but the style of these shows less plasticity.

These works mark the end of early Byzantine painting. In 725 Leo III launched his assault against images. Earlier religious paintings were destroyed and nothing new was created. Not until 843 did the controversy finally end with victory over the Iconoclasts. The anniversary of the restoration of images is to this day solemnly celebrated in the Eastern Church as the Feast of Orthodoxy. *220*

The great losses in monumental painting and sculpture of the sixth century are partly compensated for by the surviving Byzantine ivories and silverwork. As for the fifth century in the West, so in Constantinople for the sixth, consular diptychs provide a chronological framework for stylistically related pieces. The earliest preserved consular diptych from Constantinople is that of Areobindus (506), the latest that of Justinus (540). The rapid stylistic development away from Western products of the fifth century can be seen from a comparison of, say, the diptych of Anastasius of 517, now in Paris, with that of the consul Sividius (488), also in Paris. The Byzantine piece shows a stronger sense of volume; the consul is seen enthroned on his *sella curulis*, wearing an embroidered *toga contabulata*, holding in his right hand a *mappa* with which he gives the signal for the circus games to begin, and in his left a scepter surmounted by a portrait of the emperor. The circus scenes with animals in the lower part of the panels have a lively sense of movement. *219*

This marked artistic revival sets in at the turn of the century, as the diptych of Areobindus shows. The rendering of the figure is still somewhat schematic but by the time of Justinian—witness the diptych of Justinus (540), now in Berlin—it gains in plasticity and characterization. At the same time frontality is more strictly observed in ivories than in painting.

Another series of ivories can be classified with these diptychs. Thus the diptych of Anastasius is stylistically so close to the triumphant emperor on the Barberini diptych, now in the Louvre, that the latter has also been thought to be Anastasius I. The lively portrayal and the articulate treatment of relief are evidence of an imitation of classical models. Alexandrian products may have been an influence here. Similar in style and technique are the six panels in high relief in the treasury of the Cathedral of Aachen. The figure of Bacchus, ensconced in vine scrolls, and those of the Nereids recall both in subject and in style Alexandrian art, especially the mass-produced Hellenistic bone carvings. The so-called Ariadne relief, now in the Musée Cluny, Paris, also fits into this group. It is a typical instance of the classicizing pieces which, like the contemporary silver, are strongly influenced by Hellenistic art. A certain mannerism in the drapery is characteristic for them, and appears already in the well-known ivory diptych in Monza of a poet and his muse. The poet has been identified both with contemporaries such as Ausonius and Claudius Claudianus, and with persons from antiquity, such as Seneca. The latter identification seems the more probable. *221* *223*

39

Whereas the Byzantine provenance of these pieces may be established easily, greater caution is indicated in the case of the five-part religious diptych from Murano now in Ravenna. Stylistically the diptych does have affinities with this group, particularly with the circus scenes on the diptychs of Areobindus and Anastasius, and there are similarities in the heads. But iconographically it is somewhat different from metropolitan works and is closer to works from Asia Minor and Syria. Thus the Murano panel cannot be localized definitely in Constantinople. The problem is similar to the one we have already encountered in connection with the three purple codices, in particular the Codex Rossanensis, and the explanation may well be that they were made in a place in Asia Minor or Syria which was under strong metropolitan influence. The panel with the Virgin from the Murano diptych, in the John Rylands Library in Manchester, is iconographically very close to the ivory relief with the enthroned Virgin and the three Magi, in the British Museum. But in the latter, as in the diptych of Anastasius or that of Magnus (518), the forms are clearer and more plastic.

226–235
224, 225

The transition in Byzantium to true Justinian style is marked by two fine panels portraying empresses, one enthroned, the other standing, now in Florence and Vienna respectively. The imperial majesty expressed in them recalls the representation of Theodora in San Vitale. The unusual panel in the cathedral treasury at Trier, depicting the translation, in 415, of the relics of Joseph and Zacharias by the patriarch Atticus, belongs to the same phase. Two other important works in this group are the diptych with Christ on one leaf, the Virgin and Child on the other, in Berlin, and the Chair of Maximian in the Museo Arcivescovile in Ravenna. A monogram on the bottom edge of the Berlin diptych, partly cut off, has been interpreted as that of Archbishop Maximian of Ravenna. If Maximian commissioned the piece, Ravenna suggests itself as the place of origin, but the style is entirely Constantinopolitan. Its eclectic, somewhat dry treatment of folds recalls distantly the wonderful panel with an archangel in the British Museum. Particularly impressive is the majestic bearing of Christ: a fully frontal, carefully balanced figure, the type showing obvious affinities with imperial portraits. One is reminded of the enthroned Christ in Sant' Apollinare Nuovo. The five figures on the front side of the episcopal throne in Ravenna belong to the same school. Though the drapery is harsher and the heads more naturalistic, the general style is the same as that of the Berlin diptych. The monogram on the front side below the seat is today generally admitted to be that of Maximian (546–556), which offers a basis for dating. The problem of provenance on the other hand has not, so far, been solved. A number of scholars incline to favor Alexandria, others have staked claims variously for Antioch, Constantinople, and Ravenna. A further complication is that three or four different styles can be distinguished among the panels comprising the chair, which suggests the participation of several artists. Iconographically too the various cycles differ from each other. However, the Byzantine style dominates.

226–229

226, 232–235

230–233

234, 235

The main artist, to whom the figures on the front side are to be attributed, was evidently a votary of Byzantine court art. The ornamental bands with their sharply cut acanthus leaves must also be the work of a master who was acquainted with sculptural decoration in Constantinople, especially in Hagia Sophia. The vine scrolls recall Egyptian bone carving. The scenes from the life of Christ on both sides of the back are in a very different, pronouncedly flat style. Iconographically, Syrian art may have been an influence. While the two artists responsible respectively for the front side figures and for the scenes on the back are contemporary, the style of the story of Joseph on the sides suggests an earlier date. These scenes have more movement, the actions have greater realism, and the rendering of space is that of an earlier generation. The same style is to be found in a group of pyxides, exemplified by the one with the sacrifice to Isis in Wiesbaden, and the one with the legend of St. Menas in the British Museum. These ivory reliefs are closely connected with the Egyptian school of the end of the fifth century. Oddly enough, the panels of the Joseph cycle are not in the correct historical sequence,

236

which suggests that they may be earlier than the chair and were incorporated in it as ready-made decoration. The presence of several styles in the carving of the chair can perhaps be accounted for by supposing that Maximian commissioned the piece from a Ravenna workshop which had several artists working for it. Had the chair been made in Constantinople, the style would probably have been more unified.

254
248
237

In these works the style of sixth-century Byzantine art, both metropolitan and as practiced in Ravenna, can be clearly recognized. It is interesting to follow its spread from Constantinople to both the East and the West. The manner of the Eastern provinces is most apparent in pieces like the five-part diptych with Christ and Mary at the Monastery of Etschmiadzin in Armenia. In the West, too, various workshops seem to have adopted the Byzantine style. Thus in Gaul a number of Byzantinizing reliefs were produced, such as the five-part diptych from St. Lupicin in the Bibliothèque Nationale in Paris, the diptych in Saulieu, and figures of individual Apostles, such as the one in Tongres and in Brussels, or the ones from Mettlach in the Metropolitan Museum. These reliefs have a harsh style and heavy folds; they are late examples of a provincial art considerably removed from their models.

The same development of sixth-century Byzantine silver parallels that of the ivories. Numerous pieces have been found in South Russia, especially near the Black Sea, most of which are today in the Hermitage in Leningrad, among them the silver dish from the district of Poltava with a cross between two angels. In the Mediterranean region important treasures have been found at Stuma, Cyprus, Lesbos, Lampsacus, Canicattini Bagni, and Canoscio. Many of these silver pieces carry official stamps, often imperial monograms, impressed on them during production in the imperial workshops. On the basis of these control marks they can be securely dated.

255

There are pieces made for secular use with the stamps of Anastasius I (491–518), Justinian (527–565), and Phocas (602–610), and the dishes from Cyprus belong to the reign of Heraclius (610–641). Other items can be identified by the names of those who commissioned them, for instance the dish of Bishop Paternus (ca. 519) in Leningrad, or the cross of Justin II (565–578) in St. Peter's in Rome. Frequently, as in Cyprus, the treasure finds contain not only stamped silver pieces, but also goldsmiths' work in which coins are used as part of the ornament, so that there are two independent sources for establishing a chronology. The rich treasure of Assiut includes very fine pieces of this type—arm bands, large collar chains with pendants (encolpia) whose coin decoration gives them their approximate date. These examples show that, about 500, Byzantine metalwork was also affected by the marked classicizing trends. As for Theodosian art, so the models for the silver pieces of the sixth century were Hellenistic works, especially those of Alexandrian origin with their marine motifs, sea animals, putti, and mythological scenes. The copying is sometimes so exact that, without the imperial stamps, one would often be reluctant to consider them later copies. Yet a comparison with their models does reveal differences: in the sixth-century pieces the chasing is harder and stands out more sharply against the background, and in the late fourth-century pieces the differences are even more pronounced, as may be seen from a comparison with pieces like the Parabiago dish.

107
246
249, 250

245
221

Works with Christian motifs, like the vase from Emesa (Homs) in Paris, also frequently imitate the Hellenistic manner. The dishes with scenes from the life of David from Cyprus most probably drew on contemporary manuscript illuminations. How close a stylistic kinship existed between these silver pieces and contemporary ivories is revealed by a comparison of, say, the dish in Leningrad representing a cross between two angels with the diptych in Monza showing a poet and his muse.

247

A number of unstamped silver pieces found in Syria, such as those from Antioch, now in New York, those from Riha, now in Dumbarton Oaks, and those from Hama, now in Baltimore, are rather different from

Byzantine works. The subjects are portrayed with greater freedom and realism, the drapery is more linear, the relief flatter. In some cases the exact provenance is still unknown. An intermediary stage is exemplified by the Communion of the Apostles on the paten from Stuma, now in Istanbul, which carries the stamps of Justin II (565–578), although the style of the figures is closest to such Syrian works as the paten from Riha. To this group of objects should also be attributed several gold pendants, although they are technically closer to coins and medals and have strong iconographic affinities with the ampullae of Monza. The most characteristic is perhaps the large pendant from the Cyprus treasure, dating after the period of Justinian, now at Dumbarton Oaks. The pendant medallion from Adana, now in Istanbul, with a series of scenes from the life of Christ, also recalls in its technique contemporary Byzantine coins. The representations are closely related to the monumental painting of Palestine which was disseminated throughout the Christian world by devotional pieces acquired by returning pilgrims.

No Byzantine silver pieces made after the reign of Heraclius have so far come to light. Their production must have declined rapidly as a result of worsening economic conditions.

The picture of early Byzantine art would not be complete without a mention of the wealth of precious textiles turned out by the imperial workshops. Contemporary authors and the *Liber pontificalis* are full of references to stuffs of rare magnificence presented to churches and palaces by the emperors in Constantinople or the popes in Rome. Agnellus tells of the gifts of Maximian to the various churches in Ravenna, and the *Liber pontificalis* gives detailed descriptions of Byzantine, Syrian, and Egyptian silk fabrics in Rome.

These textiles offer rich comparative material, which has not so far been exploited, for the study of painting and mosaics. Frequent cases of borrowing can be established. In Constantinople the silk industry had enjoyed special imperial encouragement and protection since Constantine's time and reached its highest development under Justinian.

Above all, Justinian introduced the silkworm into Byzantium, thus making raw silk obtainable locally and avoiding the expense of the long trip from China and the duties levied in Persia. Persian weavers seem to have been employed in Constantinople, which may account for the frequent copying of Persian fabrics during the sixth and seventh centuries; the imperial piece from Mozac, now in Lyons, is an example. At the same time Hellenistic patterns of scattered foliage were also very popular down to the time of Justinian. It has not, so far, been possible to make a clear distinction between the Byzantine products and those manufactured elsewhere, especially in Syria. The motifs on the fabric from the Sancta Sanctorum at St. John Lateran, now in the Vatican, strongly recall Byzantine miniature painting. The heavy silk twill with a red background belonging to this group—to which the piece with Samson fighting the lion, preserved in several copies, also belongs—could equally well be a product of the celebrated Syrian workshops.

After the period of Justinian, Hellenistic motifs disappear progressively from Byzantine textiles, the dominant influence becoming that of Eastern, especially Persian, workshops, so that in textiles particularly there is a complete break with the classical tradition.

With this break the last chapter of antique art comes to a close. A great era of world history has come to an end. The change is marked by the Iconoclastic controversy which is to be accounted for partly by the preponderance of the Eastern spirit. New peoples, above all Islam, appear on the historical scene. Economic conditions in the Christian East and in Italy are transformed, new political and artistic trends come to the surface, and the Carolingian renaissance in the North and the end of the Iconoclastic controversy in the East bring forth a new world.

1   Istanbul, Archeological Museum. Emperor Diocletian from Nicomedia (284–305)

2  Salonika, Arch of Galerius with triumphs from the Emperor's Persian campaign, 297. S. pillar, E.side. c. 297–305

3   Salonika, Arch of Galerius with triumphs from the Emperor's Persian campaign, 297. S. pillar, N. side. c. 297–305

4   Rome, Santa Maria Antiqua. Sarcophagus, c. 270. Above: general view. Below: middle section, Orans and Philosopher

5 Rome, Santa Maria Antiqua. Sarcophagus, c. 270. Above: left half, Jonah. Below: right half, the Good Shepherd and Baptism of Christ

6 Rome, Lateran Museum. Sarcophagus, second half of IVth century. The Good Shepherd and the Vintage

7 Above: Rome, Catacomb of St. Callixtus. The Good Shepherd, middle of IIIrd century.
Below: Rome, Catacomb of St. Domitilla. Christ and the Twelve Apostles, middle of IVth century

8  Above: Rome, Catacomb of St. Callixtus. Orans, beginning of IVth century.
Below: Rome, Catacomb of St. Priscilla. Orans and Mary with Christ-Child (?), end of IIIrd century

9   Above: Rome, Catacomb of St. Priscilla. The three youths in the furnace, beginning of IVth century.
Below: Rome, Catacomb of St. Callixtus. Moses striking the rock, end of IVth century

10    Above: Rome, Catacomb of St. Domitilla. Christ, middle of IVth century. Cf. Pl. 7 below.
Below: Rome, Catacomb of Vigna Massimo. Portrait of a deceased woman, first half of IVth century

11 Gilded glasses, IVth. century. Above, left: Paris, Petit Palais. Double portrait.
Below, left: London, British Museum. Double portrait. Right: Paris, Cabinet des Médailles. Pope Callixtus

12   Florence, Archeological Museum. Two oil-lamps, IVth century.
Left: Moses striking the rock. Right: Christ and St. Peter in a boat

13 Hartford (Conn.), Wadsworth Atheneum. Lamp, IVth century

14   Rome, Arch of Constantine from the North. 312–315

15  Rome, Arch of Constantine, 312–315. Relief frieze with scenes from the Emperor's political and military achievements

16 Rome, Palace of the Curators. Constantine the Great (306–337). Head of a seated portrait, marble, from the Basilica of Maxentius

17  Rome, Palace of the Curators. Constantine the Great (306–337). Head of a seated portrait, marble, from the Basilica of Maxentius

18   Rome, Palace of the Curators. Colossal bronze head of Constantius II (324–361). c. 360

19   Rome, Palace of the Curators. Colossal bronze head of Constantius II (324–361). c. 360

20  Paris, Cabinet des Médailles. Constantine the Great (?). Chalcedony bust, IVth century

21  Coin-portraits. Above, centre: Constantius I Chlorus (293-305). Aureus. Above, left and right: Constantine the Great (306-337).
Gold solidus. Centre: Helen, Constantine the Great's mother (d. 336). Gold medallion. Below: Constantine the Great (306-337).
Gold medallion, obverse and reverse.

22 Rome, Vatican. Museo Pio-Clementino. Porphyry sarcophagus of St. Helen (d. 356).
Roman equestrians and captive Barbarians, second quarter of IVth century

25    Rome, Vatican. Museo Pio-Clementino. Porphyry sarcophagus of St. Helen (d. 336),
mother of Constantine the Great, second quarter of IVth century

24   Rome, Vatican. Museo Pio-Clementino. Porphyry sarcophagus of Constantina, daughter of Constantine the Great, IVth century

25   Venice, St. Mark's, S. side. Porphyry group of the Emperor's Diocletian, Maximianus, Galerius and Constantius I. Chlorus, c. 300

26   Rome, Baptistery of the Lateran, IVth and Vth centuries

27  Rome, Baptistery of the Lateran, interior

28  Rome, Santo Stefano Rotondo from the West, Vth century

29  Rome, Santa Costanza from the West, first half of IVth. century

50   Rome, Santa Costanza, interior. View from the entrance looking East, first half of IVth century

31  Rome, Santa Costanza, interior. View of the S. ambulatory

32 Rome, Santa Costanza. Part of the mosaics in the N. ambulatorium, with a portrait of Constantina (d. 354) and Bacchic scenes

33 Rome, Santa Costanza. Above: mosaic in apse of S. ambulatorium, Christ enthroned upon the globe.
Below: mosaic in apse of N. ambulatorium, the giving of the Law, Christ between SS. Peter and Paul

34   Rome, Santa Costanza. Part of a mosaic in the vault of the S. ambulatorium

35   Rome, Santa Costanza. Mosaics in the vault of the E. ambulatorium

56   Rome, National Museum. Christ enthroned, statuette. c. 350–360

37   Syracuse, National Museum. Sarcophagus of Adelphia. c. 340. Below: detail, with Adoration of the Magi

38   Syracuse, National Museum. Sarcophagus of Adelphia. Above: Feeding of the Five Thousand and Raising of the Widow's son
Below: Christ's entry into Jerusalem

39  Syracuse, National Museum. Sarcophagus of Adelphia. Double portrait of Adelphia and her husband. c. 340

40    Above: Rome, Lateran Museum. Sarcophagus with Biblical scenes, end of IIIrd century.
Below: Paris, Louvre. Chest-sarcophagus, VIth–VIIth century

41    Vatican, Grottoes of St. Peter's. Sarcophagus of the Roman Prefect Junius Bassus (d. 359)

42    Vatican, Grottoes of St. Peter's. Sarcophagus of Junius Bassus.
Above: Christ as Judge between SS. Peter and Paul. Below: Christ's entry into Jerusalem

43   Vatican, Grottoes of St. Peter's. Sarcophagus of Junius Bassus. Adam and Eve

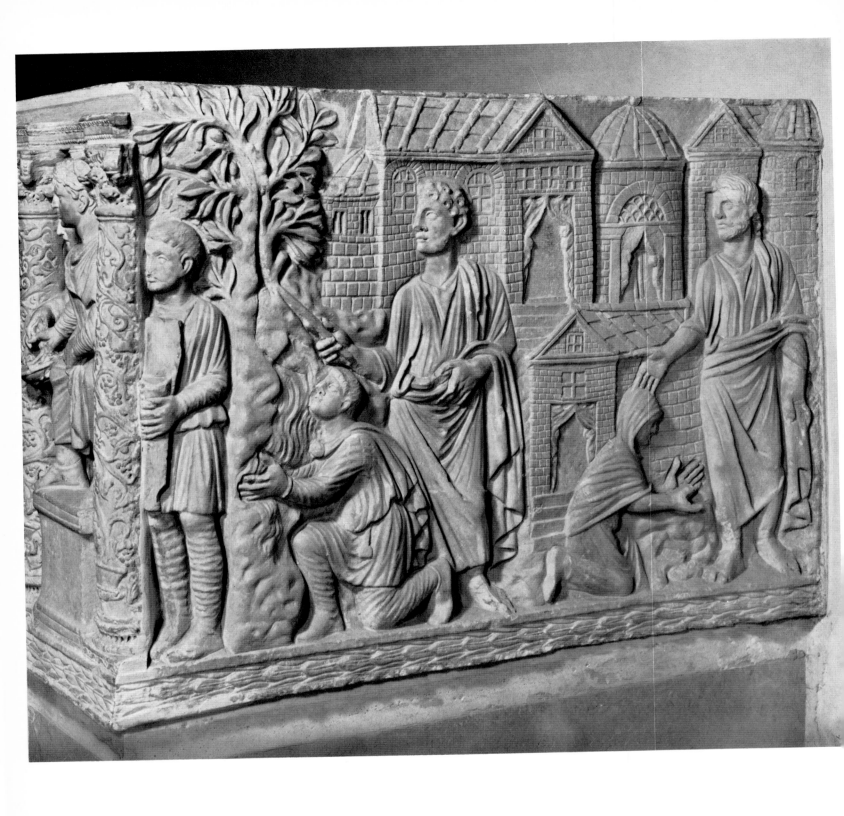

44    Vatican, Grottoes of St. Peter's. Narrow end of a sarcophagus, right side.
Healing of the woman with an issue of blood and cursing of the fig-tree, middle of IVth century. Cf. Pl. 45

45   Vatican, Grottoes of St. Peter's. Central part of sarcophagus. Christ gives St. Peter the Law, middle of IVth century

46  Milan, Sant'Ambrogio. Sarcophagus, end of IVth century. Narrow end: Ascension of Elijah. Back: Christ teaches the Apostles

47    Milan, Sant'Ambrogio. Sarcophagus, end of IVth century. Narrow end: Sacrifice of Isaac. Front: Christ giving the law

48 Paris, Louvre. Emperor Julian the Apostate (361–365)

49   Paris, Louvre. Emperor Julian the Apostate (361–363)

50   Istanbul, Archeological Museum. Emperor Valentinianus II (375–392), from Aphrodisias. c. 390

51    Istanbul, Archeological Museum. Emperor Valentinianus II (375–392), from Aphrodisias

52    Coin-portraits. Above, left and right: Constantius II (337-361). Gold solidus. Above, centre: Julian the Apostate (361-363). Gold
solidus. Centre. left: Theodosius I (379-395). Gold solidus. Centre, right: Aelia Flaccilla, wife of Theodosius I (d. 388). Bronze.
Below, centre: Galla Placidia (d. 450). Gold solidus (above) and silver siliqua (below). Below, left: Honorius (393-423). Gold solidus.
Below, right: Constantius III, husband of Galla Placidia (407-411). Gold solidus

53  Madrid, Academy. Missorium of Emperor Theodosius I. 388.

54 Istanbul, Hippodrome, Obelisk of Theodosius. Base-relief on S.E. side with Emperor Theodosius and sons watching chariot-race. c. 390

55  Istanbul, Hippodrome. Obelisk of Theodosius. Base-relief on N.W. side, with Emperor Theodosius,
his two sons Arcadius and Honorius and Valentinianus II. at chariot-race; also Persians and Dacians bearing tribute. c. 390

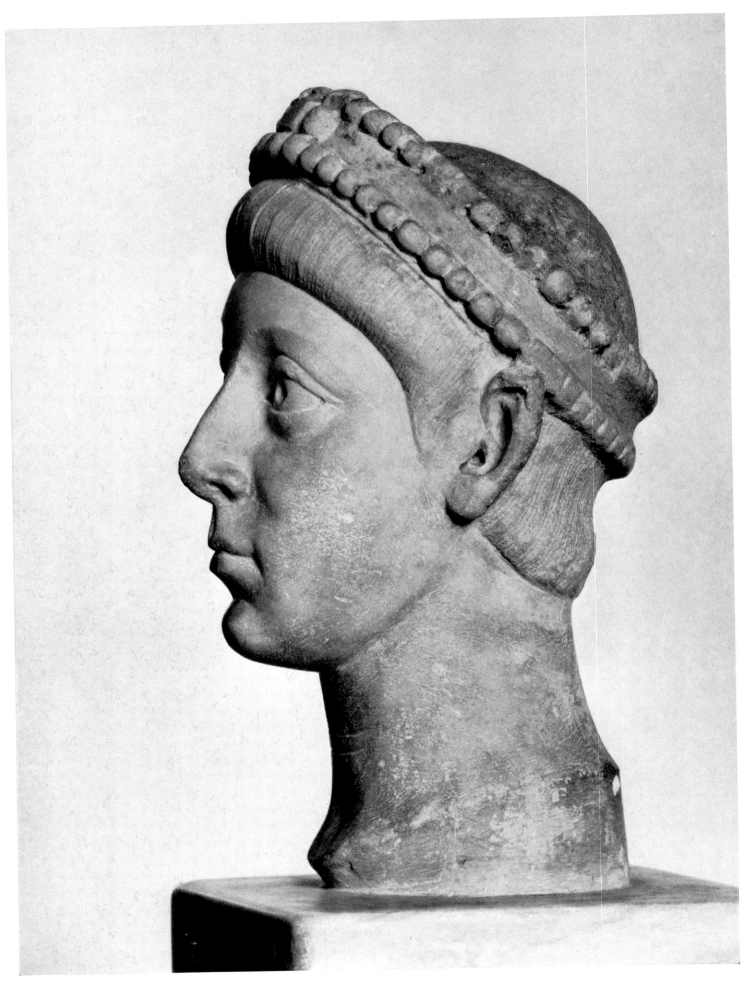

56   Istanbul, Archeological Museum. Emperor Arcadius (383–408)

57   Istanbul, Archeological Museum. Emperor Arcadius (383–408)

58    Paris, Cabinet des Médailles. Aelia Flaccilla (d. 388), wife of Emperor Theodosius I (?)

59   Paris, E. de Rothschild Collection. Cameo with Honorius and Mary. 398

60   Brescia, Museo Civico. Cross (VIIth–VIIIth century) with gilded glass portrait (IVth century). Cf. Pl. 61

61   Brescia, Museo Civico. Gilded glass with portrait of mother and two children, IVth century

62   Monza, Cathedral Treasury. Serena with her son Eucherius. Ivory diptych, left panel. c. 400. Cf. Pl. 63

63   Monza, Cathedral Treasury. Stilicho (c. 360–408) Ivory diptych, right panel. c. 400. Cf. Pl. 62

SPQR
RINVENUTA NEL VIALE PRINCIPESSA MARGHERITA
IL DC III GIUGNO MDCCCLXXIX

64   Rome, Palace of the Curators. Roman Consul. c. 400

65   Istanbul, Archeological Museum. High official from Aphrodisias, c. 410

66   Istanbul, Archeological Museum. Head of high official from Aphrodisias, beginning of Vth century. Cf. P. 67

67  Istanbul, Archeological Museum. High official from Aphrodisias, beginning of Vth century

68   Milan, Castello Sforzesco. Head of an Empress, middle of Vth century

69  Barletta. Colossal Statue of Emperor Marcianus (450–457)

70   Barletta. Head of Emperor Marcianus. Cf. Pl. 69

71   Barletta. Head of Emperor Marcianus. Cf. Pl. 69

72   Istanbul, Archeological Museum. Victory. Constantinople, Vth century

73   Berlin, State Museums. Fragment of a sarcophagus (?) from Constantinople. Christ between two Apostles. c. 400

74 Istanbul, Archeological Museum. Bust of an Evangelist from Constantinople. c. 450

75   Istanbul, Archeological Museum. Child's sarcophagus, second half of IVth century

76    Istanbul, Archeological Museum. Part of drum of a column with vine and ornamental figures, Vth century
Above: Pair with sacrifical animals. Below: Baptism of Christ

77   Istanbul, Archeological Museum. Part of drum of a column with vine and ornamental figures. Shepherd with dog, goat and bull,
Vth century

78  Istanbul, Archeological Museum. Chancel from Salonika. Details from left and right sides of chancel:
One of the three Magi and Mary with the Christ-child, second half of Vth century

79  Istanbul, Archeological Museum. Chancel from Salonika. Side of right half of chancel: Mary with the Christ-child and Angels,
second half of Vth century

80    Istanbul, Archeological Museum. Balusters with acanthus and ivy leaves. Mythological scenes at the ends, middle of Vth century

81   Istanbul, Archeological Museum. Relief.
Entry into Jerusalem, from the Church of St. John the Baptist in the Studios Cloister, Constantinople, late Vth century

82   Venice, St. Mark's, Vth century (?). Left front column of ciborium, three lower scenes from left to right.
Lowest scene : Visitation and Birth of Christ. Second scene : St. Joseph and the Good Tidings to the Shepherds.
Third scene : Adoration of the Magi

85    Venice, St. Mark's. Vth century(?). Right front column of ciborium.
Below: The Maries and the Angel at the Sepulchre. Above: Christ in Limbo

84   Bobbio, San Colombano. Ivory pyxis with Orpheus, end of IVth century

85   Brescia, Museo Civico. Ivory casket. General view, second half of IVth century

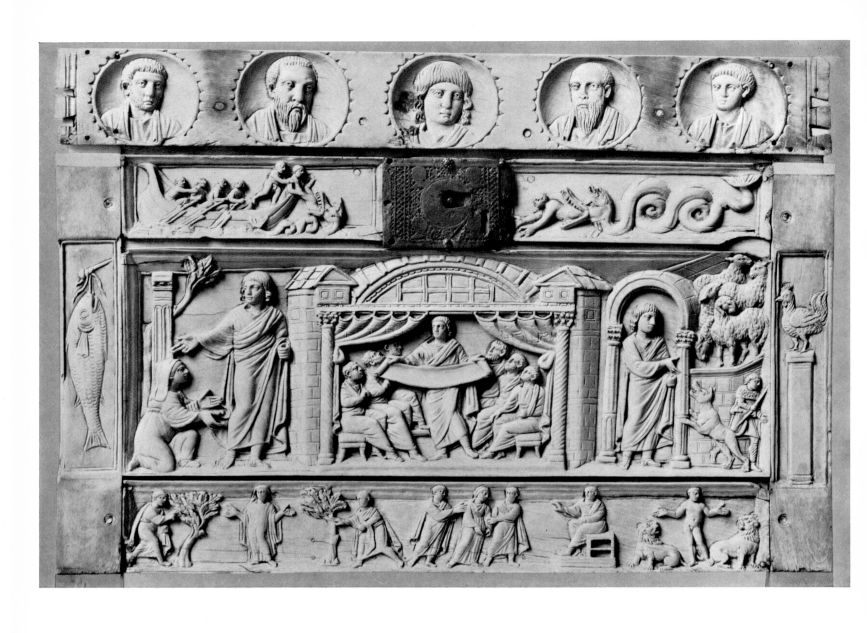

86　Brescia, Museo Civico. Ivory casket. Front, Christ among the Apostles, (centre). Christ as Good Shepherd (right).
Healing of the woman with an issue of blood (left)

87  Brescia, Museo Civico. Ivory casket. Back, Christ with two Apostles on the lake (left). Ananias and Sapphira (right and centre)

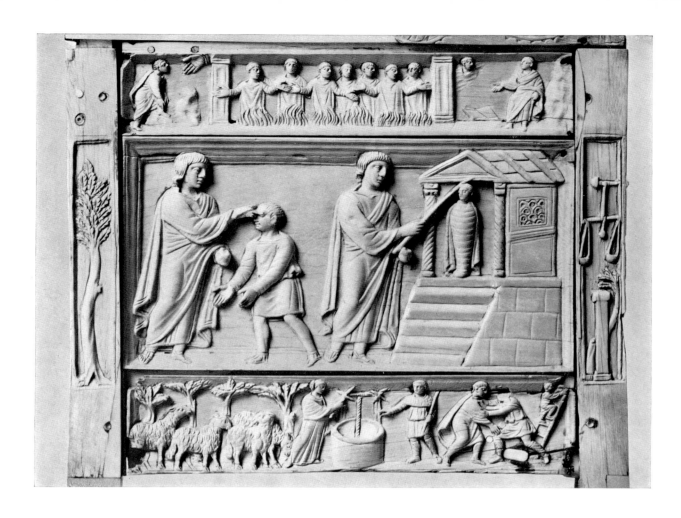

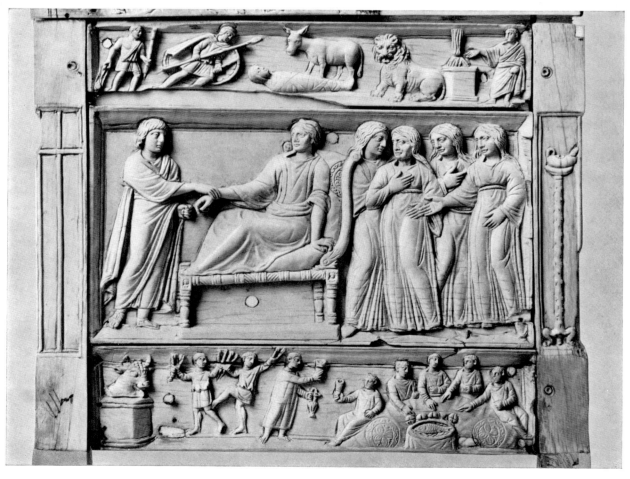

88   Brescia, Museo Civico. Ivory casket. Above (right side of casket): Healing of the Blind and Raising of Lazarus.
Below (left side of casket): Jairus' Daughter.

89   Brescia, Museo Civico. Ivory casket. Lid.
Upper part: Christ in Gethsemane, Taking of Christ and Peter's Denial. Lower part: Christ before Caiaphas and Pilate

90 Paris, Cluny Museum. Ivory diptych of the Nicomachi and Symmachi, end of IVth century. Left panel: Ceres-priestess before the altar of Cybele.

SYMMACHORVM

91    London, Victoria and Albert Museum. Ivory diptych of the Nicomachi and Symmachi, end of IVth century.
Right panel: Bacchus-priestess with handmaid before altar

92   Milan, Castello Sforzesco. Leaf of ivory diptych. Women at the Sepulchre. c. 400

SYMMACHORVM

91   London, Victoria and Albert Museum. Ivory diptych of the Nicomachi and Symmachi, end of IVth century.
Right panel: Bacchus-priestess with handmaid before altar

92    Milan, Castello Sforzesco. Leaf of ivory diptych. Women at the Sepulchre. c. 400

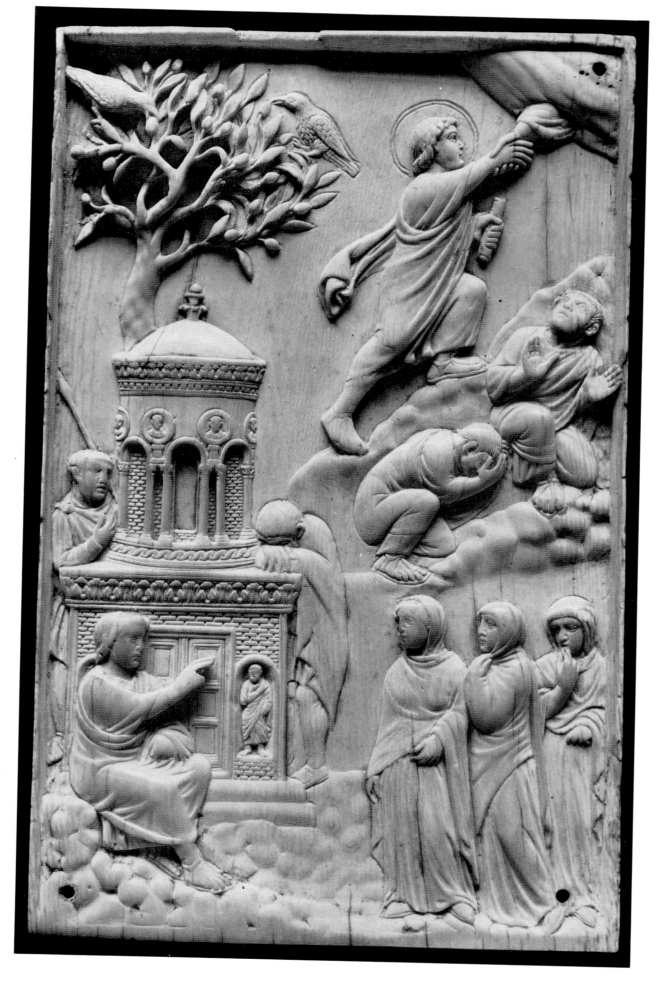

93   Munich, Bavarian National Museum. Ivory panel. Women at the Sepulchre and Ascension of Christ. c. 400

94   London, British Museum. Ivory panel. Bellerophon, Vth century

95   Berlin, State Museums. Ivory pyxis. Christ among the Apostles and Abraham's Sacrifice. c. 400

96  Paris, Cabinet des Médailles. Ivory diptych panel. Consul Felix, Rome, 428

97   Left: Paris, Cabinet des Médailles. Ivory diptych panel. Consul Sividius, Rome, 488
Right: Florence, National Museum. Ivory diptych panel. Consul Basilius, Rome, 480

98   London, British Museum. Two sides of an ivory casket with scenes of the Passion. c. 420–430.
Below: Death of Judas and Crucifixion. Above: Pilate, Christ carrying the Cross, Peter's Denial

99   Paris, Louvre. Ivory panel. Apostle, first half of Vth century

100    Milan, Cathedral Treasury. Five-part ivory diptych, second half of Vth century. Left panel, cf. Pl. 101.
Above: Birth of Christ. Left: Annunciation; the Magi gazing at the Star; Baptism of Christ.
Right: Mary at the Temple; Christ among the Doctors; Entry into Jerusalem. Below: Massacre of the Innocents

101    Milan, Cathedral Treasury. Five-part ivory diptych, second half of Vth century. Right panel, cf. Pl. 100.
Above: Adoration of the Magi. Left: Healing of the Blind; Healing of the Lame; Raising of Lazarus.
Rigth: Christ between two of the Blessed; the Last Supper; the Widow's Mite. Below: The Miracle of Cana

102    Milan, Museum of Sant'Ambrogio. Fragments of the wooden doors of Sant'Ambrogio, end of IVth century. Scenes from the life of David

105    Rome, Santa Sabina. Wooden doors of W. portal. c. 430

104 Rome, Santa Sabina. Details from wooden doors of W. portal. c. 450
Two reliefs. Left: Crossing of the Red Sea; Bronze Serpent. Right: Ascension of Elijah

105 Rome, Santa Sabina. Details from wooden doors of W. portal. c. 450. Relief: Zacharias is struck dumb before the Temple

106   Berlin, State Museums. Silver plate with Artemis. End of IVth century

107  Milan, Castello Sforzesco. Silver plate from Parabiago with Cybele and Atthis, end of IVth century

108    Cesena, Biblioteca Malatestiana. Silver plate, end of IVth century. Feast of the Gods

109  Florence, Archeological Museum. Missorium of Consul Ardabur Aspar. 434

110   Milan, San Nazaro Maggiore. Silver reliquary casket, end of IVth century. General view.

111 Milan, San Nazaro Maggiore. Silver reliquary casket, end of IVth century. Lid: Christ and the Apostles

112    Milan, San Nazaro Maggiore. Silver reliquary casket, end of IVth century. Front: Adoration of the Magi

115 Milan, San Nazaro Maggiore. Silver reliquary casket, end of IVth century. Back: Joseph forgives his Brethren

114   Milan, San Nazaro Maggiore. Silver reliquary casket, end of IVth century. Left side: The three youths in the furnace and an Angel

115    Milan, San Nazaro Maggiore. Silver reliquary casket, end of IVth century. Right side: Judgment of Solomon

116    London, British Museum. Part of Esquiline Treasure.
Silver bridal casket of Secundus and Proiecta. Lid with portrait of couple, three mythological scenes and betrothal. c. 380

117   London, British Museum. Part of Esquiline Treasure. c. 380. Below: general view of casket. Above: betrothal scene from lid

118   Paris, Petit Palais. Part of Esquiline Treasure. c. 380. Dish with Venus' toilet

119   Left: London, British Museum. Part of Esquiline Treasure. c. 380. Personification of Antioch.
Right, above and centre: London, British Museum. Ornamental gold buckle, front and back, IVth century.
Below: Berlin, State Museums. Gold bracelet. c. 400

120   Paris, Louvre. Silver pyxis, Vth century. Below: view from front with Adoration of the Magi. Above: lid with the Raising of Lazarus

121  Left: Vatican, Christian Museum. Silver jug with medallions of the Apostles, beginning of Vth century.
Right: London, British Museum. Silver flagon with Healing of the Blind, beginning of Vth century

122   Salonika, Hagios Georgios. View from the apse of the presbyterium looking N.W. Beginning and end of IVth century

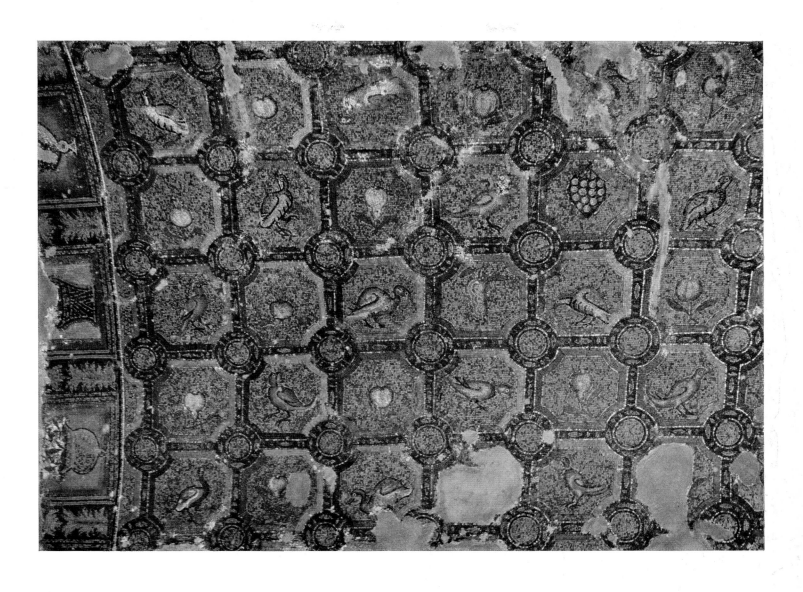

123   Salonika, Hagios Georgios. Mosaic of the barrel-vault above the S. niche, c. 400

124    Salonika, Hagios Georgios. Part of mosaic frieze in dome. Left: St. Onesiphoros, right: St. Porphyrios, c. 400

125  Salonika, Hagios Georgios. Part of mosaic frieze in dome.
Left: an unknown saint (name destroyed), right: St. Damian, c. 400

126   Salonika, Hagios Georgios. St. Onesiphoros. Cf. Pl. 124

127 Salonika, Hagios Georgios. St. Porphyrios. Cf. Pl. 124

128   Rome, Santa Maria Maggiore. Part of mosaic frieze in central nave. The Jews rebel against Moses, second quarter of Vth century

129   Rome, Santa Maria Maggiore. Part of mosaic frieze in central nave. Crossing of the Red Sea, second quarter of Vth century

130   Rome, Santa Pudenziana. Mosaic in the apse. Christ teaching the Apostles in the Heavenly Jerusalem. 401–417

131   Rome, Santa Maria Maggiore. View of interior, second quarter of Vth century

AMBROSIVS          NAVOR

152    Milan, Sant'Ambrogio: San Vittore in Ciel d'Oro. Part of a mural mosaic: SS. Ambrose and Nabor, beginning of Vth century

133   Salonika, Hosios David. Part of mosaic in apse. Ezechiel and the Lion of St. Mark, middle of Vth century

134    Salonika, Hosios David. Mosaic in apse. Christ and the Symbol of St. Matthew, middle of Vth century

135   Salonika, Hosios David. Part of mosaic in apse. Majestas Domini, with Ezechiel and Habakkuk, middle of Vth century

136    Milan, Sant'Aquilino and San Lorenzo from the S. E., middle of Vth century

157   Milan, San Lorenzo. Interior from the South, Vth century

138    Milan, Sant'Aquilino. Mosaic in apse. Christ with the Apostles, middle of Vth century

139    Ravenna, Orthodox Baptistery. (Battistero Neoniano) consecrated c. 458. Exterior from the East

140   Ravenna, Orthodox Baptistery. Consecrated c. 458. Interior seen from the entrance

141   Ravenna, Orthodox Baptistery. Dome, Baptism of Christ in the centre, surrounded by the Apostles. Below, architectural motives with
altars and thrones. c. 430–458

142   Ravenna, Orthodox Baptistery.

Above: from the dome, the Apostles Paul, Peter and Andrew. Below: mosaic ornament of the marble facing on the lower wall

143   Ravenna, Orthodox Baptistery. Stucco figures (Prophets) around the windows

144   Ravenna, Mausoleum of Galla Placidia (d. 450), from the S. W.

145  Ravenna, Mausoleum of Galla Placidia (d. 450). Interior seen from entrance

146    Ravenna, Mausoleum of Galla Placidia (d. 450). Mosaic lunette on back wall with St. Lawrence going to martyrdom

147   Ravenna, Mausoleum of Galla Placidia (d. 450). Mosaic lunette on the entrance wall with Christ as Good Shepherd

148    Ravenna, Archiepiscopal Chapel. c. 494–519. Mosaic in ceiling.
Four floating angels with sacred monogram, also the symbols of the four Evangelists

149    Ravenna, Arian Baptistery. c. 500Mosaic in the dome, Baptism of Christ, the twelve Apostles before the throne of the Apocalypse.

150   Ravenna, Sant'Apollinare Nuovo. Part of upper mosaic frieze in nave. Christ blesses the loaves and fishes. c. 500–526

151   Ravenna, Sant'Apollinare Nuovo. Part of upper mosaic frieze in nave. Christ separates the sheep from the goats. c. 500–526

152    Ravenna, Sant'Apollinare Nuovo. Part of lower mosaic frieze in nave. Palace of Theodoric. c. 500–526 (above)
below: Female Saints and the Magi (c. 568), Mary with Angels (c. 500–526)

+SCS BALTHASSAR +SCS MELCHIOR +SCS GASPAR

153    Ravenna, Sant'Apollinare Nuovo. Part of lower mosaic frieze in nave. The three Magi. c. 568

154   Ravenna, Mausoleum of Theodoric (d. 526)

155    Ravenna, San Vitale from the South. c. 525–547, consecrated in 547

156   Ravenna, San Vitale, interior, ambulatorium N.

157 Ravenna, San Vitale. View of interior looking towards the presbyterium. c. 525–547, consecrated in 547

158  Ravenna, San Vitale. Mosaic in apse. Christ between two Angels and SS. Vitalis and Ecclesius

159   Ravenna, San Vitale. View of the N.E. side of the presbyterium with mosaic. Abraham's Sacrifice

160   Ravenna, San Vitale. S.W. wall and ceiling of presbyterium, looking upwards. In the lunette: Sacrifice of Abel and of Melchisidech

161    Ravenna, San Vitale. Vault of presbyterium and middle of wall arch

162     Ravenna, San Vitale. Above: Arch and capitals from upper triphorium on N. E. side of the presbyterium.
Below: Arch and capitals from upper triphorium on S. W. side of the presbyterium

163   Ravenna, San Vitale. View of the columns of the  S.W. wall of the presbyterium

164   Ravenna, San Vitale, consecrated 547. Mosaic. Emperor Justinian with Bishop Maximianus and his suite

165    Ravenna, San Vitale, consecrated 547. Mosaic. Empress Theodora and her Ladies

166   Ravenna, San Vitale. Part of mosaic: Emperor Justinian with Bishop Maximianus and suite

167    Ravenna, San Vitale. Part of mosaic: Empress Theodora and her suite

168   Ravenna, Sant'Apollinare in Classe. Between 535 and 549. E. view

169   Ravenna, Sant'Apollinare in Classe. Between 535 and 549. W. view

170   Ravenna, Sant'Apollinare in Classe. View through the N. side-aisle

171　Ravenna, Sant'Apollinare in Classe, consecrated 549. View through the central nave

172    Ravenna, Sant'Apollinare in Classe. Mosaic in the presbyterium. St. Ursus

173   Ravenna, Sant'Apollinare in Classe. Presbyterium. c. 549

174   Ravenna, San Francesco. Sarcophagus. Christ among the Apostles and the giving of the Law to St. Paul. c. 400

175 Ravenna, San Francesco. Sarcophagus of Bishop Liberius (d. 378?). Giving of the Law to St. Paul. c. 400

176 Ravenna, National Museum. Sarcophagus with the Giving of the Law; below: detail from left side: tree with birds, beginning of Vth century

177    Ravenna, Cathedral. Sarcophagus with Christ between SS. Peter and Paul. c. 420-430

178    Ravenna, Santa Maria in Porto fuori. Sarcophagus. Giving of the Law to St. Paul, beginning of Vth century

179   Ravenna, San Vitale. Sarcophagus. The three Magi with Mary and the Christ-child. c. 400-410. Below: Mary with the Christ-child.

180   Ravenna, National Museum. Hercules chasing the hind. Low relief, Vth-VIth century

181   Ravenna, Sant'Apollinare Nuovo. Three slabs in the presbyterium, middle of VIth century

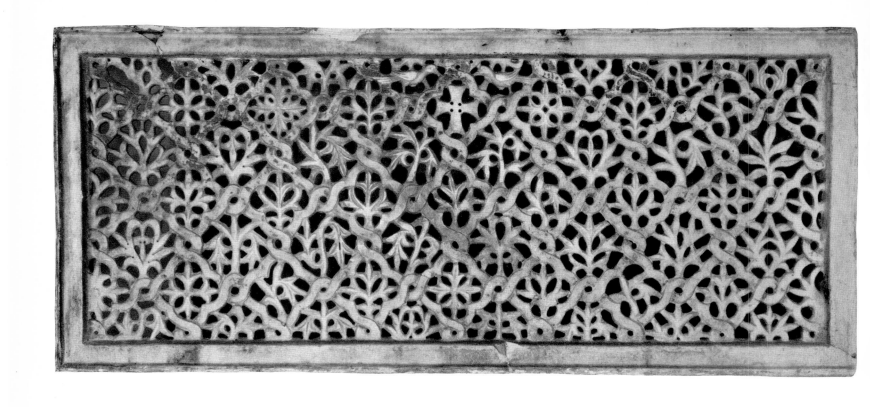

182    Ravenna, National Museum. Two slabs from the presbyterium of San Vitale, middle of VIth century

185   Ravenna, Cathedral. Marble chancel of Archbishop Agnellus (556–569)

184    Rome, San Lorenzo fuori le Mura. General view

185   Rome, San Lorenzo fuori le Mura. View from the presbyterium into the W. basilica. Mosaics on triumphal arch, end of VIth century

186  Istanbul, Hagios Sergios and Hagios Bacchos. 527. Interior looking N.W.

187   Istanbul, Hagios Sergios and Hagios Bacchos. 527. Interior looking East

188 Istanbul, Hagios Sergios and Hagios Bacchos. 527.
Above: decoration of architrave in N.W. octagon. Below: capitals from the upper gallery

189    Istanbul, Hagios Sergios and Hagios Bacchos. 527. Two columns and architrave of the lower ambulatorium in the N. octagon

190   Istanbul, Hagios Sergios and Hagios Bacchos. 527. View from N.W.

191   Istanbul, Hagia Sophia. 532–537. View from S.W. taken from a minaret of the Sultan Achmet Mosque

192    Istanbul, Hagia Sophia. 532–537. View from the East

193  Istanbul, Hagia Sophia. 532–537. View from N.W. Front of main entrance at the period of the Byzantine Empire

194    Istanbul, Hagia Sophia. 552–557. View from the middle of the N.W. gallery (reserved for the Byzantine Empresses),
looking S. E. through the church

195   Istanbul, Hagia Sophia. 532–537. View from the apse looking W.

196   Istanbul, Hagia Sophia. 532–537. Capitals and columns from the S. corner of the S.W. gallery

195  Istanbul, Hagia Sophia. 532–537. View from the apse looking W.

196 Istanbul, Hagia Sophia. 532–537. Capitals and columns from the S. corner of the S.W. gallery

197   Istanbul, Hagia Sophia. 532–537. Arcades and wall on N.E. side

198   Istanbul, Hagia Sophia. 532–537. Above: ornament on lower arcades in N. corner. Below: details of the ornament

199   Istanbul, Hagia Sophia. 532–537. View looking upwards from the S. corner of the lower ambulatorium towards the main dome and wall in the N.E.

200    Istanbul, Hagia Sophia. 532–537. Stone ornament in lower S.W. ambulatorium

201  Istanbul, Hagia Sophia. 552–537. Stone ornament in E. part of the interior, with the Sultan's Gallery resting on antique columns

202   Istanbul, Hagia Sophia. 532–557. Stone ornament in lower W. ambulatorium

203 Istanbul, Hagia Sophia. 532–537. Capital with the monogram of Justinian and architrave on S. pillar

204     Istanbul, Hagia Sophia. 532–537. Middle part of S.W. gallery with view of N.E. wall

205    Istanbul, Hagia Sophia. 532–537. S. part of S.W. gallery

206   Istanbul, Cistern Basilica. Various types of capitals

207   Istanbul, Cistern Basilica, built under Justinian I (527–565)

208   Venice, before St. Mark's. One of the two columns from San Giovanni d'Acri, VIth century

207  Istanbul, Cistern Basilica, built under Justinian I (527–565)

208　Venice, before St. Mark's. One of the two columns from San Giovanni d'Acri, VIth century

209    Above: Venice, St. Mark's. Architrave and capitals from r. side-entrance on the W. facade.
Below, left: Istanbul, Archeological Museum. Capital from Constantinople, VIth century.
right: Ravenna, National Museum. Capital from San Michele in Africisco, shortly before the middle of the VIth century

210    Venice, St.Mark's. Architrave and capitals on the N.side, VIth century

211   Venice, St. Mark's. Two ornamental slabs on the N. facade, VIth century

212　Ravenna, Theodoric's Palace (so-called), VIIth-VIIIth century

215   Salonika, Hagios Dimitrios. View of exterior from the West.
Building commenced at end of Vth century, renewed after 629. Renovated after the fire of 1917

214  Salonika, Hagios Dimitrios. Left: Capital and warriors in N. transept. Right: Capital on the W. wall

215   Salonika, Hagios Dimitrios. View through central nave from N.W. Building commenced at end of Vth century. Renewed after 629.
Renovated after the fire of 1917

216  Salonika, Hagios Dimitrios. Mosaics on pillars c. 629 – 643. Left: St. Demetrius as patron-saint of children. Right: St. Sergius

217     Salonika, Hagios Dimitrios. St. Demetrius between Prefect Leontius, founder of the church and Bishop Johannes (d. 649) who renewed it after the fire of 629. Pillar-mosaic

218  Paris, Cluny Museum. Ivory. Ariadne (so-called). c. 500

219 Paris, Louvre. Ivory. Barberini diptych (so-called). Emperor Anastasius I (491-518), beginning of VIth century

220    Paris, Cabinet des Médailles. Ivory diptych. Emperor Anastasius I (491–518). 517

221  Monza, Cathedral Treasury. Ivory diptych with Muse and Poet. c. 500

222    London, British Museum. Ivory. Adoration of the Magi. Detail: Birth of Christ, VIth century

225   Ravenna, National Museum. Five-part panel of an ivory diptych, VIth century.
Middle: Christ among Saints and Apostles, among them the three youths in the furnace. Left: Healing of the Blind and the Possessed.
Right: Raising of Lazarus and Healing of the Lame. Below: Scenes from the history of Jonah

224   Berlin, State Museums. Left panel of an ivory diptych. Cf. Pl. 225. Christ between SS. Peter and Paul. Middle of VIth century

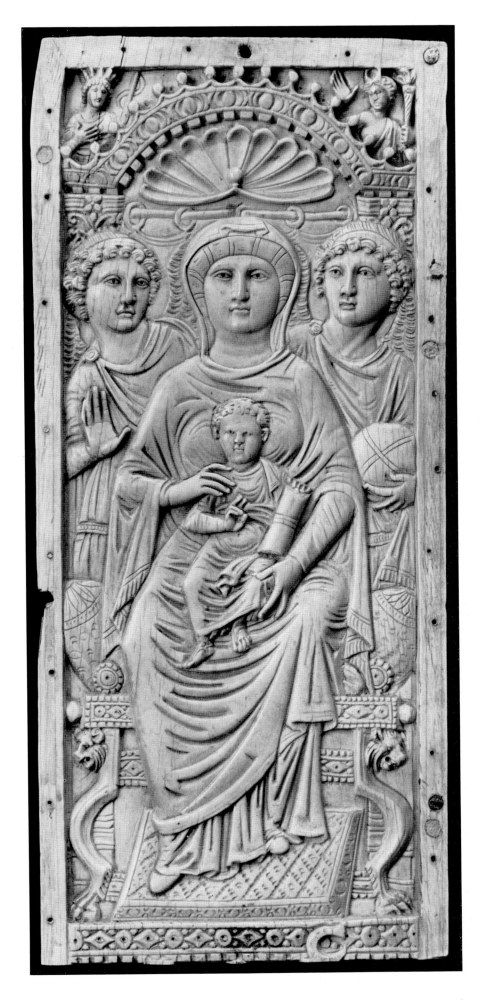

225   Berlin, State Museums. Right panel of an ivory diptych. Cf. Pl. 224. Mary with Angels. Middle of VIth century

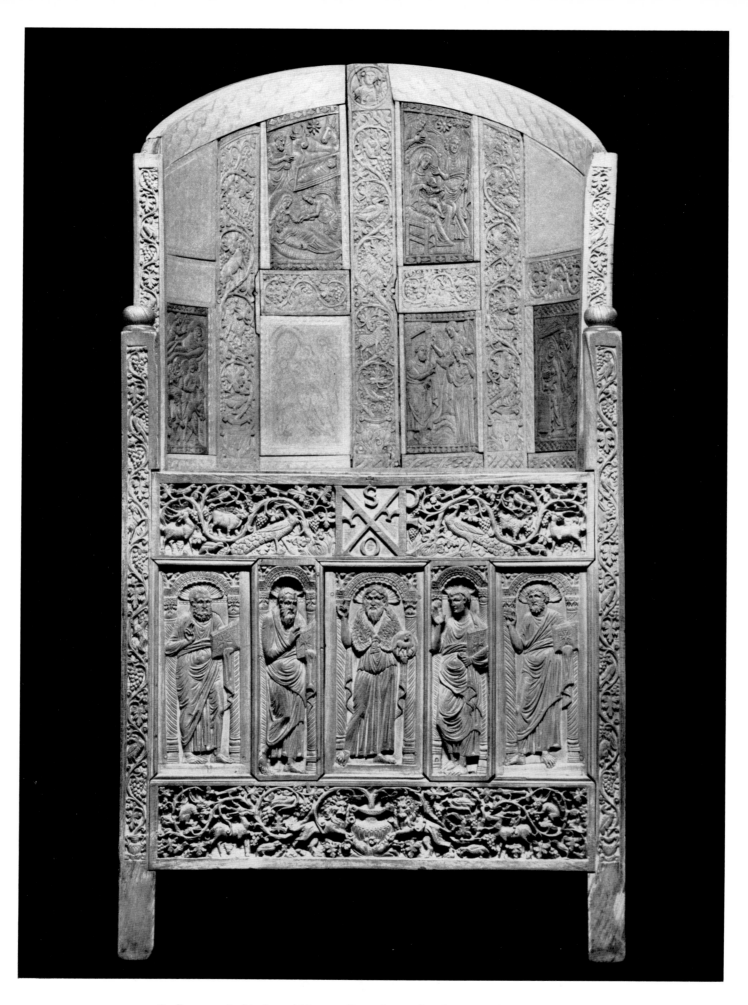

226    Ravenna, Archiepiscopal Museum. Ivory throne of Archbishop Maximianus (545-553)

227   Ravenna, Archiepiscopal Museum. Detail from ivory throne of Archbishop Maximianus. St. John the Baptist

228   Ravenna, Archiepiscopal Museum. Detail from ivory throne of Archbishop Maximianus. Two Evangelists

229   Ravenna, Archiepiscopal Museum. Detail from ivory throne of Archbishop Maximianus. Two Evangelists

250    Ravenna, Archiepiscopal Museum. Detail from ivory throne of Archbishop Maximianus.
Front surface of back of throne, Joseph's Dream and Flight into Egypt

231  Ravenna, Archiepiscopal Museum. Detail from ivory throne of Archbishop Maximianus. Front surface of back of throne, Annunciation

232   Ravenna, Archiepiscopal Museum. Detail from ivory throne of Archbishop Maximianus. Behind the throne, Baptism of Christ

233    Ravenna, Archiepiscopal Museum. Detail from ivory throne of Archbishop Maximianus. Behind the throne, Miracle of loaves and fishes

234    Ravenna, Archiepiscopal Museum. Detail from ivory throne of Archbishop Maximianus.
Upper half of left side, Joseph receives his Brethren and the Measuring of the Corn

235   Ravenna, Archiepiscopal Museum. Detail from ivory throne of Archbishop Maximianus.
Right side, looking downwards: Joseph's Brethren tell of his death; Joseph in the Well and the Killing of the kid; Joseph sold into slavery

236    Above: Washington, Dumbarton Oaks Collection. Ivory pyxis, VIth century.
Moses receiving the Tables of the Law, Daniel in the Lions' Den.
Below: London, British Museum. Ivory pyxis with scenes from the legend of St. Menas, VIth century

235   Ravenna, Archiepiscopal Museum. Detail from ivory throne of Archbishop Maximianus.
Right side, looking downwards: Joseph's Brethren tell of his death; Joseph in the Well and the Killing of the kid; Joseph sold into slavery

236    Above: Washington, Dumbarton Oaks Collection. Ivory pyxis, VIth century.
Moses receiving the Tables of the Law, Daniel in the Lions' Den.
Below: London, British Museum. Ivory pyxis with scenes from the legend of St. Menas, VIth century

257    New York, Metropolitan Museum. Ivory panel. St. Paul, VIth–VIIth century

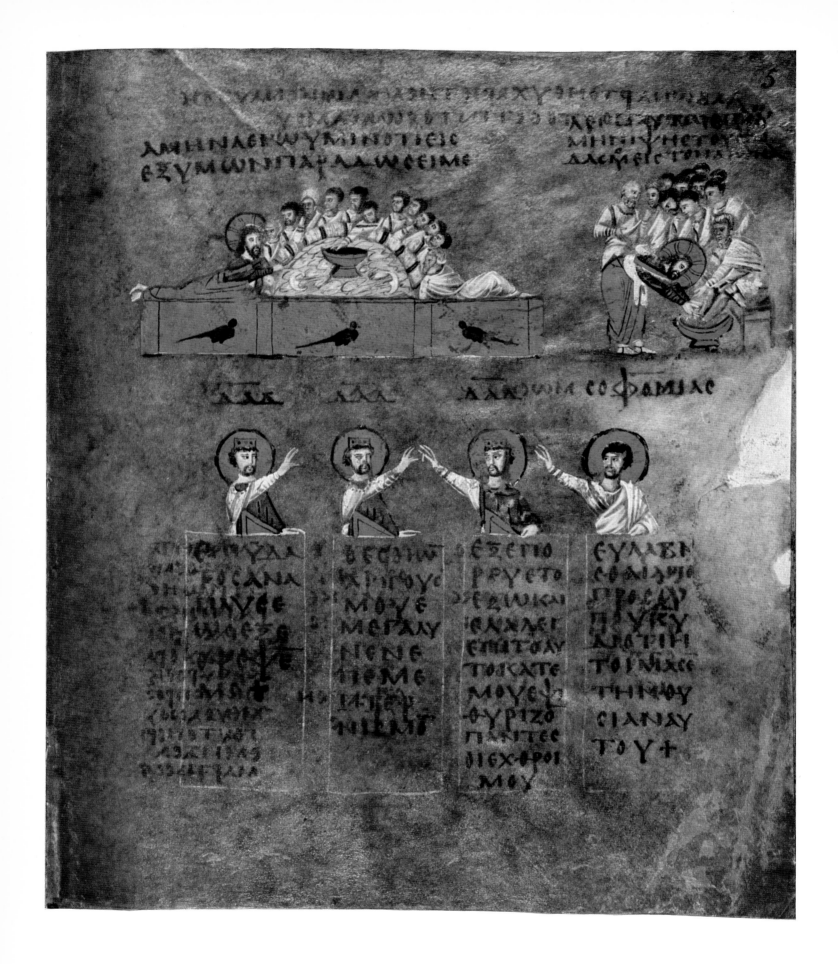

238    Rossano, Archiepiscopal Museum. Codex Purpureus: the Last Supper and Christ washing the Disciples' feet, VIth century

239    Rossano, Archiepiscopal Museum. Codex Purpureus: Pilate invites the Jews to choose between Christ and Barabbas,
VIth century

240    Rossano, Archiepiscopal Museum. Codex Purpureus: Communion of Bread, VIth century

241   Rossano, Archiepiscopal Museum. Codex Purpureus: the Wise and the Foolish Virgins, VIth century

242   Castelseprio, Santa Maria Foris Portas. Fresco: Birth of Christ and the Good Tidings to the Shepherds, VIth-VIIth century ( ?)

243    Castelseprio, Santa Maria Foris Portas. Fresco: Presentation in the Temple, VIth–VIIth century (?)

244   Gold  medallion with portrait of Emperor Justinian I. (527–565). From a cast of the lost original

243  Castelseprio, Santa Maria Foris Portas. Fresco: Presentation in the Temple, VIth–VIIth century (?)

244   Gold  medallion with portrait of Emperor Justinian I. (527–565). From a cast of the lost original

245    Leningrad, Hermitage. Silver plate from the neighbourhood of Poltawa.
Cross upon the starry heavens, with guardian angels, VIth century

246    Paris, Louvre. Silver vase with medallions of Christ and the Apostles, from Emesa. Constantinople, VIth century

247   Istanbul, Archeological Museum. Silver paten with Communion of the Apostles, VIth century

248   Washington, Dumbarton Oaks Collection. Gold jewellery from Cyprus.
Two necklaces and medallion. Above: Baptism of Christ. Below: Mary with Angels and Adoration of the Magi. c. 600

249   London, British Museum. Detail of a silver bowl from Cyprus. St. Sergius. c. 600

250   New York, Metropolitan Museum. Detail from Cyprus Treasure. Silver plate with David and lion. c. 600

251　Paris, Cabinet des Médailles. Silver plate. Hercules with lion, VIth century

252    Leningrad, Hermitage. Silver dish. c. 500

253    Leningrad, Hermitage. Silver flagon with mythological scenes. Byzantine, first half of VIIth century

254   Monza, Cathedral Treasury. Silver vial for oil, from Palestine, with scenes:
Adoration of the Shepherds and Magi (below) and Ascension of Christ (above). c.600

255  Berlin, State Museums. Detail from Assiut Treasure. Golden neckband and medallion with the Annunciation, VI–VIIth century

256   Washington, Dumbarton Oaks Collection. Silk textile with lion-hunt, VIIth–VIIIth century

255   Berlin, State Museums. Detail from Assiut Treasure. Golden neckband and medallion with the Annunciation, VI–VIIth century

256  Washington, Dumbarton Oaks Collection. Silk textile with lion-hunt, VIIth–VIIIth century

257   Vatican, Museo Cristiano. From Sancta Sanctorum. Silk textile with Annunciation, VIIth–VIIIth century

258    New York, Cooper Union Museum, Textile with cock, beginning of VIIth century

# NOTES TO THE PLATES

# BIBLIOGRAPHICAL ABBREVIATIONS

The titles of certain publications which are cited frequently in the notes to the plates are given in an abbreviated form. The following is a complete list of these abbreviations:

Ainalov, *Foundations*  AINALOV, D. V. *Ellinisticheskiye osnovy vizantinskovo iskusstva* [The Hellenistic Foundations of Byzantine Art], St. Petersburg, 1900

Ammann, *Pittura*  AMMANN, A. M. *La pittura sacra bizantina*, Rome, 1957

van Berchem and Clouzot, *Mosaïques*  VAN BERCHEM, M. and CLOUZOT, E. *Mosaïques chrétiennes du IV^me au X^me siècle*, Geneva, 1924

Bovini, *Avori*  BOVINI, G. and OTTOLENGHI, L. *Catalogo della mostra degli avori dell'alto medio evo*, Ravenna, 1956

Bovini, *Guida del Museo*  BOVINI, G. *Guida del Museo Nazionale di Ravenna*, Ravenna, 1951

Bovini, *Monumenti*  BOVINI, G. *Monumenti figurati paleocristiani conservati a Firenze*, Vatican City, 1950

Bovini, *Sarcofagi*  BOVINI, G. *I sarcofagi paleocristiani*, Vatican City, 1949

Bréhier, *Sculpture*  BRÉHIER, L. *La sculpture et les arts mineurs byzantins*, Paris, 1936

Cabrol and Leclercq, *Dictionnaire*  CABROL, F. and LECLERCQ, H. *Dictionnaire d'archéologie chrétienne et de liturgie*, Paris, 1924–53

*Catalogue*, Baltimore  *Early Christian and Byzantine Art* (exhibition catalogue), The Walters Art Gallery, Baltimore, 1947

*Catalogue*, Paris  *Trésors d'art du Moyen-âge en Italie* (exhibition catalogue), Paris, 1952

Cecchelli, *Vita*  CECCHELLI, C. *La vita di Roma nel medioevo*, Rome, 1951–60

Coche de la Ferté, *Antiquité*  COCHE DE LA FERTÉ, E. *L'antiquité chrétienne au Musée du Louvre*, Paris, 1958

Colasanti, *Arte bisantina*  COLASANTI, A. *L'Arte bisantina in Italia*, Milan, 1923

Dalton, *Byzantine Art*  DALTON, O. M. *Byzantine Art and Archaeology*, Oxford, 1911

Dalton, *Catalogue Antiquities*  DALTON, O. M. *Catalogue of Early Christian Antiquities in the British Museum*, London, 1901

Dalton, *Catalogue Ivories*  DALTON, O. M. *Catalogue of the Ivory Carvings of the Christian Era... in the British Museum*, London, 1909

Dalton, *East Christian Art*  DALTON, O. M. *East Christian Art*, Oxford, 1925

Deichmann, *Kirchen*  DEICHMANN, F. W. *Frühchristliche Kirchen in Rom*, Basel, 1948

Delbrueck, *Konsulardiptychen*  DELBRUECK, R. *Die Konsulardiptychen und verwandte Denkmäler*, Berlin, 1929

Delbrueck, *Porphyrwerke*  DELBRUECK, R. *Antike Porphyrwerke*, Berlin, 1932

Delbrueck, *Kaiserporträts*  DELBRUECK, R. *Spätantike Kaiserporträts*, Berlin, 1933

Diehl, *Manuel*  DIEHL, C. *Manuel d'art byzantin*, 2 vols., 2nd ed., Paris, 1925–26

Dütschke, *Studien*  DÜTSCHKE, H. *Ravennatische Studien*, Leipzig, 1909

Ebersolt, *Arts somptuaires*  EBERSOLT, J. *Les Arts somptuaires de Byzance*, Paris, 1923

von Falke, *Seidenweberei*  VON FALKE, O. *Kunstgeschichte der Seidenweberei*, Berlin, 1921

Firatli, *Guide*  FIRATLI, N. *A Short Guide to the Byzantine Works of Art in the Archaeological Museum of Istanbul*, Istanbul, 1955

Galassi, *Roma o Bizanzio*  GALASSI, G. *Roma o Bizanzio*, Rome, 1953

Garrucci, *Storia*  GARRUCCI, R. *Storia dell'arte cristiana nei primi otto secoli della chiesa*, Prato, 1873–81

Garrucci, *Vetri*  GARRUCCI, R. *Vetri ornati di figure in oro*, 2nd ed., Rome, 1864

Gerke, *Christus*      GERKE, F. *Christus in der spätantiken Plastik*, Mainz, 1940

Gerke, *Sarkophage*      GERKE, F. *Die christlichen Sarkophage der vorkonstantinischen Zeit*, Berlin, 1940

Goldmann, *Sarkophage*      GOLDMANN, K. *Die ravennatischen Sarkophage*, Strasbourg, 1906

Grabar, *L'Empereur*      GRABAR, A. *L'Empereur dans l'art byzantin*, Paris, 1936

Grabar, *Martyrium*      GRABAR, A. *Martyrium*, Paris, 1946

Haseloff, *Vorromanische Plastik*      HASELOFF, A. *Die vorromanische Plastik in Italien*, Berlin, 1930

Helbig and Amelung, *Führer*      HELBIG, W. and AMELUNG, W. *Führer durch die öffentlichen Sammelungen klassischer Alterthümer in Rom*, Leipzig, 1891

Kautzsch, *Kapitellstudien*      KAUTZSCH, R. *Kapitellstudien*, Berlin, 1936

Kitzinger, *Early Mediaeval Art*      KITZINGER, E. *Early Mediaeval Art in the British Museum*, London, 1955

Kollwitz, *Plastik*      KOLLWITZ, J. *Oströmische Plastik der theodosianischen Zeit*, Berlin, 1941

Kollwitz, *Sarkophage*      KOLLWITZ, J. *Die Sarkophage Ravennas*, Freiburg i.B., 1956

*Kunstschätze der Lombardei*      *Kunstschätze der Lombardei* (exhibition catalogue), Zurich, 1948

Lasareff, *Byzantine Painting*      LASAREFF, V. *History of Byzantine Painting*, Moscow, 1947–48

Lawrence, *Sarcophagi*      LAWRENCE, M. *The Sarcophagi of Ravenna* (College Art Association Monographs), New York, 1945

Longhurst, *Catalogue*      LONGHURST, M. H. *Catalogue of Carvings in Ivory, Victoria and Albert Museum*, London, 1927

L'Orange, *Studien*      L'ORANGE, H. P. *Studien zur Geschichte des spätantiken Porträts*, Oslo, 1933

L'Orange and von Gerkan, *Bildschmuck*      L'ORANGE, H. P. and VON GERKAN, A. *Der spätantike Bildschmuck des Konstantinsbogens*, Berlin, 1939

Lucchesi Palli, *Ciboriumsäule*      LUCCHESI PALLI, E. *Die Passions- und Endszenen Christi auf der Ciboriumsäule von San Marco in Venedig*, Prague, 1942

Marucchi, *Catacombe*      MARUCCHI, O. *Le catacombe romane*, Rome, 1933

Matzulewitsch, *Byzantinische Antike*      MATZULEWITSCH, L. *Byzantinische Antike*, Berlin, 1929

Maurice, *Numismatique*      MAURICE, J. *Numismatique Constantinienne*, 2 vols., Paris, 1908–12

Mendel, *Catalogue*      MENDEL, G. *Musées Imperiaux Ottomans, catalogue des sculptures grecques, romaines et byzantines*, 3 vols., Constantinople, 1912–14

Morey, *Early Christian Art*      MOREY, C. R. *Early Christian Art*, Princeton, 1953

Nordström, *Ravennastudien*      NORDSTRÖM, C. O. *Ravennastudien*, Stockholm, 1953

Peirce and Tyler, *L'Art byzantin*      PEIRCE, H. and TYLER, R. *L'Art byzantin*, Paris, 1932–34

Ricci, *Tavole*      RICCI, C. *Tavole storiche dei mosaici di Ravenna*, Rome, 1930–37

Rodenwaldt, *Kunst*      RODENWALDT, G. *Die Kunst der Antike*, Berlin, 1927

Rosenberg, *Merkzeichen*      ROSENBERG, M. *Der Goldschmiede Merkzeichen*, 4 vols., 3rd ed., Frankfurt, 1928

Rosenberg, *Niello*      ROSENBERG, M. *Niello bis zum Jahre 1000*, Frankfurt, 1924

Rumpf, *Stilphasen*      RUMPF, A. *Stilphasen der spätantiken Kunst*, Cologne, 1957

Schneider, *Byzanz*      SCHNEIDER, A. M. *Byzanz*, Berlin, 1936

von Simson, *Fortress*      VON SIMSON, O. *Sacred Fortress*, Chicago, 1948

Smith, *Iconography*      SMITH, E. B. *Early Christian Iconography*, Princeton, 1918

Strong, *Scultura*      STRONG, E. *La scultura romana da Augusto a Costantino*, 2 vols., Florence, 1923–26

Styger, *Katakomben*      STYGER, P. *Die römischen Katakomben*, Berlin, 1933

Swift, *Roman Sources*      SWIFT, E. H. *Roman Sources of Christian Art*, New York, 1951

Talbot Rice, *Byzantine Art*, 1958      TALBOT RICE, D. *Masterpieces of Byzantine Art* (exhibition catalogue), Edinburgh, 1958

Toesca, *Storia*      TOESCA, P. *Storia dell'arte italiana*, Vol. I, *Il Medioevo*, Turin, 1927

Venturi, *Storia*      VENTURI, A. *Storia dell'arte italiana*, Vols. I, II, Milan, 1901–2

Volbach, in Bossert, *Geschichte*      VOLBACH, W. F. "Das christliche Kunstgewerbe der Spätantike und des frühen Mittelalters im Mittelmeerraum," in Bossert, H., *Geschichte des Kunstgewerbes*, Vol. V, Berlin, 1932

Volbach, *Elfenbeinarbeiten*      VOLBACH, W. F. *Elfenbeinarbeiten der Spätantike und des frühen Mittelalters*, Mainz, 1952

Volbach, *Metallarbeiten*      VOLBACH, W. F. *Metallarbeiten des christlichen Kultes*, Mainz, 1921

306

Volbach, *Tessuti*                                   VOLBACH, W. F. *I Tessuti del Museo Sacro Vaticano*, Vatican City, 1942

Volbach, Salles, and Dutuit, *Art byzantin*         VOLBACH, W. F., SALLES, G., and DUTUIT, G. *Art byzantin*, Paris, n. d.

Vopel, *Goldgläser*                                  VOPEL, H. *Die altchristlichen Goldgläser*, Freiburg i. B., 1899

Weibel, *Textiles*                                   WEIBEL, A. C. *Two Thousand Years of Textiles*, New York, 1952

Wilpert, *Malereien*                                 WILPERT, J. *Die Malereien der Katakomben Roms*, Freiburg i. B., 1901

Wilpert, *Mosaiken*                                  WILPERT, J. *Die römischen Mosaiken und Malereien der kirchlichen Bauten vom IV bis XIII. Jahrhundert*, 4 vols., 2nd ed., Freiburg i.B., 1916

Wilpert, *Sarcofagi*                                 WILPERT, J. *I sarcofagi cristiani antichi*, 4 vols., Rome, 1929

Wirth, *Wandmalerei*                                 WIRTH, F. *Römische Wandmalerei*, Berlin, 1934

de Wit, *Bildnismalerei*                             DE WIT, J. *Spätrömische Bildnismalerei*, Berlin, 1938

Wulff, *Altchristliche Kunst*                        WULFF, O. *Altchristliche und byzantinische Kunst*, 2 vols., Berlin, Neubabelsberg, 1914-18. Bibliographisch-kritischer Nachtrag, Potsdam, 1935

Wulff, *Beschreibung*                                WULFF, O. *Beschreibung der Bildwerke der christlichen Epochen*, Berlin, 1909

# NOTES

*Publisher's note:* The captions which appear with the illustrations in this book could not be read and edited before they were printed. Since it was entirely impracticable to reprint all the plates because of the stylistic irregularities and errors in some of the captions, we have placed the corrected and expanded information at the head of each of the entries in these notes to the plates. The reader is asked to refer to that material rather than to the formulations under the illustrations.

## 1

THE EMPEROR DIOCLETIAN (284–305). Marble, slightly damaged, part of an over life-size statue. Height 15⅜ in. (39 cm.). Found in Nicomedia (Izmit). Istanbul, Archaeological Museum.

A bearded man, wearing a wreathlike diadem, his identification with Diocletian may be seen from similarities with his portraits on coins and medals, a double herma in Solin (H. Fuhrmann in *Römische Mitteilungen*, 1938, p. 35) and the double cameo with Maximianus Herculius in the Dumbarton Oaks Collection (G. Richter, *Greek and Roman Antiquities in the Dumbarton Oaks Collection*, Cambridge, Mass., 1956, pl. VI, a-c). The head was made before Diocletian's abdication in 305 in Nicomedia, where he had assumed the imperial dignity in 284.

For the iconography of Diocletian's portraits, see L'Orange, *Studien*, p. 100 ff. V. Poulsen in *Antidoron M. Abramič*, I, Vjesnik, Split, 1954–57, p. 188; also: R. O. I. Arik in *Archaeologischer Anzeiger*, 1939, p. 166, figs. 36–39; F. K. Dörner in *Die Antike*, 1941, p. 139, fig. 2.

## 2, 3

TRIUMPHAL ARCH OF THE EMPEROR GALERIUS. ca. 298. SALONIKA.
[2] East side of south pier: triumphs from the Emperor's Persian campaign of 297.
[3] North side of south pier: triumphs from the same campaign.

Erected about 298 to commemorate his victory over the Persians and long campaigns in Mesopotamia and Armenia. Only half of the vaulted archway is extant. It is situated on the Via Egnatia, but not strictly in its east-west axis; to the north an oblong peristyle led to the Emperor's mausoleum, not far to the south stood the palace and the Hippodrome. The friezes begin on the east side of the south pier with the first Victory in Armenia and end on the north pier with the final stage of the campaign, the Crossing of the Euphrates. In the upper zone of the south pier the Emperor, still without armor, addresses his Dacian troops in Serdica; next is the reception of Armenian envoys asking for protection; underneath, Diocletian and Galerius attend the solemn sacrifice before the opening of the

campaign; in the lowest zone, Persian peace envoys appear bearing costly gifts. The reliefs on the side [3] have scenes of war. Above, the Emperor in a vehicle approaching an Armenian city, marked by a shrine to Anaïtis; underneath, the decisive battle: in the center the emperor, high on horseback, protected by the Jovian eagle; in the third zone, the Emperors Diocletian and Maximian enthroned, after the victory, the river gods Euphrates and Tigris beneath their feet; in the lowest zone, trophy-bearing victories. Though the portrait heads are badly damaged, probably intentionally by later Christians, a stylistic kinship with the portraits of the First Tetrarchy, such as the porphyry pieces in Rome [22, 23] and Venice [25], is still discernible.

F. K. Kinch, *L'Arc de triomphe de Salonique*, Paris, 1890; Wulff, *Altchristliche Kunst*, I, p. 161, figs. 157–159; L'Orange, *Studien*, p. 28, figs. 61–63; H. von Schönebeck in *Byzantinische Zeitschrift*, 1937, p. 361; P. E. Arias, *La scultura romana*, Messina, 1943, p. 205; E. Dyggve in *Studia orientalia Ioanni Pedersen dicata*, Copenhagen, 1953, p. 69, fig. 7; Rumpf, *Stilphasen*, p. 9, figs. 3-4.

## 4–6

The most comprehensive publication on EARLY CHRISTIAN SARCOPHAGI is Wilpert, *Sarcofagi*. The connection between the earliest Christian and pagan sarcophagi has been studied by Rodenwaldt, *Kunst*, Gerke, *Sarkophage*, and F. Gerke in *Zeitschrift für Kirchengeschichte*, 1940, p. 1 ff. A general survey appears in Wulff, *Altchristliche Kunst*, I, p. 100, Nachtrag, p. 13. For Ravenna sarcophagi: Lawrence, *Sarcophagi;* Bovini, *Sarcofagi;* Kollwitz, *Sarkophage.* For sarcophagi from Gaul: E. Le Blant, *Les Sarcophages chrétiens de la Gaule*, Paris, 1886; F. Benoit, *Sarcophages paléochrétiens d'Arles et de Marseille*, Paris, 1954.

## 4, 5

SARCOPHAGUS. ca. 270. Rome, Santa Maria Antiqua.
[4] Above: front. Below: center part of front, *orans* and philosopher.
[5] Above: left side of front, *Jonah and the Whale*. Below: right side of front, *The Good Shepherd* and *The Baptism of Christ*.

The oval sarcophagus is plain on the back but decorated on the other sides. On the left: a river god, scenes from the story of Jonah; in the middle: the deceased as philosopher between an *orans* and the Good Shepherd; on the right: *The Sacrifice of Abraham*, two fishermen with a net. A close connection with pre-Constantinian sculpture permits a secure dating about 270. For a later development of this type of sarcophagus see the one in the Musei Lateranensi [40 above].

Wilpert, *Sarcofagi*, I, p. 7, pls. 1–2; Wulff, *Altchristliche Kunst*, I, p. 103, fig. 183; H. von Schönebeck in *Rivista di Archeologia Cristiana*, 1937, p. 311; Gerke, *Sarkophage*, p. 259, pls. 52, 59.

## 6

SARCOPHAGUS. ALLEGORICAL GRAPE HARVEST AND THE GOOD SHEPHERD. 2nd half of the 4th century. From the Catacomb of Praetextatus. Rome, Musei Lateranensi.

The figure of the Good Shepherd, bearded, appears three times. Although the sarcophagus is purely Hellenistic in its iconography, it must be assigned to the Theodosian period on stylistic grounds.

Wilpert, *Sarcofagi*, I, p. 142, pl. 117; Toesca, *Storia*, I, fig. 23; Gerke, *Sarkophage*, p. 247, n.l.

## 7–10

CHRISTIAN CATACOMBS with painted decorations are to be found from the end of the 2nd century onward in the East and above all in Italy. The interesting catacomb in Alexandria has, unfortunately, been destroyed, but an important Eastern type, probably a borrowing from Jewish models, has been preserved in the funerary chambers of the Seven Sleepers in Ephesus. In the western Mediterranean the best examples of this type of chamber (hypogeum) have been preserved in Syracuse, Naples, and Rome (Wulff, *Altchristliche Kunst*, I, p. 17, Nachtrag, p. 2). The Roman catacombs, their very existence forgotten during the Middle Ages, were first rediscovered and investigated by Antonio Bosio between 1593 and 1629. Modern research began with Joseph Wilpert who published the most important monuments in his fundamental work, *Die Malereien der Katakomben Roms* (Freiburg i. B., 1901). Applying modern archaeological methods, P. Styger (*Katakomben*, and *Die römischen Märtyrergrüfte*, Berlin, 1935) tried to work out a system for dating the construction of the vaults, and from them their paintings. He concluded that no Christian monument could be dated before 200. There seem to have been no communal cemeteries in the 2nd century nor any larger sepulchral units, either Jewish or Christian. Only about eleven cemeteries can be dated to the period before Constantine (A. M. Schneider, "Die ältesten Denkmäler der römischen Kirche," *Festschrift zur Feier des 200jährigen Bestehens der Akademie der Wissenschaften in Göttingen*, II, *phil.-hist. Kl.*, 1951, p. 166). Gradually, with the growing cult of martyrs, the cemeteries developed out of former small family vaults. The earliest and most important catacombs are named after Callixtus, Domitilla, Praetextatus, and Priscilla, and that of Callixtus already existed under Pope Zephyrinus (198–217). The Catacombs of Priscilla and Domitilla show how the vault of a rich Christian family was extended from more general use. For the catacombs in Naples, see H. Achelis, *Die Katakomben von Neapel*, Leipzig, 1936.

A comparison with secular painting throws some light on the development of the decoration in the catacombs (Wirth, *Wandmalerei*), and it has become increasingly evident that Christian painting generally follows the contemporary style. Thus the wall decoration and especially the manner of dividing the ceiling into compartments, as in the funerary chambers of the Catacomb of Lucina, reproduce patterns common in earlier Roman houses.

C. M. Kaufmann, *Handbuch der christlichen Archäologie*, 2nd ed., Paderborn, 1913, p. 123 ff.; Wulff, *Altchristliche Kunst*, I, p. 50 ff., Nachtrag, p. 2 ff.; Marucchi, *Catacombe;* Wirth, *Wandmalerei;* de Wit, *Bildnismalerei;* Morey, *Early Christian Art*, p. 60 ff.; J. Kollwitz, *Das Christusbild des 3. Jahrhunderts*, Münster, 1953; R. Bianchi Bandinelli in *Rivista dell'Istituto Nazionale Archeologia e Storia dell'Arte*, 1953-54, p. 1; L. Hertling and E. Kirschbaum, *Die römischen Katakomben und ihre Märtyrer*, Vienna, 1950; C. Cecchelli in *Corsi di cultura*, Ravenna, 1958, p. 45.

## 7 ABOVE

GOOD SHEPHERD. Fresco. 3rd century. Detail from the ceiling of the Vault of Lucina. Rome, Catacomb of Callixtus.

The construction of the vault has been dated in the second half of the 2nd century (Styger, *Katakomben*, pl. 4), and its decoration has therefore also been attributed to this early period. But the use of lines (red, or red and green) to divide the space geometrically into fields similar to those in the chambers underneath San Sebastiano (Wirth, *Wandmalerei*, fig. 83) suggests instead the first half, or perhaps even the middle of the 3rd century.

Wilpert, *Malereien*, pl. 66, 2; Wirth, *Wandmalerei*, p. 170, pl. 40.

## 7 BELOW

CHRIST AMONG THE APOSTLES. Fresco. 4th century. In an *arcosolium* of the Crypt of Ampliatus. Rome, Catacomb of Domitilla.

The extent to which the type of the apostolic group has been developed suggests a 4th-century origin.

Wilpert, *Malereien*, pl. 148, 2; Wulff, *Altchristliche Kunst*, I, p. 82, fig. 65; de Wit, *Bildnismalerei*, p. 55, pl. 47.

## 8 ABOVE

THE DECEASED AS ORANS IN PARADISE. Fresco fragment; the lower part destroyed by a tomb added later. Early 4th century. Rome, Catacomb of Callixtus.

On the left an inscription: DIONYSAS IN PACE (Dionysus rest in peace).

Wilpert, *Malereien*, pl. 111.

## 8 BELOW

ORANS AND VIRGIN AND CHILD. Fresco in lunette above a tomb. Rome, Catacomb of Priscilla, Crypt of "Velatio virginis."

The deceased as *orans*, on her left a teacher with two pupils, on her right a mother holding her child, thought to be either the Virgin or *Ecclesia Mater*. Datable by its location to the 3rd century.

Wilpert, *Malereien*, pl. 79; Wulff, *Altchristliche Kunst*, I, p. 81, fig. 63; Peirce and Tyler, *L'Art byzantin*, I, p. 52, pl. 51.

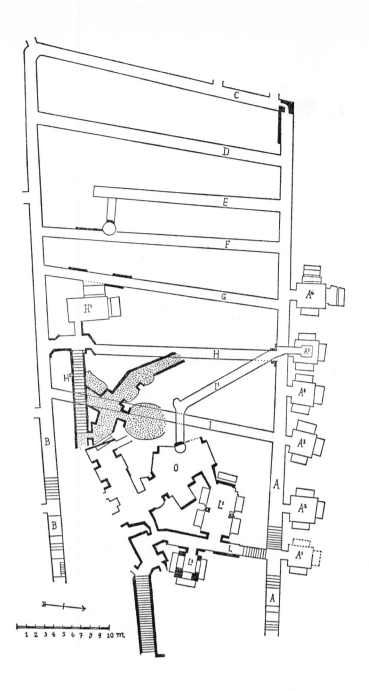

FIGURE 7. Catacomb of Callixtus, oldest part (area I). The system of two main galleries, A and B, linked by lateral galleries from L in the east to C in the west shows that here, as in the oldest parts of other catacombs, the ground allotted for burial was strictly delimited, since the boundaries of the surface lot could not be exceeded. As a result, such allotments were intensively exploited, by means of a network of galleries known, from its resemblance to a gridiron, as the grid system. The oldest part (Area I), measuring 29.6 m. × 70 m. (96 ft. × 230 ft.) (older reckoning: *in fronte pedes* C, *in agro pedes* CC), was created in the reign of Marcus Aurelius (161–80) for Christian members of the family of Caecilii. Galleries A and B, both about 12 m. (40 ft.) below ground level originally, could be approached by two stairs. In this earliest period there were five chambers: $L^1$ (later a papal vault), $L^2$ (the *cubiculum* of Orpheus), and the three so-called Chambers of the Sacrament: $A^1$, $A^2$, $A^3$. In the second period, soon after, the area was extended, beginning with Gallery B, continuing across Gallery C and along Gallery A, and chambers $A^4$– $A^6$ were added. In the third period, during the reign of Commodus (180–92), an attempt was made to enlarge the cemetery by excavating a lower floor which seems, however, to have collapsed; the stairs $H^2$ were to have led to it. After: P. Styger, *Die römischen Katakomben*, Berlin, 1933.

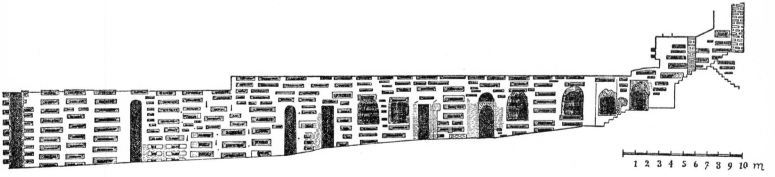

FIGURE 8. Catacomb of Callixtus, oldest region (Area I). Cross section: right wall of Gallery B.
After: P. Styger, *Die römischen Katakomben*, Berlin, 1933.

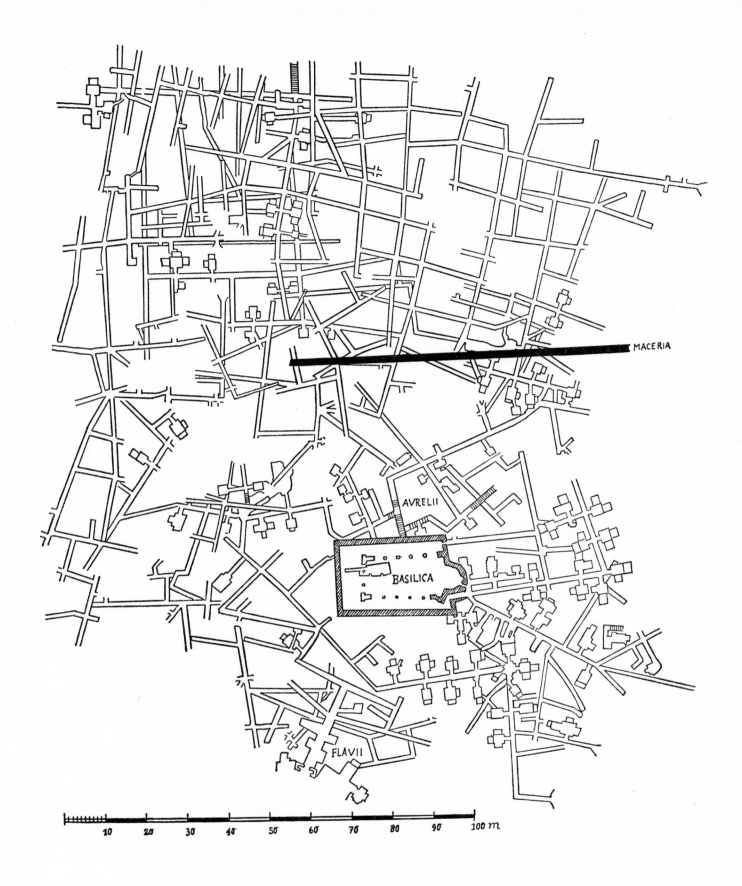

MACERIA

AVRELII

BASILICA

FLAVII

10   20   30   40   50   60   70   80   90   100 m

FIGURE 9. Catacomb of Domitilla. Plan of the oldest regions including the basilica and the underground burial sites *(hypogea)* of the Flavii and the Aurelii. The heavy line represents the remains of the enclosure *(maceria)* of a pagan funerary site with *columbaria* under which the oldest part of the catacomb was situated. After: P. Styger, *Die römischen Katakomben*, Berlin, 1933.

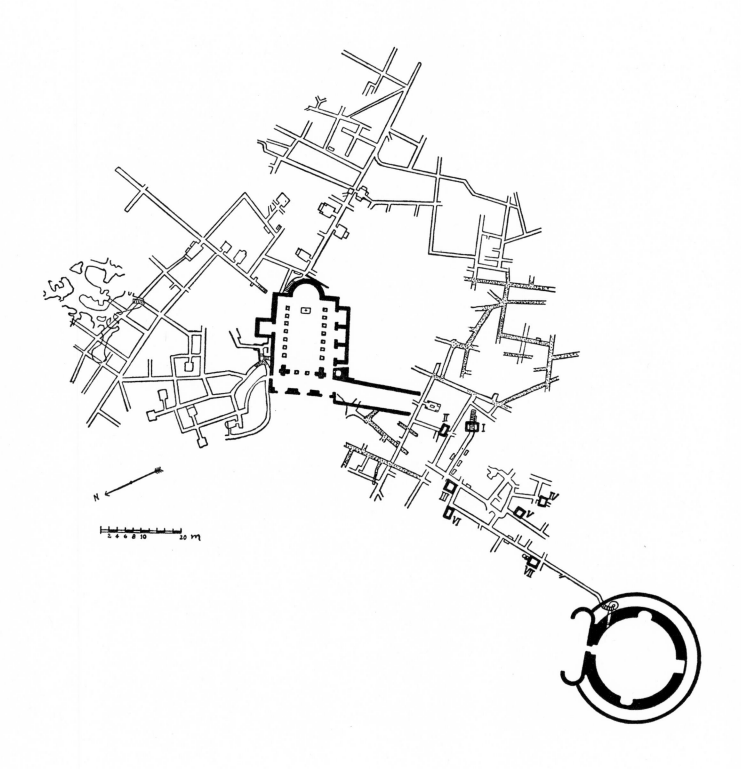

FIGURE 10. Catacomb of St. Agnes with the basilica of Sant' Agnese fuori le Mura (see fig. 25) over the tomb of the martyr and the Mausoleum of Constantina (known today as Santa Costanza; see figs. 12, 13, and plates 29–35). After: P. Styger, *Die römischen Katakomben*, Berlin, 1933.

**9 ABOVE**

THE THREE HEBREWS IN THE FIERY FURNACE. Fresco. Early 4th century. Rome, Catacomb of Priscilla, Capella Greca.

According to Styger (*Katakomben*, p. 141), the Capella Greca dates from the 2nd century. The paintings cannot be earlier than the beginning of the 4th. Besides *The Three Hebrews in the Fiery Furnace*, there are Noah as *orans*, *The Sacrifice of Abraham*, *Moses Striking the Rock*, scenes from the story of Susanna, and others.

Wilpert, *Malereien*, pl. 78, 1; Wulff, *Altchristliche Kunst*, I, p. 68, fig. 53, pl. III, 1, Nachtrag, p. 8; K. Pfister, *Katakombenmalerei*, Potsdam, 1924, pl. XXI.

**9 BELOW**

MOSES STRIKING THE ROCK. Fresco. 4th century. Rome, Catacomb of Callixtus.

Dated in the 4th century on stylistic grounds.

Wilpert, *Malereien*, pl. 237, p. 2; de Wit, *Bildnismalerei*, p. 61, pl. 53; Marucchi, *Catacombe*, p. 209, fig. 67.

**10 ABOVE**

CHRIST. Detail from the fresco in the Crypt of Ampliatus, plate 7 below. 4th century. Rome, Catacomb of Domitilla.

Wilpert, *Malereien*, pl. 148, 2.

**10 BELOW**

ORANS. Fresco fragment. First half of the 4th century. Rome, Catacomb of Vigna Massimo.

De Wit (*Bildnismalerei*, p. 51, pl. 41) describes it as late Constantinian (ca. 337). This type of *orans* is very frequent; for examples see Wilpert, *Malereien*, pl. 174, and Toesca, *Storia*, I, fig. 17.

Wilpert, *Malereien*, pl. 175; K. Pfister, *Katakombenmalerei*, Potsdam, 1924, pl. XXVII.

**11–13**

MINOR ARTS IN THE EARLY CENTURIES OF OUR ERA. Very little has survived. Christian clay lamps, numerous in the Roman catacombs and elsewhere in the East and West, do not go back further than the middle of the 3rd century. On the oldest lamps syncretistic representations, such as the Good Shepherd, are frequent. Under Constantine the Great, workshops of all kinds throughout the empire become very active. Very few works in precious metals have survived [110–121], which is all the more to be regretted as written sources, such as the *Liber pontificalis* (the papal annals), tell of a great many presents made by emperors and popes to palaces and churches. Bronze works have, naturally, survived in much larger quantities. Here too, in the earliest pieces of the 4th century, elements of pagan art are still frequent, especially on lamps [13], and a noticeable change in style occurs only in the 5th century. Beside the lamps, the successive styles of censers offer an uninterrupted line of development. Bronze weights with human and animal representations also occur.

Furniture and caskets were often decorated with ivory and bone. The latter is common in the early imperial period, as finds in Pompei, Naples (Museo Nazionale), and Rome (Musei del Vaticano) show, while ivory carving did not reach its full flower until after the time of Constantine [84–101].

Only a few textiles have survived from the early Christian centuries, most of them preserved by the hot sands of Egypt. A few isolated pieces in Italy, mainly from reliquaries, can be securely attributed to the first five centuries, and perhaps also a few undecorated dress relics, such as the one from the Sancta Sanctorum, now in the Vatican, and various *brandea* (pieces of material with relic value; *Reallexikon für Antike und Christentum*, ed. T. Klauser, Stuttgart, 1950ff., II, p. 522), may be early. Silk did not become important until the time of Justinian when Byzantium ceased to depend on imported raw material (256–58).

Dalton, *Catalogue Antiquities;* Wulff, *Beschreibung;* Volbach, *Metallarbeiten;* W. F. Volbach, *Spätantike und frühmittelalterliche Stoffe*, Mainz, 1932; Volbach, *Tessuti; Kunst der Spätantike, Catalogue*, Berlin, 1939; *Catalogue*, Baltimore; Cecchelli, *Vita;* Coche de la Ferté, *Antiquité*.

**11 ABOVE**

DOUBLE PORTRAIT OF A MAN AND WIFE. Gold-glass medallion. Diameter 3¼ in. (8.3 cm.). 4th century. Paris, Petit Palais, Collection Dutuit.

The man wears a *toga contabulata*, the woman, a diadem. Inscription: PIE ZESES. For this type of representation with a similar inscription, see H. Vopel, *Goldgläser*, p. 18. Glasses of this type have been found mainly in the stucco decoration of catacombs.

W. Froehner, *Collection Dutuit*, II, Paris, 1901, no. 223, pl. 168; *Catalogue sommaire des Collections Dutuit*, Paris, 1925, no. 238.

**11 CENTER**

PORTRAIT OF POPE CALLIXTUS. Gold-glass medallion. 4th century. Paris, Cabinet des Médailles.

Inscription: CALLIXTUS.

Garrucci, *Vetri*, pl. 19,1; Vopel, *Goldgläser*, p. 85, no. 402.

**11 BELOW**

DOUBLE PORTRAIT OF A MAN AND WIFE WITH A FIGURE OF HERCULES. Gold-glass medallion. Diameter 4¼ in. (10.7 cm.). 4th century. London, British Museum.

The man wears a *toga contabulata*, the woman, a diadem. Inscription around edge: ORFITUS ET CONSTANTIA IN NOMINE HERCVLIS; above the heads: ACERENTINO FELICES BIBATIS (In the name of Hercules Acheruntius may Orfitus and Constantia live happily). Similar gold-glass medallions of the 4th century with portraits of couples have been found in large quantities, especially in Rome. Most of them are today in the Museo Sacro in the Vatican.

Garrucci, *Vetri*, p. 35, 1; O. Pelke, *Altchristliche Ehedenkmäler*, Strasbourg, 1903; Vopel, *Goldgläser*, no. 113, pl. 1; Dalton, *Catalogue Antiquities*, no. 608., pl. XXIX; Cecchelli, *Vita*, I, 1951, p. 146; Kitzinger, *Early Mediaeval Art*, p. 4, pl. V.

**12 LEFT**

LAMP. Bronze. 4th century. Florence, Museo Archeologico.

Inside the handle formed by a wreath is the scene of Moses Striking the Rock; this type of lamp has affinities with the sculpture of the sarcophagi.

Toesca, *Storia*, I, p. 67, fig. 49; Bovini, *Monumenti*, p. 13, fig. 9.

**12 RIGHT**

LAMP IN THE FORM OF A BOAT. Bronze. 4th century. Found in Rome, near Santo Stefano Rotondo. Florence, Museo Archeologico.

Above the sail, an inscription: DOMINVS LEGEM DAT VALERIO SEVERIO EUTROPI VIVAS. The figures have been identified as St. Peter at the rudder and St. Paul speaking, intended perhaps as a symbol of the church, though they are more likely to be Christ at the rudder and an *orans* at the bow (C. M. Kaufmann, *Handbuch der christlichen Archäologie*, Paderborn, 1913, p. 324, fig. 117).

Lamps with reflectors that are decorated with figures are frequent and there are numerous examples in the Vatican and in the Staatlichen Museen, Berlin (Wulff, *Beschreibung*, I, p. 169).

Garrucci, *Storia*, I, p. 469; Leclercq, *Manuel d'archéologie chrétienne*, II, Paris, 1907, p. 555; Toesca, *Storia*, I, p. 67, fig. 50; Volbach, in Bossert, *Geschichte*, V, fig. p. 73; Bovini, *Monumenti*, p. 8, figs. 5–8; L. Voelkl in *Miscellanea*, ed. G. Belvederi, 1954–55, p. 396, fig. 3.

**13**

LAMP. Bronze. Length 6¾ in. (17.2 cm.). 4th century. From Caltagirone (Sicily). Hartford, Conn., Wadsworth Atheneum.

Chain lost; handle is in the shape of a griffin's head, but the lamp is identified as Christian by monogrammatic crosses on the body. Griffin lamps of this type are very frequent; for examples in Berlin: Wulff, *Beschreibung*, I, no. 763; London: Dalton, *Catalogue Antiquities*, no. 502; the Vatican: Garrucci, *Storia*, VI, no. 470, 3, 8; and innumerable other places.

*Catalogue*, Baltimore, no. 238, pl. 39.

**14, 15**

ARCH OF CONSTANTINE. ROME. 312–15.
[14] View from the north.
[15] Details of reliefs. About 315. Above: the rostrum. Below: Roman troops.

The senate had the arch erected after Constantine's victory at the Milvian Bridge (312) for his decennial in 315. Reliefs from the times of Trajan, Hadrian, and Marcus Aurelius were incorporated, and without them it would not have been possible to complete the work in such a short space of time and with the few qualified artists available. In structure, the arch follows earlier Roman examples such as those of Titus and Severus. For the earlier sculptures, see Strong, *Scultura*, pp. 144, 219, 250; L'Orange and von Gerkan, *Bildschmuck*; Rodenwaldt, *Kunst*, pp. 602–605.

There are six contemporary reliefs on the arch (height, ca. 40 in.), two on each of the principal faces (immediately above the side arches) and one on each of the lateral faces. They represent, beginning on the western lateral face and moving counterclockwise, the Departure of the Troops (*profectio*), the Siege of Verona (*obsidio*), the Battle at the Milvian Bridge (*proelium*), the Entry into Rome (*ingressus*), the Emperor Addressing the Citizens (*oratio*), and the Emperor Distributing Largesse (*liberalitas*). The tondi on the lateral faces are also contemporary. Two have the Sun and Moon riding chariots, respectively. In the spandrels and on the coping stones there are personifications of rivers and seasons, victories and other omens of public felicity. The prisoners of war and the victories on the pedestal reliefs are harsher in style.

Numerous reliefs from Rome, securely dated by inscriptions, serve as stylistic forerunners; for example: the Orfitus Altar with Cybele in the Villa Albani, carrying a consular inscription of 295 (Gerke, *Sarkophage*, p. 99, pl. 44, 1–2), or the sacrificial relief on a column base in the Forum commemorating the decennial of 303 (L'Orange, *Studien*, fig. 242). A large number of Christian sarcophagi of the Constantinian period are close to the triumphal arch and seem to have been decorated by artists working in the same or closely related workshops (H. von Schönebeck in *Römische Mitteilungen*, 1936, p. 306).

L'Orange and von Gerkan, *Bildschmuck*, p. 225; Gerke, *Christus*, p. 24; H. Brunn and W. Arndt, *Denkmäler griechischer und römischer Skulptur*, Munich, 1888–1947, p. 500; F. Grossi-Gondi, *L'arco di Costantino*, Rome, 1913; Wulff, *Altchristliche Kunst*, I, p. 165, figs. 160–161, Nachtrag, p. 19; G. Rodenwaldt in *Römische Mitteilungen*, 1921–22, p. 58; G. von Kaschnitz-Weinberg in *Die Antike*, 1926, p. 48, fig. 7; Strong, *Scultura*, p. 335; L'Orange, *Studien*, p. 284, figs. 235–237; A. Alföldi in *Römische Mitteilungen*, 1934, p. 118, pls. 4–5; H. Kähler in *Jahrbuch des deutschen archäologischen Institutes*, 1936, p. 180, 1952, p. 1; H. Kähler, *Rom und seine Welt*, Munich, 1958, p. 42, pls. 261–262; G. Becatti in *Critica d'arte*, 1940, p. 41; W. Technau, *Die Kunst der Römer*, Berlin, 1940, p. 286, figs. 235–238; A. Grabar in *Cahiers archéologiques*, 1949, p. 156; Bovini, *Sarcofagi*, p. 41, figs. 27–31; Swift, *Roman Sources*, pl. 1; B. Berenson, *The Arch of Constantine*, London, 1954; L. Voelkl, *Der Kaiser Konstantin*, Munich, 1957, figs. 26–31; Rumpf, *Stilphasen*, p. 8, figs. 1, 5.

**16–25 AND 48–71**

LATE ANTIQUE PORTRAIT SCULPTURE. Important new finds have increased our knowledge in this field but the starting point is still the securely dated official monuments [2, 3, 14, 15, 25, 54, 55], votive platters [53, 109], coins [21, 52], medallions [244], and ivory diptychs [90, 91, 96, 97, 220]. R. Delbrueck (*Porphyrwerke*) has dealt systematically with imperial monuments in porphyry from the First Tetrarchy to Justinian II. New finds in the East have enriched our knowledge, particularly of Theodosian sculpture [50 ff.]. Nonetheless, many problems in this field remain unsolved.

H. Koch in *Antike Denkmäler*, 1912–13, p. 20; Wulff, *Altchristliche Kunst*, I, p. 151, Nachtrag, p. 19; R. Delbrueck in *Römische Mitteilungen*, 1914, p. 71; Delbrueck, *Kaiserporträts*; G. Rodenwaldt in *76. Winckelmannsprogramm*, Berlin, 1919; L'Orange, *Studien*; C. Cecchelli in *Rivista di Archeologia Cristiana*, 1951, p. 199; *Actes du VIme congrès internationale des études byzantines*, 1951, p. 85; J. Kollwitz, in *Annales archéologiques de Syrie*, 1951, p. 200; H. Kähler in *Jahrbuch des deutschen archäologischen Institutes*, 1952, p. 1; W. Alzinger, in *Jahreshefte des österreichischen archäologischen Institutes*, 1955, p. 27; G. C. Picard in *Monuments Piot*, 1957, p. 83; Rumpf, *Stilphasen*.

**16, 17**

CONSTANTINE THE GREAT (306–37). Marble. Head from a colossal statue. Height 8 ft., 6 in. (2.60 m.). Rome, Palazzo dei Conservatori.
[16] Full face.
[17] Profile.

Complete, this statue of the seated Emperor must have been over 30 ft. high. It was found in the Basilica of Constantine during the 15th century, and fragments, a part of the chest and one shoulder, are still behind the west apse. The identification is secured by a comparison with the portraits of Constantine on his coins and on the triumphal arch. It probably dates as early as about 313 and not 324-30, as R. Delbrueck (*Kaiserporträts*, p. 121) and H. P. L'Orange (*Studien*, p. 137, no. 86) assume; A. Rumpf (*Stilphasen*, p. 18) dates it about 360-70.

Helbig and Amelung, *Führer*, no. 887; Delbrueck, *Kaiserporträts*, p. 121, pls. 37-39; L'Orange, *Studien*, p. 63, fig. 163; H. Kähler in *Jahrbuch des österreichischen archäologischen Institutes*, 1952, p. 9, figs. 16-17; G. C. Picard in *Monuments Piot*, 1957, p. 83; Rumpf, *Stilphasen*, p. 18, fig. 55.

## 18, 19

CONSTANTIUS II (337-61). Cast bronze. Height 5 ft., 9½ in. (1.77 m.). Rome, Palazzo dei Conservatori.
[18] Profile.
[19] Full face.

About 1200 the statue was put up on two columns in front of the Lateran Palace but in 1471 Sixtus IV transferred it to the Palazzo dei Conservatori. Probably a standing figure, perhaps wearing a chlamys. Original height over 30 ft. The identification with Constantius II was put forward by E. Petersen (in *Diss. Pontificia Accademia Romana di archeologia;* 1900, p. 175); K. Kraft (in *Jahrbuch für Numismatik und Geldgeschichte*, 1954-55, p. 177) has suggested Constantine. According to R. Delbrueck (*Kaiserporträts*, p. 139, pls. 52-54), it was possibly erected to celebrate the triumph of Constantius II in 357.

C. Gradara in *Roma e l'Oriente*, 1914, p. 40; L'Orange, *Studien*, no. 87, fig. 164; Peirce and Tyler, *L'Art byzantin*, I, pl. 26; Rumpf, *Stilphasen*, p. 17, fig. 54.

## 20

HEAD OF AN EMPEROR. Constantine the Great (?). Chalcedony. Height 3¾ in. (9.5 cm.), with the later scepter, 6¾ in. (17 cm.). 4th century. Paris, Cabinet des Médailles.
From Sainte-Chapelle, where it served as a scepter ornament. Arm and drapery restored during the 15th century. A. Venturi (*Storia*, I, p. 556, fig. 489) guardedly suggests Valentinian III.

E. Babelon, *Le Cabinet des antiquités à la Bibliothèque Nationale*, Paris, 1887, pl. p. 115; E. Babelon, *Le Cabinet des Médailles et antiquités*, I, Paris, 1924, p. 128, fig. 52; Cabrol and Leclercq, *Dictionnaire*, vol. III, pt. 2, col. 2643, figs. 3228-3229; Volbach, in Bossert, *Geschichte*, V, p. 98, fig. p. 99.

## 21

COINS.

Above center: FLAVIUS VALERIUS CONSTANTIUS CHLORUS. Aureus with the bust of the Emperor wearing a laurel wreath; struck in Antioch, 293-96; gold, 5.34 gr. (LH. 1957).

Constantius I Chlorus was Caesar from March 1, 293, and Augustus from May 1, 305, the beginning of the Second Tetrarchy, till his death on July 25, 306.

Second row: FLAVIUS VALERIUS CONSTANTINUS, better known as Constantine the Great.

Left: Solidus with the bust of the Emperor wearing the imperial diadem; struck in Constantinople; gold, 4.37 gr. (LH 1957). See Maurice, *Numismatique*, II, p. 498, pl. XV, 9.

Right: Solidus with the bust of the Emperor, age about forty, wearing a jeweled diadem; struck in Salonika between 324 and 326; gold, 4.22 gr. (MMB. 1958). See Maurice, *Numismatique*, II, p. 468.

Constantine the Great became Caesar in the Third Tetrarchy, on July 25, 306, and Augustus in 307, after his marriage with Fausta, daughter of M. Aurelius Valerius Maximianus. He was born on February 27, 286 or 287, the son of Constantius Chlorus and his first wife, Helena (see below), and died in May, 337, in Ancyrona soon after receiving the sacrament of baptism.

Center: FLAVIA JULIA HELENA, Mother of Constantine the Great. Double solidus with the bust of St. Helena as Augusta, wearing the diadem; struck in Ticinum (Pavia), probably for presentation as a gift on the occasion of Constantine's vicennial on July 25, 325; gold, 8.80 gr. Paris, Cabinet des Médailles.

Maurice, *Numismatique*, II, p. 281; F. Gnecchi, *I medaglioni romani*, I, Milan, 1912, p. 13, pl. 6, 1; J. Lafaurie in *Revue numismatique*, 1955, p. 227ff., pls. IX-XI.

The mother of the Emperor was a native of Bithynia where she was an innkeeper. She became the wife of Constantius Chlorus (see above) in 274 but was divorced by him on dynastic grounds, and he then married Flavia Maximiana Theodora, stepdaughter of Maximianus Herculius, thus fortifying his position in the tetrarchic system. Constantine first raised his mother to patrician status, then made her *nobilissima femina*, and later *Augusta*. After her death she was canonized.

Bottom row: CONSTANTINE THE GREAT AND C. FLAVIUS VALERIUS LICINIANUS LICINIUS. Medallion; struck at Ticinum (Pavia) in 313; gold, 39.78 gr., i.e., a ninefold solidus. Paris, Cabinet des Médailles.

The medallion commemorates the entry of Constantine and Licinius into Milan where the two emperors met in conference and agreed to proclaim religious peace, thus giving Christianity official recognition and incorporating it as a new constructive factor in the fabric of the state. Legend on the reverse: FELIX ADVENTUS AUGUSTORUM NOSTRORUM.

Maurice, *Numismatique*, II, p. 238ff.; E. Babelon in *Mélanges Boissier*, Paris 1903, pp. 49ff.; J. M. C. Toynbee, *Roman Medallions*, New York, 1944, pp. 64, 108, 178.

Licinius was born in 250 or 264, became Augustus in 308, and married Constantina, Constantine's half sister (the daughter of Constantius Chlorus and Theodora). He was strangled in 325 on a charge of high treason.

M. Bernhart, *Handbuch zur Münzkunde der römischen Kaiserzeit*, Halle, 1926; P. H. Webb in H. Mattingly and E. A. Sydenham, *The Roman Imperial Coinage*, V, London, 1927-33; J. W. E. Pearce in H. Mattingly and E. A. Sydenham, *The Roman Imperial Coinage*, IX, London, 1951; E. S. G. Robinson, *A Guide to the Exhibition of Roman Coins*, London, 1952.

The first four coins are enlarged 3 times, the last 2.25 times; the first four reproduced by courtesy of Messrs. A. G. Leu & Co., Zurich, Adolph Hess AG., Lucerne (LH.), and Münzen und Medaillen AG., Basel (MMB.).

**22, 23**

SARCOPHAGUS OF SAINT HELENA. Porphyry, carved and polished on all sides. Height 7 ft., 11 in. (2.42 m.), length 8 ft., 9½ in. (2.68 m.), width 6 ft., ½ in. (1.84 m.). Early 4th century. Almost certainly from the Mausoleum of St. Helena, called Torre di Pignattara. Rome, Musei del Vaticano; some fragments are also preserved in the museum's storerooms.

[22] Detail: Roman horsemen with captive barbarians.

[23] Detail: Romans and barbarians fighting.

The sarcophagus was re-used for Pope Anastasius IV (d. 1154) and placed in St. John Lateran. Represented are Roman horsemen fighting barbarian soldiers on foot and the capture of the barbarians. Made in Egypt. The imperial portrait (original in storage, see Delbrueck, *Porphyrwerke*, pl. 101) recalls the Emperor Constantius Chlorus, as he is portrayed on the porphyry column now in the Vatican Library (Delbrueck, *Porphyrwerke*, pl. 27) which suggests 306, the year of Constantius' death, as a likely date.

P. Franchi de' Cavalieri, *Nuovo Bulletino di archeologia cristiana*, 1921, p. 15; G. Rodenwaldt in *Jahrbuch des deutschen archäologischen Institutes*, 1922, p. 31; G. Rodenwaldt in *Scritti in onore di B. Nogara*, Rome, 1937, p. 389; J. Ebersolt in *Byzantinische Zeitschrift*, 1929–30, p. 582; Helbig and Amelung, *Führer*, no. 312; E. Sjökvist and A. Westholm in *Opuscula archaeologica*, 1935, p. 1; Rumpf, *Stilphasen*, p. 16, fig. 50.

**24**

SARCOPHAGUS OF CONSTANTINA. Porphyry. Height 7 ft., 4⅝ in. (2.25 m.), length 7 ft., 7¾ in. (2.33 m.), width 5 ft., 1 in. (1.55 m.). Early 4th century. From Santa Costanza. Rome, Musei del Vaticano.

Known during the Renaissance as "Sepolcro di Bacco." The putti gathering grapes are similar to those of the mosaics in the Mausoleum [32]. That it was probably made in Egypt is supported by the fragments found there (K. Michailowski in *Römische Mitteilungen*, 1928, p. 131). There are fragments of other imperial porphyry sarcophagi in Istanbul (J. Ebersolt, in *Byzantinische Zeitschrift*, 1930, p. 582). The date is probably close to that of the sarcophagus of St. Helena.

Helbig and Amelung, *Führer*, no. 209; Delbrueck, *Porphyrwerke*, p. 219, pl. 104; Wulff, *Altchristliche Kunst*, I, p. 141, fig. 128, Nachtrag, p. 16; E. Strong, *Art in Ancient Rome*, London, 1929, fig. 538; Rumpf, *Stilphasen*, p. 16, fig. 51.

**25**

TWO PAIRS OF EMPERORS: DIOCLETIAN AND MAXIMIAN (right), CONSTANTIUS I CHLORUS AND GALERIUS (left). Porphyry. Height 4 ft., 3⅛ in. (1.30 m.). About 300. Probably from Akkon, possibly brought to Venice by Lorenzo Tiepolo in 1258. Venice, San Marco, set into the south corner.

The emperors, in tunics, chlamydes and armor, carry swords; their headgear consists of cylindrical caps. The piece is close to the Tetrarchs in the Vatican Library (Delbrueck, *Porphyrwerke*, pls. 35–37) so that it probably dates 295–305. An Egyptian origin is suggested by similarities with a head in Cairo, possibly the Emperor Licinius (Delbrueck, *Porphyrwerke*, pls. 38, 39).

R. Delbrueck, *Bildnisse römischer Kaiser*, Berlin, 1914, pl. 39; Delbrueck, *Porphyrwerke*, p. 84, pls. 31–34; Wulff, *Altchristliche Kunst*, I, p. 155, fig. 148, Nachtrag, p. 19; L'Orange, *Studien*, p. 16, figs. 32, 34, 41; Peirce and Tyler, *L'Art byzantin*, I, p. 83, pls. 2, 3; Rumpf, *Stilphasen*, p. 9, fig. 29.

**26–31**

For CONSTANTINIAN ARCHITECTURE the most important general works on Early Christian art are Wulff, Toesca, and Swift.

Important specialized studies are: R. Krautheimer, *Corpus basilicarum christianarum Romae*, Vatican City, 1927 ff.; *Reallexikon für Antike und Christentum*, ed. T. Klauser, Stuttgart, 1950 ff.; *Kunstchronik*, 1951, p. 115 and 1953, p. 242; Grabar, *Martyrium*; E. Kirschbaum in *Rivista di Archeologia Cristiana*, 1936, p. 271 ff.; R. Krautheimer in *Review of Religion*, 1939, p. 127; E. Dyggve in *Zeitschrift für Kirchengeschichte*, 1940, p. 103; P. Lemerle in *Bulletin de l'Académie Royale de Belgique, cl. de lettres*, 1948, p. 306; L. Voelkl in *Rivista di Archeologia Cristiana*, 1953, p. 49; K. J. Conant in *Speculum*, 1956, p. 1; C. Delvoye in *Annuaire de l'Institut de Philologie et d'Histoire Orientales et Slaves*, 1954–57, p. 205.

**26, 27**

BAPTISTERY OF ST. JOHN LATERAN (San Giovanni in Fonte). ROME.

[26] Exterior.

[27] Interior.

Excavations of 1923–25 (G. B. Giovenale, *Il Battistero Lateranense*, Rome, 1929), and more recent research by A. Tschira (in *Römische Mitteilungen*, 1942, p. 116), show that parts of the external wall are all that remains of the original Constantinian structure. This Early Christian edifice, erected on the remains of baths belonging to the adjacent palace, was a simple round structure. Under Sixtus III (432–40), it was completely rebuilt and given its present octagonal form (interior diameter ca. 65 ft. [19–20 m.]) with the eight porphyry columns around the piscina [fig. 11]. From this period also dates the entablature over the columns and the eight pedestals for pillars in the corners of the exterior wall designed to carry the barrel vault that formerly covered the ambulatory. The present drum is later. In the original narthex there are still remains of old decoration. The baptistery was partly rebuilt in the Baroque style by Pope Paul III.

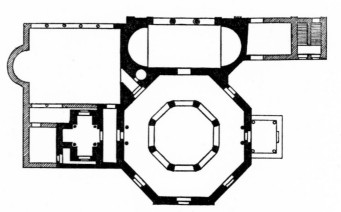

FIGURE 11. Baptistery of St. John Lateran (San Giovanni in Fonte), Rome. Plan. Present entrance from northwest (on plan at bottom). On the right, the Chapel of St. John the Baptist; opposite on the left, the Chapel of St. John the Evangelist, both added by Pope Hilarus (461–68). To the southeast, facing the entrance, the original narthex of the baptistery, with remains of the old entrance, transformed in the 12th century into the Capella di Santi Seconda e Rufina (or Santi Cipriano e Giustino). After: G. Dehio and G. von Bezold, *Die kirchliche Baukunst des Abendlandes*, Stuttgart, 1887–1901.

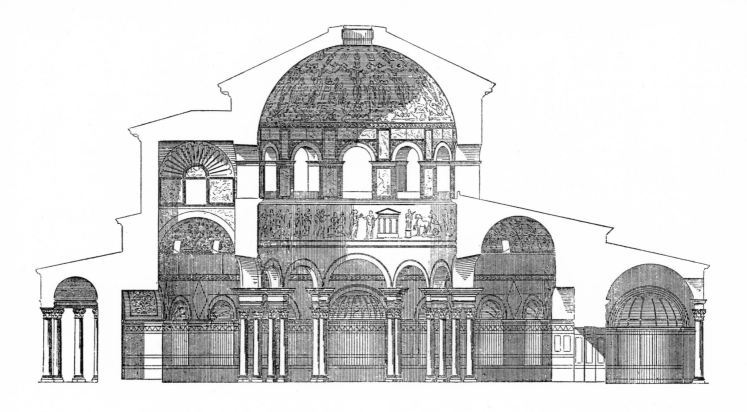

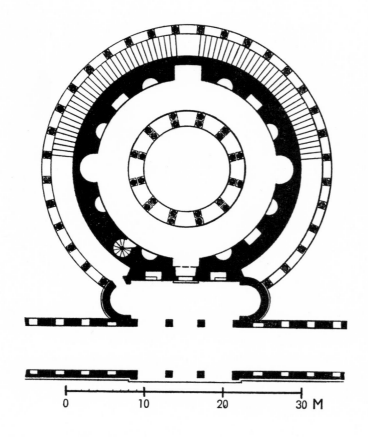

FIGURES 12 AND 13. Santa Costanza, Rome. Mausoleum of Constantina, daughter of Constantius Chlorus, as well as of other members of the imperial family. Consecrated as a church by Pope Alexander IV in 1256. Central space surrounded by 12 radially disposed pairs of columns, each united by an entablature supporting the high drum with 12 windows. Concrete dome with central skylight. Circular enclosing wall with small niches for sarcophagi and three larger ones for altars. The groundplan shows the parts no longer extant: the external peristyle with a stair leading down to a hypogeum, the vestibule and the oblong hall in front of it, which may have been used for funeral celebrations. To the left of the longitudinal section the destroyed external ambulatory; on the right, the narthex-like vestibule and, in front of it, the oblong hall. The interior decoration of the cupola and the frieze below the drum, sketched in the longitudinal section, follow Ciampini, *Vetera monumenta*. After: G. Dehio and G. von Bezold, *Die kirchliche Baukunst des Abendlandes*, Stuttgart, 1887–1901.

A. von Gerkan in *Deutsche Literaturzeitung*, 1930, col. 1659; Wulff, *Altchristliche Kunst*, I, p. 250, fig. 241, Nachtrag, p. 36; M. Armellini, *Le chiese di Roma del. sec. IV al XIX*, 2nd ed., Rome, 1942, I, p. 133; R. Krautheimer in *Journal of the Warburg and Courtauld Institutes*, 1942, p. 24, pl. 4b; Deichmann, *Kirchen*, p. 40, figs. 57–59.

## 28

### SANTO STEFANO ROTONDO, ROME.

This centralized building, erected under Pope Simplicius (468–83), follows Eastern models, most probably the Church of the Holy Sepulcher in Jerusalem. Of the original edifice all that has survived are the inner circle of columns with a plain architrave, the drum, and the wide ambulatory. The arcades of the outer circle of columns have been incorporated into the wall except for a few free standing intercolumniations on the east side. Structurally Sant'Angelo in Perugia is very close to this church.

W. Altmann, *Die italienischen Rundbauten*, Berlin, 1906; Wulff, *Altchristliche Kunst*, I, p. 248, fig. 240, Nachtrag, p. 35; R. Krautheimer in *Rivista di Archeologia Cristiana*, 1935, p. 51; Grabar, *Martyrium*, I, p. 260.

## 29–35

### SANTA COSTANZA, ROME. First half of the 4th century.
[29] Exterior, view from the west.
[30] Interior, facing east.
[31] Ambulatory.
[32] Mosaics in the vault of the ambulatory. Vintage scenes and a portrait, possibly of Constantina (died 354).
[33] Mosaics. Above: south apse, *Christ Enthroned*. Below: north apse, *Christ Giving the Law to SS. Peter and Paul*.
[34] Detail of a mosaic in the vault of the ambulatory.
[35] Mosaics in the vault of the ambulatory.

Intended perhaps as a baptistery by Constantina, but used as a mausoleum after her death (354). The interior has retained its original structure. The mosaics in the ambulatory have undergone extensive restorations [32–35]; those in the dome have been lost, but are known from earlier drawings by Antonio San Gallo, Francesco Ollanda, and others. The exterior still clearly reflects the articulation of the interior, though it has suffered considerable alterations. Of the original vestibule all that has survived are the marble door frame and a part of the originally vaulted apsidial terminals. A similar narthex-like vestibule was part of the Lateran Baptistery and of the mausoleum adjoining San Sebastiano (R. Lanciani in *Diss. Pontificia Accademia Romana di archeologia*, 1920, p. 55). The vaulted peristyle originally surrounding the building and open to the outside [plan fig. 13] is already absent from the Renaissance drawings (C. Hülsen, *Il libro di Giuliano di San Gallo*, Leipzig, 1910, pls. 16, 39). External colonnades of this type, however, have survived in the mausoleum at Split.

Wulff, *Altchristliche Kunst*, I, p. 246, fig. 239; C. Cecchelli, *Sant'Agnese e Santa Costanza*, Rome, 1924; R. Krautheimer in *Journal of the Warburg and Courtauld Institutes*, 1942, p. 26, pl. 5d; M. Stettler in *Römische Mitteilungen*, 1943, p. 76; Deichmann, *Kirchen*, p. 25, figs. 5–16; K. Lehmann in *Art Bulletin*, 1955, p. 193. For the mosaics see Wilpert, *Mosaiken*, p. 272; Wulff, *Altchristliche Kunst*, I, p. 321; J. Kollwitz in *Römische Quartalschriften*, 1936, p. 55; Grabar, *Martyrium*, pl. III, 1; F. W. Deichmann in *Rivista di Archeologia Cristiana*, 1946, p. 214.

## 36

### CHRIST AS A YOUTHFUL PHILOSOPHER. Marble.
Right forearm broken off. Height 28¼ in. (72 cm.). 4th century. Rome, Museo Nazionale Romano.

The seated figure wears a long robe. Stylistically it is close to the sarcophagus of Junius Bassus [40–42] and related post-Constantinian sarcophagi such as the one in the Musei Lateranensi, no. 174 [44].

J. Wilpert in *Art Bulletin*, 1926–27, p. 35; O. Thulin in *Römische Mitteilungen*, 1929, p. 201; Wulff, *Altchristliche Kunst*, I, Nachtrag, p. 18, fig. 533; Gerke, *Christus*, p. 38, figs. 56–59.

## 37–47

For the general literature on EARLY CHRISTIAN SARCOPHAGI, see the note to 4–6.

## 37–39

### SARCOPHAGUS OF ADELPHIA. Traces of old paint.
About 340–45. Syracuse, Museo Nazionale.
[37] Above: front. Below: detail of *The Adoration of the Magi*.
[38] Above: *The Multiplication of Loaves and Fishes* and *The Raising of the Widow's Son*. Below: *The Entry into Jerusalem*.
[39] Double portrait of Adelphia and her husband.

Probably made in Rome, and according to Wilpert (*Sarcofagi*, p. 102, pls. 92, 93), in a workshop near the Catacomb of St. Callixtus.

Inscription in the center of the cover: IC ADELPHIA C F POSITA CONPAR BALERI COMITIS. On either side scenes from the life of the Virgin, *The Nativity*, and *The Adoration of the Magi*. Front: in the center, the deceased couple within a conch. In the upper register, *Christ with Adam and Eve after the Fall*, *Christ Foretelling the Denial of Peter*, *The Woman with the Issue of Blood*, *Moses Receiving the Law*, *The Sacrifice of Abraham*, *The Healing of the Blind*, *The Multiplication of Loaves and Fishes*, and *The Raising of the Widow's Son*. In the lower register, *The Three Hebrews Refusing to Worship Nebuchadnezzar's Image*, *The Marriage at Cana*, *The Adoration of the Magi*, *The Fall of Man*, and *The Entry into Jerusalem*.

According to S. L. Agnello (in *Amici delle Catacombe*, Vatican City, 1956), the *comes* Valerius, husband of Adelphia, is perhaps to be identified with L. Aradius Valerius Proculus, consularis of Sicily and consul in 340. The sarcophagus is a late example of the style of the reliefs on the Arch of Constantine. Closest to it among Roman frieze sarcophagi is the one of the Brothers (Wilpert, *Sarcofagi*, pl. 91; F. Gerke in *Rivista di Archeologia Cristiana*, 1933, p. 307) and the so-called "Dogmatic" or Trinity sarcophagus (Wilpert, *Sarcofagi*, pl. 96), both in the Musei Lateranensi; they are typical of late Constantinian sculpture.

Wulff, *Altchristliche Kunst*, I, p. 124, fig. 110; Toesca, *Storia*, I, p. 51, fig. 32; H. von Schönebeck in *Römische Mitteilungen*, 1936, p. 271; A. C. Soper in *Art Bulletin*, 1937, p. 159, fig. 7; Gerke, *Sarkophage*, pp. 208, 353; Bovini, *Sarcofagi*, p. 218, fig. 233.

## 40 ABOVE

### SARCOPHAGUS WITH BIBLICAL SCENES. Late 3rd century. Rome, Musei Lateranensi.

Upper register: *The Raising of Lazarus*, *Moses Striking the Rock*, and *Moses in Distress* (?). Lower register: scenes from the story of Jonah, *Noah in the Ark*, and a fisherman. Landscape elements are still prominent and show Hellenistic traits. Moreover, similarities with the pagan Endymion-sarcophagi warrant an early dating, probably at the end of the 3rd century. A Jonah sarcophagus in Copenhagen, Ny Carlsberg Glyptotek (Wilpert, *Sarcofagi*, pl. 59, p. 3), is related to it.

Ainalov, *Foundations*, p. 89; Wulff, *Altchristliche Kunst*, I, p. 101, pl. V, 2; L. von Sybel, *Christliche Antike*, Marburg, 1901, II, pl. V, p. 2; Wilpert, *Sarcofagi*, I, p. 17, pl. 9, 3; Gerke, *Sarkophage*, p. 38 ff., pl. I, 1–3.

## 40 BELOW

SARCOPHAGUS WITH CHRIST BETWEEN SS. PETER AND PAUL. Early 6th century. From Castelnau-de-Guers (Dépt. Hérault). Paris, Louvre.

Four fields with decorative vine scrolls alternate with three niches with figures, Christ in the central one and SS. Peter and Paul, each turning toward Christ, in the side ones. On the cover, scallop motifs, and in the center a medallion with the monogram of Christ between trees of life. The piece is typical of a large group of Aquitanian sarcophagi, of which there are excellent examples at Moissac, Bordeaux, and Soissons. The sarcophagus from Valbonne, now in the Museum in Nîmes (J. Baum, *Sculpture figurale en Europe*, Paris, 1937, no. 185, pl. 70), which also dates from the beginning of the 6th century, is particularly closely related.

E. Le Blant, *Les Sarcophages chrétiens de la Gaule*, Paris, 1886, p. 119, pl. 32; J. B. Ward Perkins in *Archaeologia*, 1938, p. 112, pl. 38, 4; D. Fossart in *Actes du V^me Congrès international d'archéologie chrétienne*, Vatican City, Paris, 1957, p. 321, fig. 7.

## 41–43

SARCOPHAGUS OF JUNIUS BASSUS (died 359). Marble. Cover partly lost. Several heads restored. Height 7 ft., 11¾ in. (2.43 m.), width 4 ft., 7½ in. (1.41 m.). Rome, Vatican Grottoes.
[41] Front.
[42] Above: *Christ Giving the Law to SS. Peter and Paul*. Below: *The Entry into Jerusalem*.
[43] *Adam and Eve*.

Inscription on upper edge: IVN BASSVS V.C. QVI VIXIT ANNIS XLII MEN. II IN IPSA PRAEFECTVRA VRBI NEOFITVS IIT AD DEVM VIII KAL. SEPT. EVSEBIO ET YPATIO CONSS. The date of death, Aug. 25, 359, determines the chronological position of the sarcophagus. From three recently found fragments of the cover, an inscription can be reconstructed that describes Junius Bassus as a most beneficent prefect of the city (B. M. Apolloni Ghetti, A. Ferrua, E. Josi, and E. Kirschbaum, *Esplorazioni sotto la confessione di San Pietro in Vaticano*, Vatican City, 1951, p. 220).

In the upper register: *The Sacrifice of Abraham, The Arrest of St. Peter, Christ Giving the Law to SS. Peter and Paul* [41], *Christ Taken to Pilate, Christ Before Pilate*. In the lower register: *Job, Adam and Eve* [43], *The Entry into Jerusalem* [42], *Daniel in the Lions' Den* (restored), *St. Paul Going to his Martyrdom*. Stylistically these sculptures are akin to the columnar sarcophagus no. 174 in the Musei Lateranensi [44, 45] as well as to the figure of Christ in the Museo Nazionale Romano [36].

Wilpert, *Sarcofagi*, I, pl. 13; J. Wilpert in *Rivista di Archeologia Cristiana*, 1938, p. 331; Wulff, *Altchristliche Kunst*, I, p. 114, pl. 7; A. Baumstark in

*Römische Quartalschriften*, 1914, p. 5; G. Rodenwaldt in *Römische Mitteilungen*, 1923–24, p. 331, and 1943, p. 23, fig. 10; M. Lawrence in *Art Bulletin*, 1932, p. 128, fig. 40; J. Roosval in *Arkeologiska Studier tillägnade H. K. H. kronprins Gustaf Adolf*, 1932, p. 273; F. Gerke in *Rivista di Archeologia Cristiana*, 1933, p. 105; Gerke, *Christus*, figs. 46–51; F. Gerke, *Der Sarkophag des Junius Bassus*, Berlin, 1936; Bovini, *Sarcofagi*, p. 21, fig. 6.

## 44, 45

COLUMNAR SARCOPHAGUS. Marble. 4th century. Formerly in the Vatican Grottoes. Rome, Musei Lateranensi.
[44] Lateral face: *Moses Striking the Rock* and *The Woman with the Issue of Blood*.
[45] Detail of front: *Christ Giving the Law to SS. Peter and Paul*.

Several heads have been restored and other parts reworked. *The Giving of the Law* is depicted in the three central niches. Christ enthroned, above the veil of heaven, hands the Scroll to St. Peter, on His left, while He looks toward St. Paul who approaches from the right. The two outer niches on the left are occupied by *The Sacrifice of Abraham* and *The Arrest of St. Peter* and those on the right by *Christ Before Pilate*. On the left lateral face is *Christ Foretelling the Denial of Peter*, on the right *Moses Striking the Rock* and *The Woman with the Issue of Blood*. The piece is close in date to the sarcophagus of Junius Bassus, though the more elegant execution suggests Eastern models. A number of other Roman Passion sarcophagi belong to the same series (F. Gerke in *Archaeologiai Ertesitö*, 1940, p. 79, fig. 16). The treatment of hair is similar to that of the Christ in the Museo Nazionale Romano [36].

Wilpert, *Sarcofagi*, I, p. 121 ff., pl. 121, 2–4; Wulff, *Altchristliche Kunst*, I, p. 115, figs. 96–98; Toesca, *Storia*, I, p. 47, figs. 28, 30; H. von Campenhausen in *Marburger Jahrbuch für Kunstwissenschaft*, 1929, p. 25, fig. 17; M. Lawrence in *Art Bulletin*, 1932, p. 133, figs. 34, 37, 39; H. von Schönebeck in *Römische Mitteilungen*, 1936, p. 326; Gerke, *Christus*, p. 41, figs. 53-55.

## 46–47

SARCOPHAGUS. (From a plaster cast in Milan, Museo di Sant'Ambrogio). Length 7 ft., 6¼ in. (2.30 m.), width 4 ft., 11 in. (1.50 m.), height 3 ft., 9 in. (1.14 m.). Late 4th century. Formerly known as the "Sarcophagus of Stilicho." Milan, Sant'Ambrogio, below the medieval pulpit.
[46] Lateral face: *The Ascension of Elijah* and *Moses Receiving the Law*.
[47] Lateral face: *The Sacrifice of Abraham* and a scene of Christ teaching. Front: *Christ Preaching to the Apostles*.

There are reliefs on all four sides with the scenes placed before a city wall pierced by gates. On the front: *Christ Preaching to the Apostles*. On the right side: *The Ascension of Elijah* and *Moses Receiving the Law* [46]. On the left side: *The Sacrifice of Abraham* and a teaching scene [47]. The back, corresponding to the front, shows Christ as teacher of the Apostles. On the front of the cover, medallion busts of the deceased couple between *The Three Hebrews Refusing to Worship Nebuchadnezzar's Image* and *The Adoration of the Magi*. Acroteria, representing heads of Christ instead of the usual pagan masks of Medusa, appear on the angles. In the left pediment is a wreath with the monogram of Christ, flanked by doves, and in the right one, the infant Jesus in the crib between the ox and the ass.

In the choice of scenes the artist follows closely the ideas expounded by St. Ambrose in his sermons (J. Kollwitz in

*Gnomon*, 1936, p. 601) so that this sarcophagus differs from others of the same type in that it has a unified iconographic scheme.

The piece belongs to the large group of city-gate sarcophagi which show a strong Eastern influence (M. Lawrence in *Art Bulletin*, 1927–28, p. 1, and 1932, p. 103). Good examples of city-gate sarcophagi in Rome are in St. Peter's (Wilpert, *Sarcofagi*, pl. 154, 4), in San Sebastiano (Wilpert, *Sarcofagi*, pl. 20, 6), in the Musei Lateranensi, and one side of a sarcophagus in the Palazzo dei Conservatori of which the other three are in the Louvre, Paris (H. von Schönebeck in *Studi di antichità*, Vatican City, 1935, figs. 14–15), as well as in Ancona (Wilpert, *Sarcofagi*, pl. 14), in Mantua (Wilpert, *Sarcofagi*, pl. 30), and elsewhere. On the basis of stylistic comparisons with such Eastern works as the Christ in Berlin [172] or with the door of Sant' Ambrogio in Milan [102], this sarcophagus can be dated toward the end of the 4th century. H. von Schönebeck (*op. cit.*, p. 115) suggests tentatively that the deceased was one of the Anicii, Q. Clodius Hermogenianus Olybrius, who died sometime before 395; the portraits of the deceased have affinities with Theodosian portraiture of the years 387–95.

Wilpert, *Sarcofagi*, pls. 188, 189; Wulff, *Altchristliche Kunst*, I, p. 119; A. C. Soper in *Art Bulletin*, 1937, p. 148, fig. 29; Gerke, *Sarkophage*, p. 354; De Chirico in *Bulletino della Commissione Archeologica*, 1941, p. 119; G. Belvederi in *Ambrosiana*, Milan, 1942, p. 177; Bovini, *Sarcofagi*, p. 232, figs. 249–250; *Storia di Milano*, I, Milan, 1953, p. 660, figs. 657–659.

## 48–51

For the general literature on LATE ANTIQUE PORTRAIT SCULPTURE, see the note to 16–25.

## 48, 49

JULIAN THE APOSTATE (?), Caesar, 355–61, Augustus, 361–63. Diadem restored. Marble. Height 5 ft., 8¾ in. (1.75 m.). From Italy. Paris, Louvre.

The bearded figure wears the sacerdotal diadem and the philosopher's cloak, and carries a scroll in his left hand. There is an almost identical statue in the Musée Cluny, Paris (Wulff, *Altchristliche Kunst*, I, p. 152, fig. 145). The identification rests on similarities with portraits on coins and gems (Delbrueck, *Kaiserporträts*, pl. 75, 2); compare also the head from Thasos (P. Lévêque in *Monuments Piot*, to be published). Furthermore it is in keeping with Julian's personality to have had himself represented as a pagan priest or a Greek orator. However, the absence of the imperial diadem is unusual, so that the identification has not gone unchallenged (J. J. Bernoulli, *Römische Ikonographie*, II, Stuttgart, 1894, p. 246).

S. Reinach in *Revue Archéologique*, 1901, p. 341; P. Kastriotes in *Archailogike ephemeris*, 1923, p. 115; Cabrol and Leclercq, *Dictionnaire*, vol. VIII, pt. 1, col. 314; Peirce and Tyler, *L'Art byzantin*, I, p. 28, pl. 28; A. Piganiol in *Comptes-rendus de l'Académie des inscriptions et belles-lettres*, 1937, p. 206; S. Pelekanidis in *Bulletin de Correspondances Hellénistiques*, 1949, p. 300.

## 50, 51

VALENTINIAN II (?). (375–92). Aphrodisian marble. Head broken off (from another statue?). Height 5 ft., 10½ in. (1.79 m.). About 390. From the Baths at Aphrodisias; found near a pedestal inscribed with the name of the Emperor. Istanbul, Archaeological Museum.

The Emperor wears a sleeveless dalmatic over a tunic, a trabea, characteristic of consular attire, draped from the right armpit to the left shoulder, on his head a diadem with a double band of pearls. Most likely this, like other statues of officials found in the neighborhood [65–67], is a local Aphrodisian product following metropolitan models. The identification is supported by parallels from Valentinian's coins and the Missorium of Theodosius [53]. Other similar portraits are the ones on the base of the Obelisk of Theodosius [55], the imperial head in the Villa Borghese, Rome (L'Orange, *Studien*, no. 95, fig. 184), and the bronze bust in Budapest (Delbrueck, *Kaiserporträts*, p. 198, pl. 93).

Mendel, *Catalogue*, II, p. 199, no. 506; G. Rodenwaldt in *76. Winckelmannsprogramm*, Berlin, 1919, p. 19, fig. 6; C. Albizzati in *Atti della Pontificia Accademia Romana*, 1922, p. 350; Wulff, *Altchristliche Kunst*, I, p. 152, fig. 144; L'Orange, *Studien*, p. 73, figs. 181–183; Delbrueck, *Kaiserporträts*, p. 195, figs. 67–68, pl. 92; J. Kollwitz, *Plastik*, p. 81, pls. 16–34; Rumpf, *Stilphasen*, p. 17, fig. 53 (considers Valens a more likely identification).

## 52

COINS.

Left row, above: CONSTANTIUS II. Solidus with a profile bust of the Emperor wearing the diadem; struck in Constantinople, about 339; gold, 4.42 gr. (MMB. 1957).

Constantius II was born August 7, 317, in Sirmium, the second son of Constantine the Great and his second wife Fausta. He was Caesar, 333–37, and Augustus, 337–61.

Left row, middle: FLAVIUS THEODOSIUS, known as Theodosius I, or Theodosius the Great. Solidus with the bust of the Emperor wearing a jeweled diadem. Gold. Paris, Cabinet des Médailles.

Theodosius I was born in 346 (?), at Cauca in Spain, son of the Roman general Flavius Theodosius, executed in 376. The Emperor of the West, Gratian, put him in command against the Goths in 378, and in 379 raised him to the dignity of Augustus. In 388 Theodosius defeated Maximus, the usurper who had overthrown Gratian, and threatened Gratian's successor, Valentinian II [50, 51]. In 394, on the Frigidus, he defeated Arbogast, who had had Valentinian II assassinated. Thereafter, he held the whole Empire under his sole rule. At his death in 395 the Empire was divided between his sons, Arcadius (377–408) [56, 57] and Honorius (see below), who succeeded to the Eastern and to the Western parts respectively.

Left row, bottom: FLAVIUS HONORIUS. Solidus with the bust of the Emperor facing front; he is in armor, wears a helmet and diadem, and carries spear and shield; struck in Constantinople; gold, 4.45 gr. (MMB. 1957).

Honorius (384–423), the son of Theodosius the Great, became West Roman Emperor in 393.

Center, above: FLAVIUS CLAUDIUS JULIANUS, called Julian the Apostate. Solidus with the bust of the Emperor wearing a pearl diadem; struck in Constantinople. Gold, 4.41 gr. (MMB. 1957).

Julian the Apostate, a nephew of Constantine the Great, was born in 332. Of the imperial family only he and his half brother Gallus escaped the dynastic assassination in Constantinople after Constantine's death. He was Caesar, 355-61, and Augustus, 361-63. Having himself renounced Christianity—hence called Apostate—Julian strove to repress the new religion and to re-establish paganism; but he died young from a wound received in a successful campaign against Persia.

Center, middle: GALLA PLACIDIA. Solidus with the bust of Galla Placidia wearing a diadem. Gold. Paris, Cabinet des Médailles.

Center, bottom: GALLA PLACIDIA. Silver siliqua with the bust of Galla Placidia; unique (H. Cohen, *Médailles impériales*, 2nd ed., VIII, 1892, p. 193) (MMB. 1957).

Galla Placidia (388-450), daughter of Theodosius the Great, was taken into captivity by Alaric, king of the Visigoths, after his sack of Rome in 410, and married in 414 to Ataulphus, Alaric's brother-in-law and successor but restored to her half brother Honorius after Ataulphus' assassination in 415. Against her will, she was married in 417 to Constantius III, then a general under Honorius. After Constantius' death in 421, she fell out with Honorius, and fled to the court of Theodosius II, the son and successor of Arcadius. Theodosius raised Galla Placidia's son by Constantius, Valentinian III (419-55) to imperial dignity in the West and made her regent during his minority. Galla Placidia died in Ravenna.

Right row, above: CONSTANTIUS II (see above). Solidus with the bust of the Emperor facing front; he is armed, wears a helmet and diadem, and carries spear and shield; struck in Rome, about 354; gold, 4.41 gr. (MMB. 1957).

Right row, middle: AELIA FLACCILLA. Maiorina with the bust of the Empress wearing a diadem; struck in Antioch, 383-86 (MMB. 1957).

Aelia Flaccilla [58] was the first wife of Theodosius the Great. She died in 386.

Right row, bottom: CONSTANTIUS III. Solidus with the bust of the Emperor wearing a diadem; struck in Ravenna; gold, 4.46 gr. (LH. 1958).

Constantius III, a military commander under Honorius and husband of Galla Placidia (see above) became co-ruler and Augustus in February 421, but died in September of that year.

Maurice, *Numismatique*, I-II; H. Cohen, *Médailles impériales*, 2nd ed., 1880-92, VII-VIII; Delbrueck, *Kaiserporträts*, p. 92, pl. 15, 4, p. 98, pl. 20, p. 104, pl. 25, 2.

All reproductions on this plate enlarged three times.

The majority of the coins are reproduced by courtesy of Messrs. A. G. Leu & Co., Zurich, and Adolph Hess AG., Lucerne (LH.), as well as Münzen und Medaillen AG., Basel (MMB.).

*Römische Münzen, Auktion XVII*, 1957. Münzen und Medaillen AG., Basel; *Antike Münzen, Auktion*, 1958. A. G. Leu & Co., Zurich, and Adolph Hess AG., Lucerne.

## 53

MISSORIUM OF THE EMPEROR THEODOSIUS I. Silver, cast, retouched, and with traces of gilding. Damaged and broken straight across. Diameter 29⅛ in. (74 cm.). 388. Found near Almendralejo (Badajoz). Madrid, Real Academia de la Historia.

Two cups found with it have been lost. Near the slightly raised edge the inscription: D(ominus) N(oster) THEODOSIVS PERPET(uus) AUG(ustus) OB DIEM FELICISSIMVM X. The X indicates the decennial, the tenth anniversary of the reign, which Theodosius celebrated at Salonika in 388. He was then 42 years old. On each side of the Emperor is one of the young Augusti, on his right Valentinian II, on his left Arcadius. On the back, the indication of weight in Greek (50 Roman pounds).

Theodosius, wearing the consular chlamys, is enthroned on the imperial tribunal in front of a tetrastyle *aedicula*. In his right hand he holds a diptychal *codicillus* which he is about to hand over to an official. The two youthful emperors, also wearing official dress and seated somewhat farther back, are smaller; two Germanic guards stand near each. In the pediment two genii; below, the personification of earth.

Silver votive platters like this one were given away by emperors on festive occasions; for votive platters see Cabrol and Leclercq (*Dictionnaire*, vol. IV, pt. 1, col. 1173, s.v. *disque*). Dated examples are in Leningrad with Constantius II (ca. 353), in Geneva with Valentinian I (364-75), in Florence with the consul Aspar Arbadur (ca. 434) [109], and in Paris, Cabinet des Médailles, with Gelimer (536-37). The fragments from Gross Bodungen, now in Halle, are close to the Madrid piece, though more provincial (W. Grünhagen, *Der Schatzfund von Gross Bodungen*, Berlin, 1954). Stylistic comparison with the Esquiline Treasure show that the platter is an Eastern product.

A. Odobesco, *Le Trésor de Petrossa*, Leipzig, 1889-1900, p. 158, fig. 72; O. M. Dalton in *Archaeologia*, 1906, p. 6, fig. 2; H. Graeven in *Römische Mitteilungen*, 1913, p. 203; Wulff, *Altchristliche Kunst*, I, p. 197, fig. 199; Volbach, *Metallarbeiten*, p. 59, no. 56; Delbrueck, *Konsulardiptychen*, p. 235, no. 62, pl. 63; Delbrueck, *Kaiserporträts*, p. 200, pls. 94-98; L'Orange, *Studien*, p. 67, pl. 171; Volbach, Salles and Dutuit, *Art byzantin*, pl. 46; Peirce and Tyler, *L'Art byzantin*, I, p. 46, pls. 35-37; Rumpf, *Stilphasen*, p. 20, fig. 73.

## 54, 55

PEDESTAL OF THE OBELISK OF THEODOSIUS IN THE HIPPODROME OF CONSTANTINOPLE. Proconnesian marble, base with limestone foundation, weathered. The plinth or upper part of the base, height 7 ft., 10 in. (2.40 m.), width 10 ft., 4 in. (3.15 m.), length 9 ft., 2 in. (2.80 m.); the lower part is slightly wider. 390. Istanbul.

[54] Relief on the southeast side: the Emperor, holding the winner's wreath, court dignitaries, and spectators at the games.

[55] Relief on the northwest side: on a tribunal, the Emperor accompanied by Valentinian II and his sons Arcadius and Honorius; below them, Persians and Dacians bearing tribute.

Latin and Greek inscriptions record the erection of the obelisk by Theodosius under the prefecture of Proculus, although his name was removed after his execution in 392. The remaining two sides have scenes showing the transport of the obelisk to Constantinople and its erection, which took place in 390.

Above, on four bronze blocks, the Obelisk of Pharaoh Thutmosis III (ca. 1504-1490 B.C.). Each side of the plinth carries reliefs with scenes. On the northwest face, three Augusti and a prince enthroned on the tribunal. The three Augusti, wearing diadems and chlamydes with imperial fibulae, hold scrolls. It can be safely assumed that they are Theodosius I, Valentinian II, and Arcadius; the prince would then be Honorius. On the assumption of an earlier date, 369, Delbrueck (*Kaiserporträts*, p. 185, pls. 85-88) suggested the Augusti Valentinian I, Valens, and Gratian, and Valentinian II or Valentinian Galates as the prince. Near the tribunal stand four military leaders and one civil dignitary, behind them the guard. In front of them kneel barbarians presenting gifts to the Emperor. On the southwest the same personages in the loggia over the circus gate, the so-called *kathisma*. On the southeast face the emperor, flanked by his two sons, bestows a wreath on the winner. Behind the senators are the bodyguard, in the foreground the spectators [54]. On the northeast face is the Emperor, enthroned between his two sons, or two high officials; in the lower register, split into two groups by the steps to the *kathisma*, are high officials. For stylistic connections with similar state monuments of the period, see O. Wulff (*Altchristliche Kunst*, I, p. 167, Nachtrag, p. 20), and H. P. L'Orange (in *XIIIme Congrès International d'histoire de l'art. Résumés*, Stockholm, 1933, p. 36). For connections with the plinth of the Column of Arcadius and the later Column of Marcian, see J. Kollwitz (*Plastik*, p. 69); for Eastern influences, see G. Rodenwaldt (in *Jahrbuch des deutschen archäologischen Institutes*, 1922, p. 35) and J. Ebersolt (*Arts somptuaires*, p. 19, fig. 1).

Dalton, *Byzantine Art*, p. 114; O. Wulff in *Kunstwissenschaftliche Beiträge, A. Schmarsow gewidmet*, Leipzig, 1907, p. 1; Wulff, *Altchristliche Kunst*, I, p. 167, fig. 163; Delbrueck, *Kaiserporträts*, p. 185, figs. 46-66, pls. 85-88; L'Orange, *Studien*, p. 66, figs. 178-180; G. Bruns, *Istanbuler Forschungen 7*, Istanbul, 1935; Morey, *Early Christian Art*, p. 134, fig. 99; L. Budde, *Entstehung des antiken Repräsentationsbildes*, Berlin, 1956, pls. 1, 2; Rumpf, *Stilphasen*, p. 23, fig. 63.

## 56, 57

ARCADIUS (383-408). Pentalic marble. Height 12¾ in. (32.5 cm.). About 395-400. Found in 1949 in Istanbul near Bayezid. Istanbul, Archaeological Museum.

The Emperor wears a diadem with a double band of pearls. Closely akin to the portrait of Valentinian II in the same museum [50, 51], and his own portraits on the pedestal of the Obelisk in the Hippodrome [55] and in Berlin (Delbrueck, *Kaiserporträts*, pl. 103), as well as to those on his coins.

N. Firatli in *American Journal of Archaeology*, 1951, p. 67, figs. 1-5; Firatli, *Guide*, no. 5028, fig. 2; Rumpf, *Stilphasen*, p. 22, figs. 65-66 (suggests Theodosius).

## 58

PORTRAIT OF AN EMPRESS, POSSIBLY AELIA FLACCILLA (died 386). From Cyprus. Marble. Right hand broken off, head attached. Height 30¾ in. (78 cm.). Paris, Cabinet des Médailles.

The Empress, who was the first wife of Theodosius the Great, wears a diadem with a double band of pearls, a tunic with long sleeves, a dalmatic, and a palla.

Because of the hair style, R. Delbrueck (*Kaiserporträts*, p. 163, pls. 62-64) thinks the statue represents the Empress Helena as she appeared at the time of her journey to Jerusalem about 326-27. But the classicizing treatment of the dress suggests Theodosian times and comparisons with portraits on coins possibly Aelia Flaccilla. A marble head in Hamburg (Delbrueck, *Kaiserporträts*, pl. 99) is close to it.

C. Albizzati in *Aréthuse*, 1928, p. 163; C. Albizzati in *Ristoris*, 1929, p. 401; Peirce and Tyler, *L'art byzantin*, I, p. 52; J. Bankö in *Jahrbuch der Kunsthistorischen Sammlungen in Wien*, Sonderheft I, 1926, p. 11; Rumpf, *Stilphasen*, p. 32, figs. 120-121.

## 59

THE EMPEROR HONORIUS AND HIS WIFE MARY. Cameo. Two-layer sardonyx. Diameter 5⅞ in. (15 cm.). 398, set in an early 13th-century quatrefoil frame with gold filigree. Paris, Collection E. de Rothschild.

The Emperor appears against a dark background wearing a diadem with the monogram of Christ in its center piece. The diadem was perhaps intended as a marriage wreath. Over his armor the Emperor wears the *paludamentum* and fibula. His bride wears the chiton and himation. A Theodosian dating is supported both by the hair style and by stylistic comparisons with works of about 400. The treatment of the drapery is very similar to that on the diptych of the Symmachi and Nichomachi [90-91]. The Emperor's head is of the same type as on the ivory diptych of Probus, dated 406 (Delbrueck, *Konsulardiptychen*, pl. 106), and the damaged marble portrait in Berlin (Delbrueck, *Kaiserporträts*, pl. 107). Thus the cameo was perhaps made on the occasion of the marriage of Honorius and Mary, the daughter of Stilicho, in Milan in 398. E. Babelon (*La Gravure en pierres fines*, Paris, 1894, p. 188) suggests a Constantinian date. E. Coche de la Ferté (*Le Camée Rothschild, un chef-d'œuvre du IVe siècle après J.-C.*, Paris, 1957) identifies the emperor as Constantius II (335). Later engraving near the edges: O HAGIOS SERGIOS and O HAGIOS BACCHOS, which may indicate that during the Middle Byzantine period the piece was kept in the Church of SS. Sergius and Bacchus in Constantinople.

S. Reinach in *Gazette des Beaux-Arts*, 1899, p. 113; H. Brunn and F. Bruckmann in *Antike Denkmäler*, IV, 1, p. 11; E. Stein, *Geschichte des spätrömischen Reiches*, Vienna, 1928, I, pl. 10; Delbrueck, *Konsulardiptychen*, p. 258, no. 66, fig. 1; Delbrueck, *Kaiserporträts*, p. 206, pl. 105; G. Battaglia in *Bulletino della Commissione archeologica comunale di Roma*, 1931, p. 131; L'Orange, *Studien*, p. 77; Volbach, Salles, and Dutuit, *Art byzantin*, p. 52, pl. 5; Peirce and Tyler, *L'Art byzantin*, I, p. 59, pl. 70; B. M. Felleti-Maj in *Critica d'arte*, 1941, p. 85, pl. 49; G. Bruns in *104. Winckelmannsprogramm*, Berlin, 1948, p. 31, fig. 27; Coche de la Ferté, *Antiquité*, pp. 30, 59.

## 60, 61

PROCESSIONAL CROSS WITH GOLD-GLASS MEDALLION. Brescia, Museo Civico.
[60] The cross. 7th century.

The large silver cross, sometimes called the Cross of Desiderius, is richly ornamented with gems, glass pastes, uncut stones, four later miniatures, and a gold-glass medallion. Various restorations were undertaken up to the 16th century. A similar though somewhat earlier processional cross with reliefs is in the Cathedral of Ravenna (Toesca, *Storia*, I, p. 352).

Venturi, *Storia*, I, p. 355, fig. 456; Toesca, *Storia*, I, p. 323; A. Morassi, *Oreficeria italiana*, Milan, 1936, no. 7, fig. 28; H. Wentzel in *Römische Mitteilungen*, 1955, p. 53.

[61] Gold-glass portrait medallion. 4th century.

The medallion, in its circular frame, is set into the lower part of the vertical arm. Diameter 2⅜ in. (6 cm.). It portrays a mother with her son and daughter. All three wear the pallium, the mother's, richly embroidered, over the tunic. Along the edge, the signature of the artist: BOUNNERI KERAMI, probably should be read as Bounnerios.

The portraits have been variously identified, most frequently as Galla Placidia with her children, Valentinian III and Honoria. But the style of the glass is clearly earlier than that of the simple Roman gold glasses of the 4th century [11]. Gold glass of this fine quality is very rare. Compare, for example, the portraits in the Museo Sacro of the Vatican (C. Albizzati in *Römische Mitteilungen*, 1914, p. 248, pl. 15, 1–2), in Cagliari (*Catalogue*, Paris, no. 37, pl. 5), or in the Louvre (Coche de la Ferté, *Antiquité*, no. 53).

H. Leclercq, *Manuel d'archéologie chrétienne*, II, Paris, 1907, p. 496, fig. 332; Venturi, *Storia*, I, p. 405, fig. 333; F. de Mély in *Aréthuse*, 1926, p. 6; H. Peirce in *Aréthuse*, 1927, p. 1; Cabrol and Leclercq, *Dictionnaire*, vol. II, pt. 1, col. 1155; M. L. Trowbridge, *Philological Studies in Ancient Glass*, Urbana, Ill., 1928; G. Mazzoti in *Felix Ravenna*, 1952, p. 72; Cecchelli, *Vita*, I, 3, p. 144; Morey, *Early Christian Art*, p. 127, fig. 132; L. Budde, *Entstehung des antiken Repräsentationsbildes*, Berlin, 1956, p. 11, fig. 18; H. Kähler, *Rom und seine Welt*, Munich, 1958, p. 272.

### 62, 63

STILICHO AND SERENA. Ivory diptych. Height 12⅝ in. (32.2 cm.), width 6⅜ in. (16.2 cm.). About 400. Monza, Cathedral Treasury.

[62] Left panel: Serena, wife of Stilicho and niece of the Emperor Theodosius I, with her son Eucherius (born 388).

[63] Right panel: most probably Stilicho as consul and *magister militum*.

As *magister militum*, the consul wears a chlamys and embroidered tunic, and holds a lance in his right hand while his left rests on a shield embellished with an imperial double portrait. On the other panel his wife is shown wearing a long tunic and sleeveless dalmatic; on her right their young son in the tunic and chlamys of a *tribunus* and *notarius*. R. Delbrueck (*Konsulardiptychen*, p. 242, no. 63, pl. 63) sees, between mother and son, traces of a girl that I have not been able to make out. It is stylistically akin to the Missorium of Theodosius [53] and the Rothschild Cameo [59]. The fashion of the dress, the cross fibula, the sword, the chlamys, and the woman's hair style are all characteristic of the period about 400. The high quality of the diptych suggests a court artist in Milan.

Dalton, *Byzantine Art*, p. 194; Peirce and Tyler, *L'Art byzantin*, I, pl. 52; Bréhier, *Sculpture*, p. 69, pl. 21; L'Orange, *Studien*, p. 78; E. Capps, Jr. in *Art Bulletin*, 1949, p. 236; W. F. Volbach, *Elfenbeinarbeiten*, no. 63, pl. 19; *Storia di Milano*, I, 1953, pl. facing p. 360.

### 64

ROMAN CONSUL HOLDING THE MAPPA. Marble. About 400. Found in Rome. Rome, Palazzo dei Conservatori.

He wears a large toga folded across the left shoulder and below the right arm, and raises the *mappa* in his right hand; the left hand, holding a scepter, is restored (not shown). The same type of toga appears on the Obelisk of Theodosius [55] and the Column of Arcadius (Delbrueck, *Konsulardiptychen*, pp. 13–15, figs. 6–8). This manner of representing officials is more frequent in the East; thus, in Istanbul there are examples from Aphrodisias [50], Smyrna, and Ephesus (Rumpf, *Stilphasen*, fig. 61). Similarities with the reliefs on the base of the Obelisk of Theodosius and the Column of Arcadius suggest a date about 400. A companion piece with a somewhat more youthful face is in the same museum.

Helbig and Amelung, *Führer*, no. 908; F. Bruckmann, H. Brunn, and W. Arndt, *Griechische und römische Porträts*, Munich, 1891–1939, pl. 314; Venturi, *Storia*, I, p. 165, fig. 155; Wulff, *Altchristliche Kunst*, I, p. 153, fig. 146; Delbrueck, *Konsulardiptychen*, p. 49, fig. 18; Toesca, *Storia*, I, p. 244; Strong, *Scultura*, II, p. 409, fig. 251; C. Albizzati in *Diss. Pontificia Accademia Romana di archeologia*, 1921, pl. 12; L'Orange, *Studien*, p. 73; Rumpf, *Stilphasen*, p. 23, fig. 60.

### 65

AN OFFICIAL. Aphrodisian marble; fingers broken off. Height 6 ft., 1⅝ in. (1.87 m.). About 400. Found in the Baths of Aphrodisias. Istanbul, Archaeological Museum.

Over the tunic he wears a chlamys fastened on the right shoulder by a fibula. This statue is comparable to the next one [66, 67], also from the Baths of Aphrodisias, as well as two portraits in Aquileia (L'Orange, *Studien*, nos. 109–110, figs. 206–207), and a head from Aphrodisias in Brussels (F. Cumont, *Catalogue des sculptures... des Musées Royaux du Cinquantenaire*, Brussels, 1913, no. 41). It can be assigned a contemporary date on the strength of similarities with the reliefs on the Obelisk of Theodosius [54, 55]; akin to the *patricius* on the ivory diptych in Novara (Volbach, *Elfenbeinarbeiten*, no. 64, pl. 20).

Mendel, *Catalogue*, vol. II, no. 507, fig. G; C. Albizzati in *Diss. Pontificia Accademia Romana di archeologia*, p. 354; Schede, *Griechische und römische Skulpturen*, Berlin, 1928, pl. 46; Rodenwaldt, in *76. Winckelmannsprogramm*, p. 16; Wulff, *Altchristliche Kunst*, vol. I, p. 153, fig. 147; L'Orange, *Studien*, no. 108, fig. 203; Kollwitz, *Plastik*, p. 84, pl. 18; H. Kähler, *Wandlungen der antiken Form*, Berlin, fig. 29; Rumpf, *Stilphasen*, p. 30, fig. 96.

### 66, 67

AN OFFICIAL. Aphrodisian marble. Back not carved. Nose damaged. Height 5 ft., 11¼ in. (1.81 m.). About 400. Found in the Baths of Aphrodisias. Istanbul, Archaeological Museum.

He wears a long-sleeved tunic and chlamys. In the lowered right hand he holds a staff, the insignia of official dignity. From the same workshop, perhaps by the same artist, as the companion piece [65]; see also the comparative material and literature cited in the previous note.

Mendel, *Catalogue*, II, p. 508, fig. G; M. Schede, *Griechische und römische Skulpturen*, Berlin, 1928, p. 21, pls. 44–45; Wulff, *Altchristliche Kunst*, I, p. 153; L'Orange, *Studien*, p. 80, figs. 202–205; C. Albizzati, *Diss. Pontificia Accademia Romana di archeologia*, p. 354; C. Albizzati in *Historia*, 1929, p. 426; Kollwitz, *Plastik*, p. 83, pl. 17; Rumpf, *Stilphasen*, p. 29, fig. 99.

### 68

HEAD OF AN EMPRESS. Marble. Nose broken off. Waved hair, pearl diadem and cap. Height 10⅝ in. (27 cm.). Mid-5th century. Milan, Castello Sforzesco.

So far the Empress has not been securely identified. Some scholars (e.g., R. Delbrueck) suggest Theodora, others Justina, with 381–91 as the likely date (Peirce and Tyler, *L'Art byzan-*

*tin*, I, p. 48, pl. 44), or Pulcheria who married Marcian in 450. The last-mentioned identification has much to be said for it because of the strong resemblance with the so-called Marcian in Barletta [69–71].

R. Delbrueck in *Römische Mitteilungen*, 1913, pls. 9–10; Delbrueck, *Konsulardiptychen*, p. 35; Wulff, *Altchristliche Kunst*, I, p. 157, fig. 154; Toesca, *Storia*, I, p. 247; Volbach, Salles, and Dutuit, *Art byzantin*, p. 37; E. Lavagnino, *Il Medioevo*, Turin, 1936, p. 62; E. Strong, *Art in Ancient Rome*, London, 1929, II, p. 195, fig. 557; A. Alföldi in *Atlantis*, 1949, p. 67; *Catalogue*, Paris, no. 8, pl. 4; Rumpf, *Stilphasen*, p. 33, fig. 135.

## 69–71

CAST BRONZE STATUE, PROBABLY OF THE EMPEROR MARCIAN (450–67) Legs, skull above diadem, fibula, and lower left part of chlamys lost. Height (without legs) 11 ft., 7¾ in. (3.55 m.); originally about 16 ft. (5 m.) Barletta, in front of the Church of San Sepolcro.

Originally the raised right hand held a scepter or a labarum, and the outstretched left hand, an orb. The Emperor wears two tunics, armor, sash, chlamys with imperial fibula, and diadem. The fibula (lost) had a pearl pendant. The use of the jeweled diadem is attested from Constantine (325–26) to Anastasius (491–518).

The identification was long in doubt and even a Carolingian origin has been suggested (A. Haseloff in *Cicerone*, 1909, p. 461). The majority favor Valentinian I (H. Koch in *Antike Denkmäler*, III, p. 20, pls. 20–21; R. Delbrueck, *Bildnisse römischer Kaiser*, Berlin, 1914, pls. 40, 41; Rodenwaldt, *Kunst*, fig. 646, pl. 42). Subsequently, Delbrueck (*Kaiserporträts*, p. 219, pls. 116–120) altered his view in favor of Marcian. Comparisons with pieces like the head of an empress in Milan [68] and also the hair style make a date toward the middle of the 5th century the most probable.

Venturi, *Storia*, I, p. 414, fig. 154; Wulff, *Altchristliche Kunst*, I, p. 158, pl. 11; J. J. Bernoulli, *Römische Ikonographie*, Stuttgart, 1894, II, p. 3, pl. 56; Grabar, *L'Empereur*, p. 16, pl. 1; Delbrueck, *Kaiserporträts*, p. 219, pls. 116–120; Kollwitz, *Plastik*, p. 93, pls. 30, 42; P. H. von Blankenhagen in *Jahrbuch des deutschen archäologischen Institutes*, 1944–45, 1949, p. 57, figs. 15–16; Rumpf, *Stilphasen*, p. 33, fig. 132.

## 72

NIKE (Winged Victory). Relief. Marble. Height 8 ft., 9½ in. (2.68 m.), width 4 ft., 9 in. (1.50 m.). About 400. Istanbul, Archaeological Museum.

Formerly the piece was in the city wall opposite Eivan Seray, allegedly a companion piece to a Virgin Annunciate. A part of the left side is lost. The winged Nike or Victory, in long, girded tunic, carrying a palm branch, strides to the left. Several scholars (Mordtmann in *Revue de l'art chrétien*, 1891, p. 22; J. Strzygowski, *Orient oder Rom*, Leipzig, 1901, p. 29; Wulff, *Altchristliche Kunst*, I, p. 174, fig. 168) have mistaken the figure for the Archangel Gabriel and therefore described it as a companion piece to a figure of the Virgin Annunciate. Datable on the strength of similarities with Theodosian reliefs, such as the sarcophagus of a prince [75] and the Obelisk of Theodosius [54, 55].

Mendel, *Catalogue*, II, p. 449, no. 667, fig. p. 450; L. Bréhier, *Etudes sur l'histoire de la sculpture byzantine* (Archives des missions scientifiques), Paris, 1911, p. 12; Kollwitz, *Plastik*, p. 77, pl. 15.

## 73

CHRIST BETWEEN TWO APOSTLES. Fragment of a sarcophagus. Proconnesian marble. Only fragment preserved. Height 4 ft., 7⅞ in. (1.42 m.), width 4 ft., 7¾ in. (1.24 m.). About 400. From Istanbul, Sulu Monastir in Psamatia. Berlin, Staatliche Museen.

A youthful Christ dressed as a philosopher, and wearing a large cloak over a tunic, stands in the center in front of a colonnaded structure. On each side, an Apostle, similarly dressed, turns toward Him.

The only preserved Christian example of the so-called Sidamara sarcophagi produced principally in Asia Minor. See the sarcophagus from Sidamara in Istanbul (Morey, *Early Christian Art*, fig. 16), and a pagan piece with a similar composition in Rome, Villa Colonna (Wulff, *Altchristliche Kunst*, I, p. 164). The fragment may be dated about 400 on the strength of similarities with the reliefs on the Obelisk of Theodosius [54, 55]. The relief foreshadows the early Ravenna sarcophagi [174].

Ainalov, *Foundations*, p. 160, pl. 4; J. Strzygowski, *Byzantinische Denkmäler*, III, Leipzig, 1903, p. XIII; Wulff, *Beschreibung*, I, no. 26; Wulff, *Altchristliche Kunst*, I, p. 172, fig. 66; Dalton, *East Christian Art*, p. 182; Strong, *Scultura*, II, p. 319; Wilpert, *Sarcofagi*, pl. 31, 2; Gerke, *Christus*, p. 68, fig. 75; Peirce and Tyler, *L'Art byzantin*, I, p. 64; Volbach, Salles, and Dutuit, *Art byzantin*, pl. 6; Kollwitz, *Plastik*, p. 166, pl. 50; D. Talbot Rice, *Byzantine Art*, rev. ed., Harmondsworth, 1954, p. 157; K. Wessel *Rom, Byzanz, Russland. Ein Führer*, Berlin, 1957, p. 123, fig. 5.

## 74

EVANGELIST. Marble medallion. Slightly damaged. Height 27⅛ in. (69 cm.). About 400. Found in Istanbul with three similar busts, also Evangelists in all likelihood. Istanbul, Archaeological Museum.

Originally in the form of a medallion, the bearded Evangelist, wearing a long cloak over a long-sleeved tunic, holds in his hands a book bearing a Greek cross. The arrangement of folds recalls the statue of Valentinian II [50], the angels on the Sarcophagus of a Prince [75], and the Victory on the Column of Marcian (Delbrueck, *Kaiserporträts*, fig. 75).

J. Strzygowski in *Byzantinische Zeitschrift*, 1892, p. 585, pl. III; Wulff, *Beschreibung*, I, no. 29, p. 18; Dalton, *Byzantine Art*, p. 153; Mendel, *Catalogue*, II, no. 661; Peirce and Tyler, *L'Art byzantin*, I, fig. 87; F. Gerke, *Das heilige Antlitz*, Berlin, 1940, p. 48, pl. 60.

## 75

SARCOPHAGUS OF A PRINCE. Marble. Height 18¾ in. (47.5 cm.), width 19¼ in. (49 cm.), length 4 ft., 5½ in. (1.36 m.). Probably about 400; with the sarcophagus were found coins of Constantine and Arcadius. Found in 1933 in the valley of the Lycos in Istanbul. Istanbul, Archaeological Museum.

Relief on all four sides. On each of the long sides, two confronting winged angels in flight, carrying a wreath containing the monogram of Christ; on each of the short sides, a large cross flanked by two Apostles (partly unfinished).

Made in all likelihood for a prince of the imperial family. Approximate date suggested by similarities with the reliefs on the Obelisk of Theodosius [54, 55]. The classicizing style recalls the drapery treatment on the diptych of Stilicho [62, 63].

Wilpert, *Sarcofagi*, III, p. 54, pl. 299; A. Müfit, *Ein Prinzensarkophag aus Istanbul*, Istanbul, 1934; H. von Schönebeck in *Römische Mitteilungen*, 1936, p. 326; A. C. Soper in *Art Bulletin*, 1937, p. 195, figs. 52, 54; Kollwitz, *Plastik*, p. 132, pls. 45, 47; Morey, *Early Christian Art*, p. 104, fig. 102.

## 76, 77

COLUMN DRUMS. Marble. First half of the 5th century. Apparently excavated near Hagia Sophia. Istanbul, Archaeological Museum.

[76] Fragments broken away at the top and bottom; height 25⅝ in. (65.2 cm.), diameter 23⅝ in. (60 cm.). Above: two women carrying sacrificial animals. Below: *The Baptism*.

[77] Roughly half the lower part is lost; height 30 in. (76 cm.), diameter 24⅝ in. (62.5 cm.). A shepherd with his dog; a bull.

Both pieces may have belonged to the same column since the technique of carving is the same. Small scenes with figures are set into vine scrolls. Of the two women, wearing long tunics, one carries a cock under her arm, the other a dog [76 above]; on their right is a goat (Mendel, *Catalogue*, II, p. 440, no. 659). In *The Baptism* [76 below] two angels carrying His clothes stand on the right of the naked Christ while St. John stands on His left. Underneath is the personification of Jordan, next to it Jonah (?), sleeping. A shepherd leaning on his staff holds a dog on a leash [77]. A charging Indian bull approaches from the right (Mendel, *Catalogue*, II, p. 435, no. 658).

The style is close to the columns of the ciborium in San Marco [82, 83] and the reliefs on the lintel of its north porch (Wulff, *Altchristliche Kunst*, I, figs. 121–122), and like these, to be dated in the first half of the 5th century. For columns, in the shape of, and decorated with vine scrolls, see E. Rosenbaum in *Journal of the Warburg and Courtauld Institutes*, 1955, p. 1.

Wulff, *Altchristliche Kunst*, I, p. 175, fig. 169; L. Bréhier, *L'Art chrétien, son développement iconographique des origines à nos jours*, Paris, 1918, fig. 99; Peirce and Tyler, *L'Art byzantin*, I, p. 81, pl. 127; *Catalogue*, Baltimore, no. 54.

## 78, 79

AMBO. Marble fragments, heavily damaged. Each half: height 5 ft., 10½ in. (1.79 m.), width 31 in. (0.79 m.). Second half of the 5th century. From Salonika. The right half (as seen when facing the ambo) formerly in Hagios Georgios, the left in Hagios Panteleimon. Istanbul, Archaeological Museum.

[78] Left: fragment, one of the Magi. Right: fragment, *The Virgin and Child*.

[79] Fragment: *The Virgin and Child with Angels*.

Each half has a stair at the back and the passage between them was originally spanned by a lintel. Portions of the upper parts have been broken off, the niches below damaged, two figures in the narrative relief half destroyed, and all the heads almost unrecognizable. The parapet above is decorated with acanthus leaves. On the outer faces are scalloped niches with columns; within these the Journey and Adoration of the Magi are developed from niche to niche. In the last niche on the outer side of the left block is a shepherd; the eagles in the spandrels indicate an imperial donation.

Though the composition recalls the Sidamara sarcophagi and the iconography follows Syrian models, it may have been produced in Salonika, as the ornament recalls the moldings in Hagios Georgios, and the somewhat later ones in Hagios Dimitrios [214]. The pulpit would thus seem to be datable to the second half of the 5th century.

Mendel, *Catalogue*, II, p. 393, no. 643; Garrucci, *Storia*, pl. 426, 1; Cabrol and Leclercq, *Dictionnaire*, vol. I, col. 1339; Wulff, *Altchristliche Kunst*, I, p. 135, figs. 124–125; G. de Jerphanion in *Atti della Pontificia Academia Romana di archeologia*, 1932–33, p. 107; G. Soteriou in *Epeteris Hetaireias Byzantinon Spoudon*, 1933, p. 418; Kollwitz, *Plastik*, p. 169; Morey, *Early Christian Art*, p. 107, fig. 111.

## 80

THREE PIERS. Marble. Height from 40½ in. to 44 in. (1.03 m.– 1.10 m.). Late 5th or early 6th century. Istanbul, Archaeological Museum.

On the lateral faces of the piers are grooves for the large, thin slabs of stone that formed the screen. For a similar piece from Top Capou, with a horseman transfixing a lion, see G. Mendel (*Catalogue*, II, p. 493, no. 694), and for three from Izmit, A. Müfit (in *Archäologischer Anzeiger*, 1931, p. 207, figs. 20–24).

Left: from Degirmendere, Izmit. On the main face an engaged round shaft decorated with vine scrolls. At the bottom a mask fashioned from leaves, within the scroll a bird, then a putto gathering grapes, and in the top loop a shepherd with a dog; on the capital an *orans*. On the lateral faces, children's heads (Firatli, *Guide*, p. 35, no. 4477, fig. 12).

Middle: decorative patterns similar to a piece from Nuruosmaniye, Istanbul, now in the Archaeological Museum (A. Müfit in *Archäologischer Anzeiger*, 1931, p. 207, fig. 24).

Right: from Izmit. The main face and engaged round shaft decorated with acanthus scrolls. In the capital Meleager and Atalanta (?) (A. Müfit in *Archäologischer Anzeiger*, 1931, p. 207, fig. 23). The pier copies antique models; compare the column decorated with vine scrolls possibly from Cyzicus, now in Istanbul (B. Ashmole in *Journal of the Warburg and Courtauld Institutes*, 1956, p. 186, pl. 39b). The putto gathering grapes recalls the reliefs on the column drums [76, 77], and the ornamentation on the door from Hagios Dimitrios in Salonika, now in the Byzantine Museum in Athens (Peirce and Tyler, *L'Art byzantin*, I, fig. 85). The pieces thus seem to date in the second half of the 5th century or perhaps the beginning of the 6th.

## 81

THE ENTRY INTO JERUSALEM. Limestone relief, damaged. Height 39¼ in. (1 m.), width 59 in. (1.50 m.). Late 5th or early 6th century. Found in Istanbul, in the Church of St. John Studion, together with two other reliefs, a fragment with Apostles and a *Maiestas Domini* (Mendel, *Catalogue*, II, p. 453, nos. 668–670). Istanbul, Archaeological Museum.

The top border is decorated with a vine scroll, the left border with acanthus leaves. Christ rides on a mule toward a city gate on the right; He is greeted by three persons. The right side has been lost.

**82, 83**

COLUMNS OF A CIBORIUM. Alabaster. Height 9 ft., 10 in. (3.01 m.). 5th century. Venice, San Marco.

[82] Front and back views of the three lower registers of the left front column. Above: *The Adoration of the Magi.* Center: *Joseph,* and *The Annunciation to the Shepherds.* Below: *The Visitation* and *The Nativity.*

[83] Detail of the right front column. Above: *Christ in Limbo.* Below: *The Marys at the Sepulcher.*

In all likelihood the four columns were brought to Venice in 1204 by the Crusaders. According to some scholars only the two front ones are original, while the two back ones are medieval Venetian copies (Morey, *Early Christian Art,* p. 105, fig. 108). For a thorough discussion of their authenticity, see E. Lucchesi Palli *(Ciboriumsäule).* Medieval inscriptions were added in Venice. Clearly the work of several hands, the front columns, by the principal masters, depict the story of the Virgin, *The Nativity,* scenes from the Life and Passion of Christ, ending with *The Ascension.* The back columns are in a coarser style.

Stylistically they are akin to the reliefs on the column drums in Istanbul [76, 77], and to those on the lintel over the north porch of San Marco (Wulff, *Altchristliche Kunst,* I, figs. 121–122). A. Venturi *(Storia,* I, p. 444, figs. 219, 272) already considered the back columns medieval Venetian copies: E. Lucchesi Palli *(Ciboriumsäule)* is even more emphatic, and some iconographic features not otherwise known before the Late Middle Ages are certainly difficult to explain. Though all four columns could be copies, the two front ones show such excellent workmanship that they can be plausibly attributed to the Eastern art of the 5th century.

H. von der Gabelentz, *Mittelalterliche Plastik in Venedig,* 1903, p. 32; Dalton, *Byzantine Art,* p. 155; Toesca, *Storia,* I, p. 266, fig. 163; G. Constantini in *Arte cristiana,* 1915, p. 8; Kollwitz, *Plastik,* p. 159, 179; Wulff, *Altchristliche Kunst,* I, Nachtrag, p. 16; A. C. Soper in *Art Bulletin,* 1938, p. 145, figs. 23, 61–64; Morey, *Early Christian Art,* p. 106, figs. 108–109.

**84–101**

LATE ANTIQUE IVORIES. Such large quantities have survived that by themselves the ivories provide sufficient material for a study of the stylistic development of the period. Ivory had been used earlier for caskets, diptychs, furniture ornaments, even doors, but it is in the middle of the 4th century that it came into full flower. Emperors, consuls, and high officials had ivory writing tablets (diptychs) made on assuming office [90, 91, 96, 97, 219, 220]; cylindrical boxes (pyxides) for jewelry and incense at first were decorated largely with pagan representations [84], though soon after the middle of the 4th century Christian scenes make their appearance [casket, 85–89; pyxis, 95]. Characteristic for the conservative Roman senatorial families are the diptychs made about 400 that still carry pagan representations [90, 91]. After the middle of the 6th century this expensive material became progressively rarer since the hunting grounds in Africa and India were depleted, and the Arab advances cut off imports.

The classification of the 5th- and 6th-century ivories according to various schools has not, so far, been entirely successful.

Among the early pieces, many diptychs dating from the late 4th and 5th centuries are clearly of Roman origin: those of the vice-prefect of the city, Rufius Probianus, now in Berlin (ca. 400), the Roman families of the Nicomachi and the Symmachi [90, 91], and of Roman consuls—Probus, 406, Felix, 428 [96], Basilius, 480, Boethius, 487, Sividius, 488 [97], and Orestes, 530. But soon Milan seems to have had its own workshops [92], and when the court moved to Ravenna, the Milanese ivory carvers probably moved with it. The five-part panel today in Milan [100, 101] was perhaps produced in Ravenna.

Other imperial residences also must have had workshops, as the pyxis found in Trier [95] indicates. Alexandria may well have been another center of some significance: reliefs such as those on the pulpit in Aachen breathe unmistakably the spirit of that city. A group of artists may also have been active in Antioch though it has not, so far, been possible to attribute specific pieces to them. In Constantinople secure attributions cannot be made until the beginning of the 6th century and consist principally of diptychs of the Constantinopolitan consuls: Areobindus, 506, Clementinus, 513, Anastasius, 517 [202], Magnus, 518, Justinian, 521, Philoxenus, 525, Apion, 539, and Justin, 540. It has become possible to distinguish the Byzantine school from various workshops active further East, especially in Asia Minor [223] and in the region of the Caucasus, mainly in Armenia. In Gaul, ivory carving seems to have continued well into Merovingian times [237].

Nearly all extant pieces have by now entered public collections and have been published, principally in the catalogues of the large museums: Paris—E. Molinier, *Catalogue des ivoires du Musée du Louvre,* Paris, 1896; London—Dalton, *Catalogue Ivories;* Longhurst, *Catalogue;* Berlin—W. F. Volbach, *Die Elfenbeinbildwerke,* 1923; the Vatican—C. R. Morey, *Gli oggetti di avorio e di osso del Museo Sacro Vaticano,* 1936. The extensive specialized literature in R. Delbrueck *(Konsulardiptychen)* and W. F. Volbach *(Elfenbeinarbeiten);* see also the catalogues of various exhibitions: the 1923 exhibition of ivories in London (Burlington Fine Arts Club); the 1931 and 1952 Byzantine exhibitions in Paris; the 1948 exhibition, *Kunstschätze der Lombardei,* in Zurich; and the 1956 exhibition of ivories in Ravenna, catalogue *(Avori)* by Bovini.

**84**

PYXIS. Ivory. Height 6¼ in. (16 cm.), width 5⅛ in. (13 cm.). End of the 4th century. Bobbio, San Colombano.

Above, left: Orpheus. Below, right: a hunting scene.

In the center Orpheus, wearing a long robe, is surrounded by wild beasts; at the back two galloping horsemen with their dogs battle against lions and tigers.

Closely akin to the Orpheus pyxis from Brioude (Haute-Loire), now in the Bargello, Florence (Volbach, *Elfenbeinarbeiten,* no. 92). G. Rodenwaldt (in *Jahrbuch des deutschen archäologischen Institutes,* 1922, p. 36) dates the Bobbio pyxis in the 4th century because of stylistic affinities to the Belgrade cameo.

Venturi, *Storia,* I, p. 444, figs. 404–405; Cabrol and Leclercq, *Dictionnaire,* vol. III, pt. 1, col. 1097, fig. 2687; O. Reichl in *Archäologischer Anzeiger,* 1932, p. 549, fig. 2; Volbach, *Elfenbeinarbeiten,* no. 91, pl. 28.

**85–89**

CASKET. Ivory, with an old silver lock. Height 8⅝ in. (22 cm.), width 9½ in. (24 cm.), length 12⅞ in. (32.7 cm.). About 360–70. From the Church of Santa Giulia. Brescia, Museo Civico, which was formerly the Church of Santa Giulia.

[85] View of the casket as a whole.

[86] Above: the front and rim of the lid. Below: detail of the rim, Christ in the center, an Apostle on each side.

[87] Above: the back and rim of the lid. Below: detail of the rim, two Apostles.

[88] The side panels.

[89] The lid.

The casket seems to have been dismembered while still belonging to the church, and the panels reassembled to form a cross. Traditionally it has been called a *lipsanotheca*, a casket for relics. On the front: Christ, inside a building, is surrounded by the Apostles; to the right, Christ, under an arcade, as the Good Shepherd; to the left, *The Woman with the Issue of Blood*, in the narrow register at the bottom, scenes from the story of Susanna and *Daniel in the Lions' Den;* in the narrow register at the top, scenes from the story of Jonah.

On the back, at the left: Christ, on the shore of the Sea of Galilee, standing between two youths; in the center, *Sapphira Before St. Peter*, and at the right, Ananias; in the narrow panel on the far right: *The Death of Judas;* in the narrow register below: *The Finding of Moses, Moses Slaying the Egyptian*, and *The Marriage at Cana* (?) or *Moses Feasted by Jethro*, according to R. Delbrueck (*Probleme der Lipsanothek in Brescia*, Bonn, 1952, p. 12); in the narrow register above: Susanna, *The Drunkenness of Noah*, and *The Brazen Serpent*.

Right side: *The Healing of the Blind* and *The Raising of Lazarus;* narrow register above: *Moses on Mount Sinai, Korah and His Band Swallowed Up* (?), and *Moses Receiving the Law* (Delbrueck, *ibid.*, p. 14); narrow register below: *Jacob and Rachel at the Well, Jacob and the Angel*, and *Jacob's Ladder*.

Left side: *The Raising of Jairus' Daughter;* narrow register above: *David and Goliath, The Man of God Slain by a Lion and Watched Over by His Ass* (I Kings 13), and *Jeroboam at the Altar of Bethel* (I Kings 13); narrow register below: *The Sacrificial Feast Before the Golden Calf*.

Lid: narrow frieze above: six doves representing souls; upper register: *Christ in Gethsemane, Christ Taken*, and *The Denial of Peter;* lower register: *Christ Before Caiaphas* and *Christ Before Pilate*. On the rims of the lid: medallions with Christ, eleven Apostles, and SS. Matthew, Paul, and Barnabas; several have been obliterated.

On the strength of stylistic parallels with columnar sarcophagi, the casket can be dated in the third quarter of the 4th century. The earlier date, about 320, put forward by Delbrueck (*ibid.*), is not acceptable, especially because of the hair styles. Close iconographic connections with gold-glass medallions and frescoes in the catacombs assure its Western origin.

Venturi, *Storia*, I, figs. 273–277; Dalton, *East Christian Art*, p. 208; Wulff, *Altchristliche Kunst*, I, p. 185, fig. 182, Nachtrag, p. 22; G. Rodenwaldt in *Römische Mitteilungen*, 1921–22, p. 103; E. Weigand in *Kritische Berichte zur kunstwissenschaftlichen Litteratur*, 1930–31, p. 53; F. Gerke in *Rivista di Archeologia Cristiana*, 1935, p. 140; A. C. Soper in *Art Bulletin*, 1938, p. 173, figs. 53, 56, 58–60; A. Alföldi in *Atlantis*, 1949, p. 80, figs. 84–86; J. Kollwitz,

*Die Lipsanothek von Brescia*, Berlin, 1933; J. Natanson, *Early Christian Ivories*, London, 1953, nos. 1–2; H. Stern in *Römische Quartalschriften*, 1955, p. 115; Volbach, *Elfenbeinarbeiten*, no. 107, pl. 31; Bovini, *Avori*, no. 8, figs. 11–15.

**90–91**

DIPTYCH OF THE NICOMACHI AND THE SYMMACHI. Ivory. Height 11¾ in. (29.9 cm.), width 4⅞ in. (12.4 cm.). 392 or 401. Formerly in the shrine of St. Bercharius in Montier-en-Der. The panel NICOMACHORUM (Musée Cluny) heavily damaged. Left panel: Paris, Musée Cluny; right panel: London, Victoria and Albert Museum.

[90] Left panel: the priestess of Ceres before the altar of Cybele. Inscription: NICOMACHORUM.

[91] Right panel: the priestess of Bacchus before the altar of Jupiter. Inscription: SYMMACHORUM.

The occasion of the panels was almost certainly a marriage alliance of these two Roman senatorial families, either about 392 or in 401. Their conservative political attitude is reflected artistically in the adoption of Augustan models. The diptych of the vice-prefect of the city, Rufius Probianus (Volbach, *Elfenbeinarbeiten*, no. 55, pl. 14), and the panel with *The Marys at the Sepulcher* in Milan [92] are very close to this diptych.

Longhurst, *Catalogue*, I, p. 26; Wulff, *Altchristliche Kunst*, I, p. 190; A. Haseloff in *Jahrbuch der preussischen Kunstsammlungen*, 1903, p. 55; Venturi, *Storia*, I, figs. 354–355; Delbrueck, *Konsulardiptychen*, no. 54, pl. 54; E. Weigand in *Kritische Berichte zur kunstwissenschaftlichen Litteratur*, 1930–31, p. 44; A. C. Soper in *Art Bulletin*, 1938, p. 164, fig. 15; E. Capps, Jr. in *Art Bulletin*, 1949, p. 233; Volbach, *Elfenbeinarbeiten*, no. 55, pl. 14.

**92**

THE MARYS AT THE SEPULCHER. Ivory leaf of a diptych. Height 12 in. (30.7 cm.), width 5¼ in. (13.4 cm.). About 400. From the Trivulzio Collection. Milan, Castello Sforzesco.

Below, in front of the decorated door of the sepulcher, the angel, seated on a rock, announces the Resurrection to the two Marys. Above, separated by an ornamental frieze, are the two sleeping soldiers in front of the sepulcher and the symbols of the Evangelists Matthew and Luke.

Closely akin to the diptych of the vice-prefect Rufius Probianus in Berlin and the panel with *The Ascension* in Munich [93]. Border ornament similar to that on the panels of the Nicomachi and the Symmachi [90, 91]. The rendering of architectural features is reminiscent of the Roman sarcophagus [44] but, in spite of these affinities with Roman pieces, it is possibly of North Italian origin.

Wulff, *Altchristliche Kunst*, I, p. 187, fig. 184; Delbrueck, *Konsulardiptychen*, no. 68; Smith, *Iconography*, p. 240; A. C. Soper in *Art Bulletin*, 1938, p. 154, fig. 16; E. P. de Loos-Dietz, *Vroeg-christelijke ivoren*, Assen, 1947, p. 103, fig. 18; Grabar, *Martyrium*, I, p. 271, pl. 16, 3; A. Ottino della Chiesa in *Bolletino d'Arte*, 1949, p. 255; Volbach, *Elfenbeinarbeiten*, no. 111, pl. 33; R. Delbrueck in *Bonner Jahrbuch*, 1952, p. 173; Bovini, *Avori*, no. 10.

**93**

THE MARYS AT THE SEPULCHER AND THE ASCENSION. Ivory. Height 7⅜ in. (18.7 cm.), width 4½ in. (11.6 cm.). About 400. From Bamberg. Perhaps the center piece of a five-part diptych. Munich, Bayerisches Nationalmuseum.

Two events are telescoped into one scene: below, the three Marys approach the angel sitting in front of the sepulcher *aedicula;* two soldiers, one of them asleep, lean against it. Higher up to the right, Christ, ascending to heaven, grasps the hand of God stretched out to Him. At His feet two Apostles.

This panel is close to *The Marys at the Sepulcher* in Milan [92] and the diptych of the Lampadii in Brescia (Volbach, *Elfenbeinarbeiten*, no. 54, pl. 18), and somewhat earlier than the Maskell casket in the British Museum [98]. Hence about 400 is a likely date; perhaps of North Italian origin.

Venturi, *Storia*, I, p. 111, fig. 60; Wulff, *Altchristliche Kunst*, I, p. 187; A. Goldschmidt, *Die Elfenbeinskulpturen aus der Zeit der karolingischen und sächsischen Kaiser*, I, Berlin, 1914, p. 69, fig. 27; R. Berliner, *Die Bildwerke des bayerischen Nationalmuseums*, IV, Augsburg, 1926, no. 1, pl. 1; H. Schrade, *Die Ikonographie der christlichen Kunst. I. Die Auferstehung Christi*, Berlin, 1932, p. 29, fig. 4; Delbrueck, *Konsulardiptychen*, p. 30; F. Gerke in *Archaeologiai Értesitö*, 1940, p. 62, fig. 75; Gerke, *Christus*, 51, fig. 88; A. C. Soper in *Art Bulletin*, 1938, p. 164, fig. 37; E. Capps, Jr. in *Art Bulletin*, 1949, p. 235; Grabar, *Martyrium*, I, p. 271, pl. 16, 2; G. H. Forsyth in *Art Bulletin*, p. 318, fig. 5; Volbach, *Elfenbeinarbeiten*, no. 110, pl. 33; R. Delbrueck in *Bonner Jahrbuch*, 1952, p. 176, pl. 28.

## 94

BELLEROPHON. Ivory, openwork; ornamental panel. Height 8¼ in. (21.2 cm.), width 3½ in. (8.8 cm.). 5th century. London, British Museum.

Bellerophon, mounted on Pegasus, slays the chimaera with his lance. Both the iconography and the horseshoe arches in the arcade of the upper border point to an Eastern origin. Stylistically it is akin to the ivory with circus scenes of lion fights in Leningrad (see Volbach, *Elfenbeinarbeiten*, no. 60, pl. 17). Datable to the 5th century.

Dalton, *Catalogue Ivories*, no. 6, pl. III; Delbrueck, *Konsulardiptychen*, p. 27, fig. 12; Peirce and Tyler, *L'Art byzantin*, vol. I, fig. 120; Volbach, *Elfenbeinarbeiten*, no. 67, pl. 20.

## 95

PYXIS. Ivory. Height 4¾ in. (12 cm.), diameter 5¾ in. (14.6 cm.). About 400. From a village near Trier. Berlin, Staatliche Museen.

Above: front, a youthful Christ enthroned, among the twelve Apostles. Below: back, *The Sacrifice of Abraham*.

A pyxis with a similar Sacrifice of Abraham was found in the arena at Trier, see W. F. Volbach (*Elfenbeinarbeiten*, no. 162, pl. 53), who suggests that this piece may be a product of the court workshops in Trier. The scene with Christ has affinities with scenes on large, ornate sarcophagi of the 4th century. On stylistic similarities to the pyxis in Bobbio [84], it is datable about 400 or shortly after.

Venturi, *Storia*, I, p. 354, fig. 395; C. R. Morey in *Art Bulletin*, 1924–25, fig. 18; Morey, *Early Christian Art*, p. 89, figs. 79–80; Delbrueck, *Konsulardiptychen*, p. 161, figs. 1–2; E. Capps, Jr. in *Art Bulletin*, 1927, p. 73; Bréhier, *Sculpture*, p. 71, pl. 25; *Kunst der Spätantike*, catalogue, Berlin, 1939, no. 156; Volbach, *Elfenbeinarbeiten*, no. 161, pl. 53; K. Wessel in *Wissenschaftliche Zeitschrift der Universität Greifswald*, 1952–53, p. 63, figs. 1a–b.

## 96

PANEL OF THE DIPTYCH OF THE CONSUL FELIX. Rome, 428. Ivory. Companion panel lost. Height 11½ in. (29.2 cm.), width 5½ in. (13.6 cm.). Formerly in Limoges. Paris, Cabinet des Médailles.

Inscription: FL(avii) FELICIS V(iri) C(larissimi) COM(itis) AC MAG(istri). In his left hand the consul holds the scepter of office surmounted by the busts of Theodosius II and Valentinian III. His *tunica palmata*, worn over a *tunica talaris*, is unornamented, the *toga contabulata* folded over the left shoulder.

Venturi, *Storia*, I, p. 488, fig. 334; Peirce and Tyler, *L'Art byzantin*, I, p. 73, fig. 110; Delbrueck, *Konsulardiptychen*, no. 3; E. Weigand in *Kritische Berichte zur kunstwissenschaftlichen Litteratur*, 1930–31, p. 33; E. Ducati, *Storia di Roma*, XXVI, Bologna, 1938, pl. 273, 1; E. Capps, Jr. in *Art Bulletin*, 1927, p. 68, fig. 6; A. C. Soper in *Art Bulletin*, 1938, p. 154, fig. 18; Volbach, *Elfenbeinarbeiten*, no. 2, pl. 1.

## 97 LEFT

PANEL OF THE DIPTYCH OF THE CONSUL SIVIDIUS. Rome, 488. Ivory. Height 5¾ in. (14.7 cm.), width 4⅛ in. (10.6 cm.). From Gerunden (Wallis). Paris, Cabinet des Médailles.

Medallion inscription: RVFIVS ACHILIVS SIVIDIVS V(ir) C(larissimus) ET INL(ustris) EX PRAEF(ecto) VRBIS. Decorated with acanthus scrolls, and in the corners, with rosettes.

Delbrueck, *Konsulardiptychen*, no. 8; Peirce and Tyler, *L'Art byzantin*, I, fig. 166a; Volbach, *Elfenbeinarbeiten*, no. 7, pl. 3.

## 97 RIGHT

PANEL OF THE DIPTYCH OF THE CONSUL BASILIUS. Rome, 480. Ivory. Height 13⅜ in. (34 cm.), width 5 in. (12.7 cm.). Florence, Museo Nazionale (Bargello).

The companion piece is in the Castello Sforzesco, Milan (Volbach, *Elfenbeinarbeiten*, no. 5, pl. 15).

Inscription: ANIC(ius) FAVST(us) ALBIN(us) BASILIVS V(ir) C(larissimus). The consul stands beside the personification of Rome who carries the *fasce*. He wears a tunic and colobium, and holds the *mappa* in his right hand and the scepter of office in his left. Below, four quadrigae on the race course; on the right, a senator. Stylistically it is akin to the diptych of the consul Boethius in Brescia which dates from 487 (Volbach, *Elfenbeinarbeiten*, no. pl. 2).

Delbrueck, *Konsulardiptychen*, no. 6, pl. 6; E. Weigand in *Kritische Berichte zur kunstwissenschaftlichen Litteratur*, 1930–31, p. 37; E. Capps, Jr. in *Art Bulletin*, 1927, p. 91, fig. 21; Cecchelli, *Vita*, I, p. 225, fig. p. 227; Volbach, *Elfenbeinarbeiten*, no. 5, pl. 3; Bovini, *Avori*, no. 29, fig. 35.

## 98

CASKET WITH SCENES FROM THE PASSION. Ivory. Height 3 in. (7.5 cm.), width 3⅞ in. (9.8 cm.). About 420. London, British Museum.

Above: *Pilate Washing His Hands*, *Christ Carrying the Cross*, and *The Denial of Peter*. Below: *The Death of Judas* and *Christ on the Cross*.

On the other sides are: *The Marys at the Sepulcher* and *The Incredulity of Thomas*. The date is suggested by stylistic relations to the diptych of the Lampadii in Brescia (Volbach, *Elfenbeinarbeiten*, no. 54, pl. 18) and the side panels of the five-part diptych in Berlin and Paris (Volbach, *Elfenbeinarbeiten*, nos. 112–113, pl. 34). In all likelihood it is a North Italian product, and shows traces of iconographic influence from Ravenna. The five-part diptych in Milan [100, 101] is also close to it but later.

Venturi, *Storia*, I, figs. 397–400; Dalton, *Catalogue Ivories*, no. 7, pl. 4; Smith, *Iconography*, p. 205; O. Reichl in *Archäologischer Anzeiger*, 1932, p.

544; A. C. Soper in *Art Bulletin*, 1938, p. 153, fig. 9; Kitzinger, *Early Mediaeval Art*, p. 100, pl. 7; F. Gerke in *Archaeologiai Értesitö*, 1940, p. 116, pl. 18, 77–78; E. Capps, Jr. in *Art Bulletin*, 1949, p. 235; K. Wessel in *Jahrbuch des deutschen archäologischen Institutes*, 1948–49, p. 125, figs. 6–9; Volbach, *Elfenbeinarbeiten*, no. 116, pl. 35; L. B. Ottolenghi in *Felix Ravenna*, 1955, p. 19, fig. 23.

## 99

AN APOSTLE. North Italy. Ivory. Height 4¾ in. (12 cm.), width 2¾ in. (7.1 cm.). Beginning of the 5th century. Paris, Louvre.

The Apostle, wearing a tunic and cloak, still recalls types known from sarcophagi and is also close to a panel with an Apostle in the Victoria and Albert Museum, London (Volbach, *Elfenbeinarbeiten*, no. 122, pl. 35), as well as a diptych leaf with a boar hunt in Liverpool (Volbach, *Elfenbeinarbeiten*, no. 59, pl. 19).

G. Migeon in *Les Arts*, 1910, p. 13; Volbach, *Elfenbeinarbeiten*, no. 123, pl. 35; E. Rosenbaum in *Art Bulletin*, 1954, p. 225, fig. 4.

## 100, 101

FIVE-PART DIPTYCH. Ivory. Height 14¾ in. (37.5 cm.), width 11⅛ in. (28.1 cm.). Second half of the 5th century. Milan, Cathedral Treasury.

[100] Center panel: within a wreath set in front of a linteled doorway, the Lamb of God, nimbed. The animal is executed in silver cloisonné inlaid with almandites. Top panel: *The Nativity* and the symbols of the Evangelists Matthew and Luke. Left panel: *The Annunciation at the Well*, the Magi, and *The Baptism of Christ*. Right panel: *The Virgin Going to the Temple*, *Christ Among the Doctors*, and *The Entry into Jerusalem*. Bottom panel: *The Massacre of the Innocents* flanked by wreaths containing busts of SS. Matthew and Luke.

[101] Center panel: in front of a linteled doorway, a jeweled cross made up of stones in raised settings is set on the Mountain of Paradise from which issue the Four Rivers. Above: *The Adoration of the Magi* flanked by wreaths containing the symbols of the Evangelists Mark and John. Left: *The Healing of the Blind*, *The Healing of the Paralytic*, and *The Raising of Lazarus*. Right: Christ on the globe between two blessed martyrs, *The Last Supper*, and *The Widow's Mite*. Below: *The Marriage at Cana* flanked by the wreaths containing the busts of SS. Mark and John.

The iconography foreshadows the mosaics in Sant'Apollinare Nuovo, Ravenna [150, 151], and it is possible that the panels are a product of Ravenna. There are also affinities with South Gallic sarcophagi. The interesting technique of inlaying recalls the cloisonné work of the lost "Harness of Theodoric" (W. A. Jenny and W. F. Volbach, *Germanischer Schmuck*, Berlin, 1933, p. 16, pl. 16).

Venturi, *Stori*, I, p. 509, figs. 388–389; Wulff, *Altchristliche Kunst*, I, p. 186; Smith, *Iconography*, p. 206; R. Delbrueck in *Antike Denkmäler*, IV, p. 5, pls. 5–6; J. Kollwitz, *Die Lipsanothek von Brescia*, Berlin, 1933, p. 48; Volbach, in Bossert, *Geschichte*, V, p. 64, figs. 155–156; Volbach, *Elfenbeinarbeiten*, no. 119, pl. 37; H. von Schönebeck in *Jahrbuch des deutschen archäologischen Institutes*, 1932, p. 120, figs. 10–11; *Kunstschätze der Lombardei*, no. 53; Delbrueck in *Bonner Jahrbuch*, 1951, p. 96, pls. 2–3, and 1952, p. 184; J. Beckwith in *Art Bulletin*, 1958, p. 3, figs. 2–3.

330

## 102

FRAGMENTS OF THE WOODEN DOORS OF SANT' AMBROGIO. Cedar. Milan.

Above: the monogram of Christ between peacocks, framed by acanthus scroll borders. Probably made during restoration in the 9th century. Height 33½ in. (85 cm.), width 49¼ in. (1.25 m.). Milan, Sant'Ambrogio, upper part of the back door. Below: scenes from the shepherd life of King David. Fragment from the original door. About 386. Height 18⅛ in. (46 cm.), width 9¾ in. (25 cm.). Milan, Museo di Sant'Ambrogio.

The door itself, still in position at the main entrance to the church, was rearranged in the 9th century, and in the restoration of 1750 the original reliefs with scenes were either partly or completely replaced. Both leaves of the door are framed by acanthus ornament in high relief. Square and rectangular fields, each with a frame of foliage, alternate. Of the original door only two pieces have been preserved, the one illustrated and another with the Anointing of David (height 18⅛ in. [46 cm.], width 13 in. [33 cm.]). The story of King David was a favorite subject of St. Ambrose in his sermons.

Stylistically the reliefs belong with other works produced in Milan under the episcopate of St. Ambrose, such as the large sarcophagus in Sant'Ambrogio [46, 47]. The division into fields recalls the door of Santa Sabina in Rome [103–105]. A similar layout occurs also on wooden doors in the East, such as the door from Mount Sinai and the one from Sitt Burbâra in Cairo (now in the Coptic Museum, Cairo).

E. Kitzinger in *Archaeologia*, 1937, p. 212; A. Particolo and U. Monneret de Villard, *The Church of Sitt Burbâra in Old Cairo*, Cairo, 1922; A. Goldschmidt, *Die Kirchentür des hl. Ambrosius in Mailand*, Strasbourg, 1902; Wulff, *Altchristliche Kunst*, I, p. 137, pl. IX; F. Reggiori in *Ambrosiana*, p. 165; *Kunstschätze der Lombardei*, p. 55, no. 47; *Storia di Milano*, I, 1953, fig. p. 693.

## 103–105

WOODEN DOOR OF SANTA SABINA, ROME. Cypress. Height of large panels 33½ in. (85 cm.), of small panels 11 in. (28 cm.), width of each panel 15¾ in. (40 cm.). About 432. Rome, Santa Sabina.

[103] The upper portion of the door.
[104] Left: *The Crossing of the Red Sea* and *The Brazen Serpent*. Right: *The Ascension of Elijah*.
[105] *Zacharias Before the Temple*.

Of the original 28 panels with scenes, 18 are preserved, but their arrangement has been altered by two restorations; the vine scroll borders in high relief are largely later replacements. Most of the scenes in the large panels are from the Gospels, those in the small ones mostly from the Passion. Old Testament scenes: incidents from the life of Moses, *The Ascension of Elijah*, *Habakkuk About to Be Transported to Babylon*. New Testament scenes: *Zacharias Before the Temple*, *The Adoration of the Magi*, *The Healing of the Blind*, *The Multiplication of Loaves and Fishes*, *The Marriage at Cana*, *The Transfiguration*, *Christ Before Caiaphas*, *Christ Foretelling the Denial of Peter*, *Pilate Washing His Hands*, *Christ Carrying the Cross*, *Christ on the Cross*, *The Marys at the Sepulcher*, *The Ascension*. Santa Sabina was begun under Pope Celestine I (422–32), and, according to the *Liber pontificalis*, completed under his successor Sixtus III (432–40; Cabrol and Leclercq, *Dictionnaire*, vol. XV, col. 229). Thus the door can be dated about 432. Its style is similar to that of sarcophagi from this period. The iconography is strongly influenced by Eastern, perhaps Syrian models. The actual Crucifixion itself is shown for one of the first, if not the first time, but it differs from that on the casket in the British Museum [98] that is in all likelihood North Italian. The high throne in *The Adoration of the Magi* is a borrowing from court ceremonial, and the interesting acclamation in the so-called Zacharias scene recalls Theodosian state monuments (R. Delbrueck in *Art Bulletin*, 1949, p. 215). A reflection of papal ideas may be discerned in the upper, large panel on the extreme right in which three figures, a female one, probably the Virgin, between SS. Peter and Paul, who represent the Jewish and pagan churches (C. Cecchelli in *Rivista di Archeologia Cristiana*, 1927, p. 133), look up to Christ above in a glory supported by the symbols of the Evangelists (E. Weigand in *Byzantinische Zeitschrift*, 1930, p. 587).

J. Wiegand, *Das altchristliche Hauptportal an der Kirche der hl. Sabina*, Trier, 1900; Venturi, *Storia*, I, p. 333, figs. 308–325; Wulff, *Altchristliche Kunst*, I, p. 138, fig. 127, pl. X, Nachtrag, p. 16; A. C. Soper in *Art Bulletin*, 1938, p. 168, figs. 40–43, 49–52; E. H. Kantorowicz in *Art Bulletin*, 1944, p. 207; Gerke, *Christus*, figs. 95–97; Deichmann, *Kirchen*, p. 57, figs. 33–36; R. Delbrueck in *Art Bulletin*, 1952, p. 138; Morey, *Early Christian Art*, p. 137, fig. 149.

## 106–121

LATE ANTIQUE SILVER WORK shows a clear return to the Hellenistic manner during the second half of the 4th and the first half of the 5th century. The material has, in recent years, been enriched by important finds, such as the Mildenhall Treasure, now at the British Museum (J. Brailsford, *The Mildenhall Treasure*, London, 1947; T. Dohrn in *Mitteilungen des deutschen archäologischen Institutes*, 1949, p. 67). The Treasure, datable to the middle of the 4th century, is earlier than other pieces found in Britain—at Corbridge (J. Haverfield in *Journal of Roman Studies*, 1914, p. 1, pl.; Rumpf, *Stilphasen*, p. 21, fig. 59), Coleraine, and Balline, all of which seem to date from the end of the 4th century (W. M. Milliken in *Bulletin of the Cleveland Museum*, Cleveland, 1958, p. 35). In Germany there is the Hassleben find (R. Zahn in W. Schulz, *Das Fürstengrab von Hassleben*, Berlin, 1933; R. Zahn in *Berliner Museen, Amtliche Berichte*, 1917, p. 263), and the fragments from Gross Bodungen (W. Grünhagen, *Der Schatzfund von Gross Bodungen*, Berlin, 1954).

The most important pieces from recent finds in Italy, such as the plate from Cesena, have been adequately published, although the Canoscio Treasure, dating from the 6th century, still awaits complete publication (*Rivista di Archeologia Cristiana*, 1935, p. 1); much of this material is discussed in: H. Odobesco, *La Trésor de Petrossa*, Leipzig, 1889–1900; Volbach, *Metallarbeiten;* Volbach, in Bossert, *Geschichte*, V, p. 56; Volbach in *Corsi di cultura*, 1958, I, p. 101.

So far it has been impossible to classify the objects by workshops or groups of workshops. In the early stages Rome was an important center, and the Esquiline Treasure was probably made there. Milan too seems to have been responsible for a number of important pieces, including the casket in San Nazaro Maggiore [110–115]. On the Italian production of this period,

see H. H. Arnason (in *Art Bulletin*, 1938, p. 193). The votive platter in Madrid [53] is in the style of the Eastern art of the Theodosian period, though no Byzantine pieces are known before 500. The votive platter of Ardabur [109] is perhaps of North African origin. Of the once famous workshops of Alexandria we know nothing in this late period. Attributions to Syrian workshops should first be made for the 6th century, the date suggested for the Antioch Chalice in the Cloisters of the Metropolitan Museum (G. de Francovich in *Commentari*, 1951, p. 14). For items in the British Museum, see Dalton, *Catalogue Antiquities;* in Berlin, the exhibition catalogue *Kunst der Spätantike*, 1939; in Paris, Coche de la Ferté, *Antiquité*.

## 106

ARTEMIS RIDING A STAG. Silver plate. Height ¾ in. (2 cm.), diameter 7⅛ in. (18 cm.). End of the 4th century. Allegedly from Ephesus. Berlin, Staatliche Museen.

Cyma border with pearls. Artemis rides through the air on a stag. There are stylistic similarities to the company of the gods on the Corbridge lanx in the British Museum (Rumpf, *Stilphasen*, fig. 59), and on both pieces the relief is obtained by chisel work from above. The elegant manner may indicate an Asiatic workshop.

R. Zahn in *Berliner Museen, Amtliche Berichte*, 1917, p. 296; F. Matz, in Bossert, *Geschichte*, IV, p. 339; *Kunst der Spätantike*, catalogue, Berlin, 1939, no. 107, pl. 29; T. Dorn in *Mitteilungen des deutschen archäologischen Institutes*, 1949, p. 115, pl. 31.

## 107

CYBELE WITH ATTIS. Cast silver plate with scorper and chisel work, traces of gilding. Diameter 15⅜ in. (39 cm.). End of the 4th century. From Parabiago. Milan, Castello Sforzesco.

In the middle, Cybele with Attis in a chariot drawn by lions, accompanied by three Corybants. Above, the Sun and Moon; on the right, the zodiac; below, personifications of the Earth and the Ocean. Because this representation is considerably more Hellenistic in spirit than dishes from Aquileia and the Farnese dish in Naples, it used to be dated in the 2nd century (A. Levi in *Journal of Roman Studies*, 1943, pl. 6, 1), but A. Alföldi (in *Atlantis*, 1949, p. 69) has classified it with late 4th-century works. It is technically akin to the casket in San Nazaro Maggiore [110–115], and compositionally to the Corbridge lanx.

*Kunstschätze der Lombardei*, p. 51, no. 37; Rumpf, *Stilphasen*, p. 20, fig. 74.

## 108

A FEAST. Central tondo of a silver plate, niello decoration, partly gilded. Border damaged. Diameter 24¾ in. (63 cm.), diameter of the central tondo 9⅞ in. (25 cm.). Late 4th century. Found in Cesena together with another, plainer dish. Cesena, Biblioteca Malatestiana.

A feast of the gods appears in the central tondo. Not shown in the illustration are the pastoral scenes on the border and the two stamps, P and L (Luguduni?) on the back.

The Ostrogothic coin found with the plate shows that it

was buried in the 6th century. Dated about 400 on the strength of affinities with the nielloed plate from Concesti in Leningrad (Matzulewitsch, *Byzantinische Antike*, pl. 47). It is also close to the plate from Hammersdorf in Königsberg (Rosenberg, *Niello*, II, p. 68, figs. 58–59) and the earlier votive platter of Constantius II (Matzulewitsch, *op. cit.*, pls. 23–25).

P. E. Arias in *Annuario della scuola archeologica Atene*, 1946–48 (1950), p. 309; R. Bianchi Bandinelli, *Hellenistic-Byzantine Miniatures of the Iliad*, Olten, 1955, p. 127.

## 109

VOTIVE PLATTER OF THE CONSUL ASPAR AR-DABUR (434). Chased silver, touched up with the scorper. External border and ring stand missing. Diameter 16½ in. (42 cm.). Found near Orbetello. Florence, Museo Nazionale (Bargello).

Circular inscription inside the slightly raised border: FL(avius) ARDABVR ASPAR VIR INLVSTRIS COM(es) ET MAG (ister) MILITVM ET CONSVL ORDINARIVS. Just inside the rim, near the left medallion: ARDABVR; near the right medallion: PLINTA; in the center above the son: ARDABVR IVNIOR PRETOR. The consul Aspar, seated slightly to the left of the center, signals the start of games with his *mappa*. The scepter of office in his left hand is surmounted by the busts of Theodosius II and Valentinian III. He wears a tunic and colobium, and, folded across the breast, the decorated trabea. His son, the praetor Ardabur, salutes with his right and holds the *mappa* in his left. Father and son are flanked by the personifications of Rome and Constantinople which carry *fasces*. In the medallions above, on the left, Aspar's father and, on the right, probably his father-in-law, Plinta, who was consul in 419. Below, winner's trophies.

Stylistically it is close to the ivory diptych of the consul Felix [96], and may be North African in origin since Aspar began his consulate in Africa, though it may have been made in Rome for the games.

A. Riegl, *Die spätrömische Kunstindustrie*, 2nd ed., Vienna, 1927, p. 227; Cabrol and Leclercq, *Dictionnaire*, vol. IV, pt. 1, col. 1187, fig. 3784; Venturi, *Storia*, I, p. 499, fig. 439; Delbrueck, *Konsulardiptychen*, p. 154, no. 35; K. Wessel in *Jahrbuch des deutschen archäologischen Institutes*, 1948–49, p. 112; H. Stern, *Le Calendrier de 354*, Paris, 1953, p. 140, pl. 28, 4.

## 110–115

RELIQUARY. Chased silver, lightly gilded. Height 6⅞ in. (17.5 cm.), width 7⅞ in. (20 cm.). Late 4th century. Milan, San Nazaro Maggiore.
[110] View of the casket as a whole.
[111] Lid: *Christ Among the Apostles.*
[112] Front: *The Adoration of the Magi.*
[113] Back: *Joseph Forgiving His Brothers.*
[114] Left side: *The Three Hebrews in the Fiery Furnace.*
[115] Right side: *The Judgment of Solomon.*

Found under the high altar, together with three leaden caskets. Made during the episcopate of St. Ambrose to enshrine the relics of the Apostles sent in 382 by Pope Damasus through the Milanese archdeacon Simplicianus (E. Villa in *Basilica Apostolorum*, 1940, p. 2; A. Ottino della Chiese in *Città di Milano*,

1949, p. 153). Bordered with rope ornament. On the lid Christ, nimbed and enthroned, appears among the Apostles, on the right St. Peter, on the left St. Paul, in front of them bread baskets and wine pitchers. Front: *The Adoration of the Magi*, with the Magi beside the Virgin's throne, wearing philosopher's cloaks, and the Christ child naked. Back: *Joseph Forgiving His Brothers.* Right side: *The Judgment of Solomon.* Left side: *The Three Hebrews in the Fiery Furnace.* A date contemporary with the translation of the relics (382) is supported by the style. Hellenistic elements both in technique and composition are to be found in contemporary secular pieces such as the Parabiago plate [107]. There are also similarities with ivories such as the diptych with *The Marys at the Sepulcher* in Milan [92], and the casket in Brescia [85–89]. The reliquary could thus be a product of the Milanese school of St. Ambrose's time. The supposition that the piece is a forgery (C. R. Morey in *American Journal of Archaeology*, 1919, p. 101) is unfounded; A. Venturi (*Storia*, I, p. 549, figs. 445–449) suggests a Roman origin, O. Wulff (*Altchristliche Kunst*, I, p. 197, fig. 200) an Eastern origin.

F. de Mély in *Römische Quartalschriften*, 1901, p. 90; Cabrol and Leclercq, *Dictionnaire*, vol. III, pt. 1, col. 1112, fig. 2694; L. Bréhier in *Gazette des Beaux-Arts*, 1920, p. 195; Volbach, *Metallarbeiten*, p. 27, no. 12; R. Delbrueck in *Antike Denkmäler*, IV, pls. 1–3; P. Toesca in *Scritti in onore di B. Nogara*, Rome, 1937, p. 503; *Storia di Milano*, I, p. 685, figs. pp. 681–685.

## 116–119 LEFT

THE ESQUILINE TREASURE. Silver. Found in 1793 on the Esquiline in Rome. London, British Museum, and Paris, Petit Palais.

Dated approximately 379–83 by the bridal casket [116, 117] with the portrait of Projecta and her husband Secundus since Pope Damasus' epitaph for her indicates that Projecta was already dead by 383 (S. Poglayen-Neuwall in *Römische Mitteilungen*, 1930, p. 124; M. T. Tozzi in *Rivista di Archeologia Cristiana*, 1932, p. 279). The Treasure also includes an ointment flask decorated with scrolls, putti, and animals, two small amphorae, a ewer with the inscription PELEGRINA VTERE FELIX, a fluted bowl, three large circular dishes, four smaller circular dishes, and four rectangular dishes, each with the monogram PROICTA TVRCI, nine spoons, one of them with the dedication IVNONI LANVVINAE SPS SVLP(icius) QVIRIN(us) (dono dedit) (Dalton, *Catalogue Antiquities*, nos. 306–330), thus originally intended as a votive offering in the temple of Juno Sospita in Lanuvium. An important item in the Treasure is the toilet casket with a domed lid and figures of the Muses on the sides (Dalton, *Catalogue Antiquities*, no. 305, pl. 19). Other items are: three hairpins; a pair of earrings; a ring; five fibulae; three amulets; a knife handle; statuettes of the city goddesses of Rome, Constantinople, Alexandria, and Antioch [119], which served perhaps as pole ends of a *sedia gestatoria* (Dalton, *Catalogue Antiquities*, nos. 332–335, pl. 20) as did two forearms holding a cylinder surmounted by a pomegranate; and horse-trappings *(phalerae)*. A pouring vessel in the shape of a female head has found its way to the Museo Nazionale in Naples (S. Poglayen-Neuwall, *op. cit.*, pl. 37); a patera came to the Petit Palais with the Dutuit Collection [118]. A bronze candelabrum and a lamp have been lost (E. Q. Visconti, *Lettera intorno ad una antica supelletile d'argento*, ed. Montagnani, Rome, 1827). The items are not all from the same workshop but seem to be contemporary.

## 116, 117

THE SILVER CASKET OF PROJECTA. Chased silver, partly gilded. Height 11 in. (28 cm.), length 21⅞ in. (55.6 cm.). About 380. London, British Museum.

[116] Lid: center, portrait of the bridal couple; sides, the *deductio* of the bride and mythological scenes.

[117] Above: detail of the lid, the *deductio* of the bride. Below: the front of the casket.

The lid has the form of a truncated pyramid; on the top in a wreath held by confronted putti is the portrait of the couple Secundus and Projecta. On the sloping panels, front: Venus combing her hair, flanked by Tritons; sides: Nereids and sea monsters; back: the *deductio* of the bride who is led by a boy into her new abode, a domed palace, and is followed by a girl carrying a large oval box; three persons approach from the right with wedding presents, the last carrying a patera. Inscription on the bottom edge: SECVNDE ET PROIECTA VIVATIS IN CHRI(sto). Each side panel of the casket is framed by scroll ornament, and decorated with arcades; in the outside arches on the front and back are peacocks. Front center: the bride at her toilet flanked by two servants with mirror and toilet casket; right lateral face: three servants with pillow (?), patera, and bucket; left lateral face: servants, the middle one carrying a box, the side ones, torches; back center: a servant holding a toilet casket suspended from three chains, flanked by similar figures with other utensils.

## 118

TOILET OF VENUS. Silver patera. Length 14½ in. (37 cm.). About 380. Paris, Petit Palais, Collection Dutuit.

The border is ornamented with small shells. The bowl is in the form of a larger shell; the goddess is at her toilet in the center, a putto with mirror on the right, and a putto with ointment casket on the left; on the handle, Poseidon. For the putti see those on the Missorium of Theodosius [53]. Most likely an Alexandrian model was used.

E. Lenormant, *La Collection A. Dutuit*, Paris, 1879, pl. 1; W. Froehner, *La Collection A. Dutuit*, Paris, 1897, pl. 108; P. Gussman, *L'Art décoratif de Rome*, I, Paris, 1908, pl. 26; Dalton, *Catalogue Antiquities*, p. 61, nos. 304-345, pls. XIII-XX; Volbach, in Bossert, *Geschichte*, V, fig. p. 57; Wulff, *Altchristliche Kunst*, I, p. 197; Toesca, *Storia*, I, p. 328, figs. 201-202; T. Dohrn in *Mitteilungen des deutschen archäologischen Institutes*, 1949, p. 129, pls. 32, 3, 33; Cecchelli, *Vita*, I, fig. p. 733; Rumpf, *Stilphasen*, p. 21, fig. 75.

## 119 LEFT

PERSONIFICATION OF THE CITY OF ANTIOCH. Silver statuette. Height 5⅛ in. (13 cm.). About 380. London, British Museum.

One of a series of four city goddesses, she wears a turreted crown and carries flowers and a cornucopia. The naked putto at her feet personifies the river Orontes. At the back is a socket for fastening the figurine to a wooden pole. Copy of a life-size statue by Eutychides (ca. 300 B.C.).

Dalton, *Catalogue Antiquities*, p. 75, no. 334.

## 119 RIGHT, ABOVE AND CENTER

ORNAMENTAL PANEL. Gold. Height 2 in. (5 cm.). London, British Museum.

Above: obverse. Center: reverse.

The square panel is in pierced work and has a pearl border. The back, soldered to the front, is decorated with a diaper pattern of leaves, framed by a pearled border. On the front, against a trellis background, a woman on horseback accompanied by a lion. For pierced work of this kind, see A. Riegl, *Die spätrömische Kunstindustrie*, Vienna, 1901, I, p. 143.

Dalton, *Catalogue Antiquities*, no. 252, pl. IV; Volbach, in Bossert, *Geschichte*, V, fig. p. 66.

## 119 RIGHT, BELOW

BRACELET. Gold, pierced work. Diameter 3⅜ in. (8.7 cm.). Found in Tartus (Syria) together with a similarly worked bell. Berlin, Staatliche Museen.

In the middle band is a Greek inscription reading, "Use it in luck as long as you live." A similar piece, from the same find, is in the City Art Museum, St. Louis, Missouri (G. O. Eisen in *Bulletin of the City Art Museum*, 1925).

R. Zahn in *Berliner Museen, Amtliche Berichte*, 1913–14, p. 85, fig. 43, 1916-17, p. 50; *Kunst der Spätantike*, catalogue, Berlin, 1939, no. 42, pl. 7.

## 120

RELIQUARY CASKET. Silver embossed and partly gilt. Height 2¼ in. (5.7 cm.), length 4¾ in. (12 cm.), width 2⅛ in. (5.5 cm.). 5th century. Found in Castello di Brivio (Lombardy). Paris, Louvre.

Above: lid, *The Raising of Lazarus*. Below: front, *The Adoration of the Magi*.

Heavy rope ornament surrounds the scenes. On the back *The Three Hebrews in the Fiery Furnace* is depicted. A similar pyxis, from Henchir Zirar near Carthage, in Rome (Musei del Vaticano), has a martyr on the lid, and on the sides, lambs adoring the Lamb of God and deer drinking from the Four Rivers of Paradise (H. H. Arnason in *Art Bulletin*, 1938, p. 216, figs. 24-25) and another, also in the Vatican, from the treasury of the Sancta Sanctorum, has *The Adoration of the Cross* on the lid and portraits of Christ and two Apostles in medallions on the back (W. F. Volbach, *Il tesoro della capella Sancta Sanctorum*, Vatican City, 1941, fig. 7). Related and probably of North Italian origin are the reliquaries in Grado, an oval one with lambs and the cross on the lid and portraits of Christ, Apostles, and saints in medallions on the sides (Arnason, *op. cit.*, p. 211, figs. 14-15), and a round one with the Mother of God Enthroned on the lid (Arnason, *op. cit.*, p. 212, figs. 15-18); these, though contemporary, are technically superior to our piece (P. L. Zovatto in *Aquileia nostra*, 1953-54, p. 119, fig. 1). For the oval pyxis in Grado, see P. L. Zovatto (*ibid.*, 1952, p. 17). These affinities suggest North Italian origin and a date in the second half of the 5th century.

P. Lauer in *Monuments Piot*, 1907, p. 229, pl. 19; Venturi, *Storia*, I, p. 521, figs. 450-52; Volbach, *Metallarbeiten*, no. 13; Cabrol and Leclercq, *Dictionnaire*, vol. III, pt. 1, col. 116, fig. 2695; E. Michon in *Syria*, 1925, p. 305; H. H. Arnason in *Art Bulletin*, 1938, p. 215, figs. 21-23; Coche de la Ferté, *Antiquité*, p. 105, no. 43, fig. p. 46.

## 121 LEFT

EWER WITH MEDALLION PORTRAITS OF CHRIST AND APOSTLES. Cast silver, lightly gilded. Oxydized. Height 7¼ in. (18.5 cm.), diameter 2¼ in. (5.7 cm.). Early 5th century. Probably found in Rome. Rome, Musei del Vaticano, from the Albani collection.

The ewer (amula) has a handle and a lid decorated with a knob, and is divided into five zones by ropelike courses. The large middle zone carries portraits in medallions of Christ, SS. Peter and Paul, and two other Apostles, the top zone, a cross flanked by four doves, the bottom zone, a lamb and four sheep. The early 5th-century phial in the Vatican with medallion portraits of Christ and St. Peter on the round middle piece (W. F. Volbach, *Guide to the Museo Sacro*, p. 11, fig. 6) is close to it. Medallion portraits are to be found on most oval *capsellae*, including the ones in Grado, in the Vatican, on the reliquary from Sebastopol in Leningrad (Rosenberg, *Merkzeichen*, IV, p. 705, no. 9965), and the vase from Emesa in the Louvre [246]. The iconography of the lamb and sheep is similar to the ivory casket in Pola (A. C. Soper in *Art Bulletin*, 1938, p. 153, figs. 1–4; Volbach, *Elfenbeinarbeiten*, no. 120, pl. 38). For a general discussion of the early Christian vessels, see J. Braun (*Das christliche Altargerät*, Munich, 1932, p. 431).

Garrucci, *Storia*, VI, pl. 460, figs. 1–4; Cabrol and Leclercq, *Dictionnaire*, vol. II, pt. I, fig. col. 1746; Volbach, *Metallarbeiten*, p. 64, no. 63; W. F. Volbach, *Guide to the Museo Sacro*, p. 11, fig. 7; H. H. Arnason in *Art Bulletin*, 1938, p. 193, fig. 1; Cecchelli, *Vita*, I, pp. 11, 699, fig. p. 700.

## 121 RIGHT

VASE WITH THE HEALING OF THE BLIND. Silver. A piece missing in the lower part on the right. Height 5 in. (12.8 cm.). About 420–30. London, British Museum, from the Leone Strozzi collection.

Rope ornament on the neck. Two scenes from the New Testament, *The Healing of the Blind* and *Christ Giving the Scroll of the Law to St. Peter* (H. H. Arnason in *Art Bulletin*, 1938, p. 208, figs. 11, 13). Its style is close to the ewer with medallion portraits [121 left] and the one formerly in the Bianchini collection, now lost (Cabrol and Leclercq, *Dictionnaire*, vol. II, pt. I, fig. 1745; Cecchelli, *Vita*, I, p. I, fig. p. 10), and the treatment of the relief recalls the flask from Traprain (A. O. Curle, *The Treasure of Traprain*, Glasgow, 1923, p. 12, no. 1, pls. 3, 5), as well as the pyxis from Pola, in Vienna (Volbach, *Metallarbeiten*, no. 11, pl. 5; Arnason, *op. cit.*, p. 219, figs. 30, 32). Like these pieces, the vase should be dated about 420–30.

Garrucci, *Storia*, VI, pl. 460, 7–8; Cabrol and Leclercq, *Dictionnaire*, vol. I, pt. 2, col. 3234, fig. 1157; Arnason, *op. cit.*, p. 208, figs. 11, 13; A. B. Tonnochy in *British Museum Quarterly*, 1952, p. 16, pl. Va.

## 122–173

WALL PAINTING AND MOSAICS in basilicas, mausoleums, and baptisteries have been destroyed in large part, and only from written records, especially the *tituli* (the accompanying inscriptions), is it still possible to gain an idea of their rich pictorial decoration. Thus the development of painting in the 4th and 5th centuries cannot here be followed as completely as in carving. Some monuments, such as the mosaics in the Church of Hagios Dimitrios in Salonika, have been partly preserved, of others, such as the magnificent cycle in the Church of the Dormition in Nicaea, nothing remains (Th. Schmidt, *Die Koimesis-Kirche in Nicäa*, Berlin, 1927; G. de Francovich in *Scritti di storia dell'arte in onore di L. Venturi*, Rome, 1956, p. 3). Material from the East is so scarce that the discovery of mosaics in the apse of Hosios David in Salonika [133–135] is particularly valuable.

In Italy some monuments have fortunately been retrieved, among them important 4th-century frescoes in the Roman Catacomb of Comodilla, and mosaics in the small mausoleum under St. Peter's and in Sant'Aquilino adjoining San Lorenzo in Milan. Despite the serious losses, damages, and heavy restorations that large portions of the mosaics have suffered, it is again possible to admire the mosaics of Santa Maria Maggiore, San Lorenzo fuori le Mura, and Santi Cosma e Damiano in Rome, Sant'Apollinare in Classe in Ravenna, and Hagios Georgios in Salonika in their original splendor, thanks to the commissions in charge of them.

In painting as in sculpture the transition from a broadly Classical style to that of Late Antiquity occurs in the time of the First Tetrarchy, during the reign of Diocletian. It is deplorable that too little has survived of post-Pompeian painting up to the end of the 3rd century, to permit the reconstruction of this important phase in art. Roman catacomb paintings, on the other hand, yield relatively adequate material for tracing the artistic development of the 3rd century [7–10]. While the *Good Shepherd* in the Catacomb of Callixtus [7] exemplifies the Hellenistic art of the 3rd century, the *orans* in the Catacomb of Priscilla [8] reflects the artistic trends of the Tetrarchy. Mosaics are represented in this group by the decoration of the small mausoleum under the Vatican Grottoes, where, beside the Sun in his chariot in the dome, representations of the Good Shepherd, Jonah, and a fisherman already appear (B. M. Apolloni Ghetti, A. Ferrua, E. Josi, and E. Kirschbaum, *Esplorazioni sotto la confessione di San Pietro in Vaticano*, Vatican City, 1951, pl. 12). The continued vigor of the Hellenistic style can be inferred also from the Renaissance drawings after the lost paintings (317) in the Basilica of Junius Bassus (C. Hülsen, *Il libro di Giuliano da San Gallo*, Leipzig, 1910, p. 47, fol. 31v). The consul in his quadriga and the animals portrayed in *opus sectile* on the wall seem more primitive, almost in the style of the popular art of the Arch of Constantine.

In North Italy this transitional style is best exemplified by the superb floor mosaics in the Cathedral of Aquileia (314–19) with the Good Shepherd, Jonah, and sea monsters (C. Cecchelli, *La basilica di Aquileia*, Bologna, 1933, pl. 30, 34; G. Brusin and P. L. Zovatto, *Monumenti paleocristiani di Aquileia e di Grado*, Udine, 1957); in Sicily, by the floor mosaics in the imperial villa at Piazza Armerina (G. V. Gentili, *La villa romana di Piazza Armerina*, Rome, 1951). In Rome the development culminates in the late Constantinian style as we know it from the mosaics in Santa Costanza [32–35], which, though heavily restored, give us a good idea of the changes in style. The differences in the stylistic development in Rome and in the East are equally apparent in painting. In the East, the Hellenistic tradition holds its own throughout the reign of Constantine and is revived in the 5th and 6th centuries, as the floor mosaics of the Great Palace in Constantinople show (G. Brett, *The Great Palace of the Byzantine Emperors*, London, 1947; D. Talbot Rice in *Revue*

334

*des arts*, 1955, p. 363). The best examples of this continuity are the numerous floor mosaics found in Antioch (D. Levi, *Antioch Mosaic Pavements*, Princeton, 1947), though many others are also known (Wulff, *Altchristliche Kunst*, I, p. 313, Nachtrag, p. 42 ff.; Galassi, *Roma o Bizanzio*). The mosaics in the dome of Hagios Georgios in Salonika, of about 400, offer another instance of this continuity of Hellenistic art. Though Rome continues to cultivate old trends, at the turn of the century strong Eastern influences penetrate into the art of Milan and especially that of Naples; witness mosaics in the Baptistery of Santa Restituta (Wilpert, *Mosaiken*, pls. 19–39), in Capua (Wilpert, *op. cit.*, pl. 77), and in Cimitile near Nola (*Atti del IV congresso internazionale di archeologia cristiana 1938*, II, Rome, 1948, p. 147; F. Weiss in *Römische Quartalschriften*, 1957, p. 1).

In miniature painting, continuous illustrations on papyrus rolls are replaced by parchment pages with isolated, framed pictures. On the whole ample material has survived, but the earlier Hellenistic miniatures are known almost exclusively through later copies, some 5th century, others Carolingian, so that research in this field is more difficult.

The Hellenistic spirit still dominates the Ambrosian Iliad, a Milanese work of the end of the 5th or beginning of the 6th century (R. Bianchi Bandinelli in *Rivista dell'Istituto Nazionale Archeologia e Storia dell'Arte*, 1953, p. 1; R. Bianchi Bandinelli, *Hellenistic-Byzantine Miniatures of the Iliad*, Bern, 1954). This Classical spirit is evident in several other manuscripts, also of Italian origin, such as the Quedlinburg Itala in Berlin, or the Vatican Virgil (Vat. lat. 3225), while the somewhat later Virgilius Romanus (Vat. lat. 3867) shows a distinctly Roman style of drawing (Cecchelli, *Vita*, I, p. 431) which persists in the later copies of the Calendar of 354 (H. Stern, *Le Calendrier de 354*, Paris, 1953, pp. 20 ff.). Even a later Roman codex, like the late 6th-century Gospels at Corpus Christi College, Cambridge (F. Wormald, *The Miniatures in the Gospels of St. Augustine*, Cambridge, 1954), shows dependence on this Roman style of drawing. In sharp contrast are the late, purple codices from the East, the one from Sinope in Paris, the Vienna Genesis, and the Codex Rossanensis [238–241]. Material on the development of miniature painting is collected most conveniently in K. Weitzmann, *Illustrations in Roll and Codex*, Princeton, 1947; C. Nordenfalk in *Beiträge für G. Swarzenski*, Berlin, Chicago, 1951, p. 9; E. Bethe, *Buch und Bild*, Leipzig, 1945.

General literature on mosaics: Cabrol and Leclercq, *Dictionnaire*, vol. XII, pt. 1, col. 57; Toesca, *Storia*, I, p. 153; Wilpert, *Mosaiken*; van Berchem and Clouzot, *Mosaïques*; C. Diehl, *La peinture byzantine*, Paris, 1933; Wulff, *Altchristliche Kunst*, I, Nachtrag, p. 40; Lasareff, *Byzantine Painting*; A. Grabar, *Byzantine Painting*, Geneva, 1953; A. Grabar and C. Nordenfalk, *Early Medieval Painting*, Geneva, 1957; Ammann, *Pittura*.

**122–127**

HAGIOS GEORGIOS, SALONIKA. 4th century.
[122] Interior, facing the entrance.
[123] Mosaics in the barrel vault of the south niche.
[124] Mosaic frieze in the dome. Detail: left, St. Onesiphoros; right, St. Porphyrios.
[125] Mosaic frieze in the dome. Detail: left, a saint (inscription destroyed); right, St. Damian.
[126] Mosaic frieze in the dome. Detail: St. Onesiphoros.
[127] Mosaic frieze in the dome. Detail: St. Porphyrios.

The original structure was erected by Galerius (305–11) together with his triumphal arch [2, 3] but transformed into a church and decorated with mosaics by Theodosius (375–94). Of these there are remains in the lower part of the dome and in the vaults of the niches. In the upper reaches of the dome only outlines have survived. Christ in eternal glory surrounded by angels occupied the center. In the comparatively well-preserved lower zone, saints stand in front of palatial structures. The saints, identified by inscriptions, make up a calendar of the monthly feasts of the church. The architectural settings recall the fourth Pompeian style. Before the restoration these mosaics were usually given a later date, E. Weigand (in *Byzantinische Zeitschrift*, 1939, p. 116) even suggesting the 6th century. The architectural features are still close to the miniatures of the Calendar of 354. In the niches are ornamental motifs with birds, fruit, and flowers.

C. Diehl, M. Le Tourneau, and H. Saladin, *Les monuments chrétiens de Salonique*, Paris, 1918, p. 23; Wulff, *Altchristliche Kunst*, I, p. 344, fig. 309, Nachtrag, p. 45; H. Hébrard in *Bulletin de Correspondance Hellénique*, 1920, p. 18; van Berchem and Clouzot, *Mosaïques*, p. 67, figs. 70–79; H. Grégoire

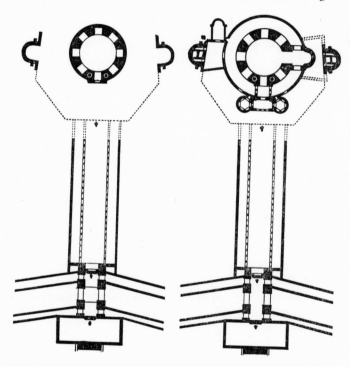

FIGURES 14 AND 15. Hagios Georgios (Mausoleum of Galerius) and the Arch of Galerius, Salonika. [14] The Emperor Galerius had his mausoleum built about 300. The internal span of the brickwork dome is 24.15 m. (79 ft., 3 in.); eight piers, 6.30 m. (20 ft., 8 in.) thick, with vaulted niches in between, carry the dome. From the mausoleum, the ceremonial avenue, 32 m. (105 ft.) wide and about 90 m. (295 ft.) long, leads to Galerius' triumphal arch [2, 3] which stands on the present—not ancient—Via Egnatia. The complete arch was a domed structure with side arches, carried by piers decorated with reliefs. [15] The mausoleum after its transformation by Theodosius into a palace church, about 390. Of the Theodosian structure only the apse has survived, the other additions having been destroyed by earthquake. The connection with the Arch of Galerius is unchanged. Both figures after E. Dyggve in *Studia orientalia Ioanni Pedersen dicata*, Copenhagen, 1953.

in *Byzantion*, 1939, p. 323; Galassi, *Roma o Bisanzio*, I, p. 50, figs. 23–24; Morey, *Early Christian Art*, p. 143, fig. 150; H. Torp in *Pepragmena tou 9 diethnous byzantinologikou Synedriou*, Athens, 1955, p. 489; Ammann, *Pittura*, p. 21.

For the architecture: E. Dyggve in *Corsi di cultura*, 1957, II, p. 79.

## 128, 129, 131

SANTA MARIA MAGGIORE, ROME. 5th century.

[128] Above: Caleb and Nun. Below: *The Stoning of Moses*. Mosaic panel in the nave. 432–40.

[129] *The Crossing of the Red Sea*. Mosaic panel in the nave. 432–40.

[131] Interior.

During the pontificate of Liberius (352–66), the pagan basilica Sicinini became Christian property and the pope transformed it into a church. Under Sixtus III (432–40) it was rebuilt as a three-aisled basilica with wide nave flanked by architraves with Ionic columns and decorated with mosaics. Those of the triumphal arch celebrate the Virgin as the Mother of God—a direct echo of the dogma promulgated at the Council of Ephesus in 431. The scenes are developed in four registers. In the center, above the founder's inscription—XYSTVS EPISCOPVS PLEBI DEI—the Apocalyptic Throne, with SS. Peter and Paul on either side. The scenes center around the Mother of God in accordance with the ideas of the Council of Ephesus, and there are subsidiary narrative scenes taken from the apocryphal gospels of the Pseudo-Matthew and the Proto-Evangelium of Jacobus.

The mosaics on the walls of the nave with scenes from the Old and the New Testament are also from the time of Pope Sixtus. On the left, scenes from the life of Abraham and Jacob, on the right, of Moses and Joshua; among them, *The Return of the Scouts from the Promised Land*, *The Stoning of Moses*, Caleb and Nun [128], and *The Crossing of the Red Sea* [129]. Of the original 42 panels, 27 have survived. During the restoration in the 1930's an earlier layer was found under some of the mosaics on the left wall; those on the right wall, however, were not made for an earlier structure. Therefore, it has now been estab-lished that the mosaics were not taken over from the earlier edifice (Wilpert, *Mosaiken*, I, p. 412) but made under Sixtus. After restoration it became apparent that they are the work of several masters who followed older models, which accounts for the occasional inclusion of two scenes in one mosaic. The mosaics on the triumphal arch are different in style, not because they are later but because they do not follow older models. Moreover, it was in the spirit of the period to borrow from the court style of state monuments, which can be seen in contemporary sculpture [64]. Sixtus' inscription on the wall above the entrance has been lost (C. Diehl, *Inscr. lat. Christ. vet.*, I, p. 182, no. 976).

Under Pope Nicholas IV (1288–92), the old apse was pulled down and replaced by a new one, further to the west, so that a transept could be introduced. The subjects depicted in the old apse—perhaps Christ and the Virgin—are not known. The coffered ceiling dates from the end of the 15th century. When the large chapels were added in the 16th century, some of the mosaics on the walls of the nave were destroyed. Those on the entrance wall have also been lost (L. De Bruyne in *Rivista di Archeologia Cristiana*, 1938, p. 305).

Venturi, *Storia*, I, p. 252, fig. 111; Wulff, *Altchristliche Kunst*, I, p. 333, figs. 302–305, pl. 20, Nachtrag, p. 44; Wilpert, *Mosaiken*, I, p. 412, pls. 8–25, 53–73; van Berchem and Clouzot, *Mosaïques*, p. 11, figs. 14–58; Cabrol and Leclercq, *Dictionnaire*, vol. XII, col. 278, figs. 8532–8535; Toesca, *Storia*, I, p. 170, figs. 100–105; E. Weigand in *Byzantinische Zeitschrift*, 1931, p. 112, 1939, p. 294; Morey, *Early Christian Art*, p. 146, figs. 156–163; Deichmann, *Kirchen*, p. 62, figs. 37–56; C. Cecchelli, *I mosaici della Basilica di Santa Maria Maggiore*, Turin, 1956; G. Bovini in *Corsi di cultura*, 1957, I, p. 45.

## 130

CHRIST AMONG THE APOSTLES. Mosaic in the apse. 401–17. Rome, Santa Pudenziana.

Above the mosaic is the inscription of Pope Innocent I (401–17). The mosaic has been cut down considerably, especially along the bottom. Most of the heads and parts of figures are restored, the outer ones almost completely. Christ raises His right hand in the gesture of address and holds in His left a book

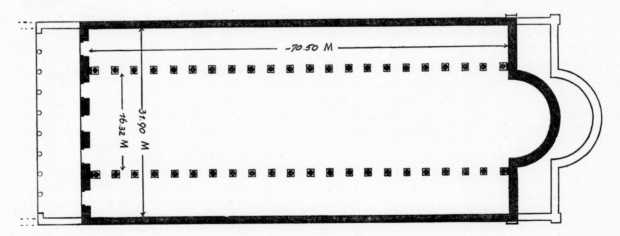

FIGURE 16. Santa Maria Maggiore, Rome. Plan. The Early Christian structure is in black; later additions, in outline, include the extension to the northwest beyond the Early Christian apse, the remains of which were found under the floor of the church. The later apse and transept were built under Pope Nicholas IV (1288–92). After the drawing by P. Marx in F. W. Deichmann, *Frühchristliche Kirchen in Rom*, Basel, 1948.

with the inscription, DOMINVS CONSERVATOR ECCLE-SIAE PVDENTIANAE (Christ the Preserver of the Church of Pudentiana). Of the twelve Apostles, only ten have survived the numerous restorations. In the background the Heavenly Jerusalem. For the restorations of 772-97, 1588, 1829, and 1832, see W. Köhler (in *Forschungen zur Kirchengeschichte und zur christlichen Kunst, J. Ficker zum 70. Geburtstag dargebracht*, Leipzig, 1931, p. 167). H. Vincent and F. M. Abel (in *Revue Biblique*, 1913, p. 531) interpret the background architecture as the historical Jerusalem with the Church of the Holy Sepulcher and the Church of the Ascension; they are followed by Wulff, *Altchristliche Kunst*, I, Nachtrag, p. 44.

Venturi, *Storia*, I, p. 118, fig. 105; Wilpert, *Mosaiken*, III, pls. 42–46; van Berchem and Clouzot, *Mosaïques*, p. 63, figs. 64–67; Toesca, *Storia*, I, pl. 169, fig. 99; Köhler, *art. cit.*; J. Kollwitz in *Römische Quartalschriften*, 1936, p. 65; K. Schefold in *Rivista di Archeologia Cristiana*, 1939, p. 300; Cabrol and Leclercq, *Dictionnaire*, vol. XII, pt. I, p. 237, fig. 8524; M. Armellini, *Le chiese di Roma dal IV al XIX secoli*, 2nd ed., Rome, 1942, p. 240; Morey, *Early Christian Art*, p. 143, fig. 152; G. Bovini in *Corsi di cultura*, 1957, I, p. 40.

## 132

ST. AMBROSE AND NABOR. Mosaic. Second half of the 5th century. Milan, San Vittore in Ciel d'Oro, adjoining Sant'Ambrogio.

The small basilica, today united with Sant'Ambrogio (F. Reggiori, *La Basilica Ambrosiana*, Milan, 1941, p. 216), is decorated with mosaics on the walls and in the dome: St. Ambrose between Gervasius and Protasius, on the opposite side Maternus between Nabor and Felix; in the center of the dome St. Victor. The representation of St. Ambrose is probably the earliest extant (A. Ratti in *Ambrosiana*, Milan, 1897, pl. p. 414). The mosaics are the final stage of the Ambrosian style that was at its best in the mosaics of Sant'Aquilino [138]. A date in the second half of the 5th century would explain the echoes of Ravenna.

Wilpert, *Mosaiken*, III, pls. 40–41; van Berchem and Clouzot, *Mosaïques*, p. III, figs. 124–126; Cabrol and Leclercq, *Dictionnaire*, vol. XII, pt. I, col. 180, fig. 8497; Galassi, *Roma o Bisanzio*, I, p. 47; F. Reggiori, *La Basilica Ambrosiana*, Milan, 1941, p. 216; *Storia di Milano*, I, p. 398; A. Grabar and C. Nordenfalk, *Early Medieval Painting*, Geneva, 1957, p. 26, fig. 2, p. 28.

## 133–135

HOSIOS DAVID, SALONIKA. Mosaic in the apse. Mid-5th century.

[133] Detail: the prophet Ezekiel and the lion, symbol of the Evangelist Mark.

[134] *Christ in Glory*, surrounded by the symbols of the Evangelists, with Ezekiel and Habakkuk.

[135] Detail: Christ.

This small edifice with three apses was formerly a monastic church. The mosaic in the middle apse was discovered in 1927 and is in an excellent state of preservation.

In the center, the youthful Christ is seated on a rainbow within a glory and flanked by the symbols of the Evangelists. Dressed in purple, He raises His right hand in the gesture of address, and holds a scroll in His left. In the lower left is Ezekiel, bending forward and covering his eyes so as not to be blinded by the vision. On the right Habakkuk holds an open book

with the dedicatory inscription. In the center below, the Four Rivers of Paradise and the personification of the river Chebar. Grabar (*Martyrium*, II, p. 198, III, pl. 40) thinks the prophet on the right is Zacharias. Christ's gesture of address is the same as in the mosaic in Sant'Aquilino [138]; the two mosaics are roughly contemporary. C. R. Morey (in *Byzantion*, 1932, p. 339, fig. 34, and *Early Christian Art*, p. 189) dates our mosaic too late (7th century).

A. Xyngopoulos in *Archaiologikon Deltion*, 1929, p. 142, figs. 22–28; V. Grumel in *Echos d'Orient*, 1930, p. 157; C. Diehl in *Comptes-rendus de l'Académie des Inscriptions*, 1927, p. 256; C. Diehl in *Byzantion*, 1932, p. 333; E. Weigand in *Byzantinische Zeitschrift*, 1931, p. 194, 1933, p. 212; Peirce and Tyler, *L'Art byzantin*, II, p. 91, figs. 63–67; Wulff, *Altchristliche Kunst*, I, Nachtrag, p. 46, fig. 537; Galassi, *Roma o Bisanzio*, II, p. 519; G. de Francovich in *Commentari*, 1951, p. 17, figs. 67, 68; S. Bettini, *La pittura bizantina*, Florence, 1939, p. 32, fig.; S. Pelekanidis, *Early Christian Memories of Salonika*, Salonika, 1949, p. 45, pls. 12–17 [in Greek]; Ammann, *Pittura*, p. 23, fig. 2.

## 136–138

SAN LORENZO AND THE CAPPELLA DI SANT'AQUILINO, MILAN.

[136] San Lorenzo and Sant'Aquilino from the southeast.

[137] San Lorenzo, interior.

[138] *Christ Among the Apostles*. Mosaic in the apse of the Cappella di Sant'Aquilino.

The church, possibly a foundation of the time of Constantius II (ca. 350), and situated in the neighborhood of the former imperial palace, was apparently an Arian church up to the time of St. Ambrose. The latest excavations have shown that, contrary to earlier assumptions, the church does not incorporate a Roman thermal establishment but is an original structure (A. Calderini, G. Chierici, and C. Cecchelli, *La Basilica di S. Lorenzo Maggiore in Milano*, Milan, 1951).

The centrally planned main body of the church was preceded by a large atrium with arcades on four sides which in turn was preceded by a portico. Of the latter, 16 columns taken over from antique buildings are still in position. Today the main entrance leads directly to the interior (diameter 148 ft. [45 m.]). Additional bays under the four towers connect the exedrae. Two side doors lead to the gallery *(matroneum)*. The octagonal Cappella di Sant'Ippolito to the east was originally flanked by the prothesis and diaconicon. The octagonal Cappella di Sant'Aquilino, perhaps originally the Arian baptistery, still retains some of its mosaic decoration [138]. The chapel also has a *matroneum*. Opinions vary as to the original form of the dome of San Lorenzo. For Sant'Aquilino, G. Chierici (in *Palladio*, 1954, p. 171) thinks that the present form of its dome more or less reflects the original one; the lower part of the walls was faced with marble. For the mosaic decoration of the upper part, see plate 138.

U. Monneret de Villard in *Il Politecnico*, 1911, p. 400; Wulff, *Altchristliche Kunst*, I, p. 249, fig. 341; Peirce and Tyler, *L'Art byzantin*, I, p. 100, pl. 174; Grabar, *Martyrium*, I, p. 408; G. Chierici in *Atti del IV Congresso internazionale di archeologia cristiana*, p. 29, figs. 1–4; A. M. Schneider in *Byzantinische Zeitschrift*, 1953, p. 184; *Storia di Milano*, I, p. 598, figs. pp. 340–341, 343.

The mosaics in an apse of the Cappella di Sant'Aquilino, the former baptistery, are the only well-preserved part of the original decoration. Against a gold background and surrounded by the twelve Apostles, the youthful Christ is enthroned. He is dressed in white, has a half open scroll in His left hand and raises His right; on either side are SS. Peter and Paul. In the apse opposite, partly lost but recognizable from outlines, probably *The Ascension of Elijah* in a chariot over the clouds; it includes a figure whose robes are blown by the wind (II Kings 2:1–12); underneath are shepherds tending their flocks (Wilpert, *Mosaiken*, pl. 41). The walls of the square atrium connecting the chapel with San Lorenzo were also decorated with mosaics: under the arcades figures of patriarchs, Apostles, and martyrs; in the upper zone, a few of them, with accompanying inscriptions, have been preserved.

The choice of scenes is inspired by the writings of St. Ambrose and suited to the character of a baptistery. The scene of Christ and the Apostles recalls catacomb paintings [7]. The treatment of the saints' heads in the atrium is still fully impressionistic and, particularly in the colors, recalls the baptistery in Naples; the heads themselves recall those in Santa Puden-

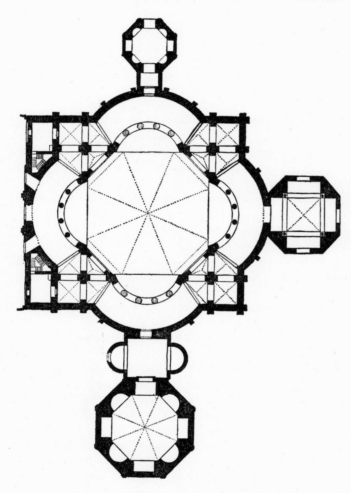

FIGURE 17. San Lorenzo, Milan. On the left, the present entrance from the west. The non-extant vaulted vestibule (originally an atrium with arcades) which preceded it is not shown; nor is the portico in front of the atrium of which a colonnade of 16 ancient columns, with a wider middle intercolumniation, is still extant. The Cappella di Sant'Ippolito to the east and the Cappella di San Sisto to the north are both from the middle of the 5th century. The octagonal structure to the south is the Capella di Sant'Aquilino. After: G. Dehio and G. von Bezold, *Die kirchliche Baukunst des Abendlandes*, Stuttgart, 1887–1901.

ziana [130]. Technically they already approach the mid-5th-century mosaics in the Mausoleum of Galla Placidia [146, 147].

Wilpert, *Mosaiken*, pls. 40–41; Toesca, *Storia*, I, p. 208, fig. 128; Wulff, *Altchristliche Kunst*, I, p. 328, pl. 19, 2, Nachtrag, p. 44; Grabar, *Martyrium*, II, p. 203; A. Grabar and C. Nordenfalk, *Early Medieval Painting*, Geneva, 1957, p. 26; van Berchem and Clouzot, *Mosaïques*, p. 59, figs. 60–63; W. F. Volbach, *Altchristliche Mosaiken*, Bern, 1947, pl. 8; Galassi, *Roma o Bisanzio*, I, p. 44, fig. 13; A. Calderini, G. Chierici, and C. Cecchelli, *La Basilica di S. Lorenzo Maggiore in Milano*, Milan, 1951, p. 674, figs. pp. 602, 604, 677.

## 139–183

RAVENNA is second only to Rome in the number of 5th- and 6th-century monuments it has preserved. In spite of many losses, it offers in terms of artistic development an almost uninterrupted series of works of architecture, sculpture, and mosaics, beginning with monuments erected soon after the imperial court was transferred there from Milan (403), that retain the Hellenistic spirit, and ending with the truly Byzantine works of the 6th century. The latter phase opens with the occupation of the city by Theodoric (March, 493) and comes to full flower between the conquest by Belisarius (May, 540) and the end of the 6th century. The importance of the art of Ravenna has, since the 18th century, given rise to an immense literature (C. Bovini in *Corsi di cultura*, 1958). Problems remain, however. The handbooks by Venturi, Wulff, Dalton, Toesca, and Morey cover the material extensively. Architecture has been treated by Verzone and Rivoira, mosaics by Wilpert, Grabar, Nordström, and Lasareff, and sculpture by Lawrence, Kollwitz, de Francovich, and Bovini. For a study of the state of preservation of the mosaics, the large album of plates begun by Ricci is indispensable. Current publications can be followed in the periodical appearing in Ravenna, *Felix Ravenna*.

Cabrol and Leclercq, *Dictionnaire*, vol. XIV, pt. 2, col. 2070, s.v. "Ravenne" with older bibliography; W. Goetz, *Ravenna*, Leipzig, 1913; O. M. Dalton, *East Christian Art*, Oxford, 1925; C. Diehl, *Ravenne*, Paris, 1928; Ricci, *Tavole*; von Simson, *Fortress*; Nordström, *Ravennastudien*.

## 139–143

BAPTISTERY OF THE ORTHODOX (San Giovanni in Fonte), RAVENNA. Built under Bishop Neon about 449–52.
[139] Exterior from the east.
[140] Interior from the entrance.
[141] Mosaics in the dome. *The Baptism*, surrounded by the Apostles, and Altars and Thrones in architectural settings.
[142] Above: detail of the mosaics in the dome: the Apostles Paul, Peter, and Andrew. Below: detail of the arcade. Marble revetments and mosaic ornamentation.
[143] Stucco decoration between the windows. Two prophets.

As Agnellus records in his *Liber pontificalis* (ed. O. Holder-Egger, Mon. German. Hist. Rer. Langob., p. 278; ed. A. Testi-Rasponi, Rev. it. SS., new ed., p. 77), the Baptistery was erected next to the old cathedral of which practically nothing remains. The present entrance is not the original door. The floor level was originally lower and the dome was probably raised subsequently (G. Gerola in *Atti del Reale Istituto Veneto di Scienze, Lettere e Arti*, 1917, p. 311). At ground-floor level arcades decorated with mosaics are projected in front of walls

FIGURES 18 AND 19. Mausoleum of Galla Placidia, Ravenna. [18] Longitudinal section. On the right, the entrance. The arms of the cross have barrel vaults, the higher middle space is covered by a dome resting on corbeled sub-arches. After: G. Dehio and G. von Bezold, *Die kirchliche Baukunst des Abendlandes*, Stuttgart, 1887–1901. [19] Reconstruction of the architectural complex to which the mausoleum belonged, including the no-longer extant cruciform palace church of Santa Croce. After: C. O. Nordström, *Ravennastudien*, Uppsala, 1953.

with marble inlay [142 below]. The climax of the mosaic decoration, *The Baptism of Christ*, in the center of the dome [141], indicates the function of the edifice. In the zone surrounding it, the twelve Apostles, in procession, bring their martyr's crowns, received in the baptism of blood, as an offering to Christ (K. Wessel in *Corsi di cultura*, 1957, I, p. 77). The outer zone of the mosaic in the dome completes this heavenly scene. Eternal Truth is represented by the four Gospels, each on an altar within a stylized sanctuary. Alternating with the altars are four thrones, images of the Apocalyptic Throne (*etimasia*). The latter is explicitly present in the mosaics of the Arian Baptistery [149]. Below, between the windows, are stucco figures of prophets and saints holding scrolls or open books [143]. In the lunettes above them small reliefs: *Daniel in the Lions' Den*, *Jonah Disgorged by the Whale*, *Christ Triumphant*, and *The Delivery of the Scroll of the Law*. The original paint on these stucco reliefs has disappeared. Mosaics of saints or prophets amid a large scroll ornament appear in the spandrels of the ground-floor arcades.

A similar doctrinal program is presented by the mosaic decoration of San Giovanni in Fonte in Naples (Wulff, *Altchristliche Kunst*, I, fig. 299). The iconographic scheme in the Baptistery of Albenga is simpler (Toesca, *Storia*, I, p. 208, fig. 127). Stylistically our mosaic recalls the apse of Sant'Aquilino in Milan [138] and the luminous figures on a blue background in the Mausoleum of Galla Placidia [145–147]. Here, as in Roman works like the apse of the Lateran Baptistery (Toesca, *ibid.*, fig. 98), the Hellenistic tradition is still clearly in evidence.

Venturi, *Storia*, I, p. 283, figs. 114–117; Wulff, *Altchristliche Kunst*, I, p. 342, fig. 307, Nachtrag, p. 45; Wilpert, *Mosaiken*, pls. 78–81; van Berchem and Clouzot, *Mosaïques*, p. 97, figs. 111–113; Galassi, *Roma o Bisanzio*, I, p. 33, pls. 11–21; E. Tea in *Felix Ravenna*, 1916, p. 939; J. Ficker in *Byzantinisch-Neugriechisches Jahrbuch*, 1921, p. 319; Ricci, *Tavole*, p. 37; S. Bettini in *Felix Ravenna*, 1950, p. 41; Morey, *Early Christian Art*, p. 157, fig. 165; Nordström, *Ravennastudien*, p. 32, pls. 7, 8; Ammann, *Pittura*, p. 28, fig. 1.

## 144–147

MAUSOLEUM OF GALLA PLACIDIA, RAVENNA. About 424–25.

[144] Exterior from the southwest.
[145] Interior from the entrance.

[146] St. Lawrence going to his martyrdom. Mosaic lunette. Mid-5th century.

[147] Christ as the Good Shepherd. Mosaic lunette. Mid-5th century.

The mausoleum was part of the first imperial palace complex, of which the palace church, Santa Croce, still remains though completely rebuilt, and lay between the palace buildings and the small 6th-century church of San Vitale [155–167]. The mausoleum was built, in the usual simple brickwork, by Galla Placidia after the death of her husband Constantius III (421) and of her brother Honorius (423), probably about 424–25, when she had returned from Constantinople to Ravenna. She died in 450 in Rome. The mausoleum has a cruciform plan and the crossing is covered by a trussed dome on pendentives [145]. The present floor (length 49 ft. [15 m.], width 42½ ft. [13 m.]) has been raised considerably (4 ft., 8 in. [1.43 m.]), so that the original effect has been destroyed. In the niches are the sarcophagi of the Empress, her husband Constantius III, and either her brother Honorius or her son Valentinian III. The sarcophagus without relief decoration or name in the middle niche is probably that of the Empress (G. de Francovich in *Corsi di cultura*, 1957, II, p. 39).

Since the chapel, not originally intended as a mausoleum, was dedicated to St. Lawrence, the saint is represented in the middle niche. From the right he approaches the gridiron on which he is to suffer martyrdom. Wearing a long white tunic with purple clavi, he shoulders a golden cross held in his right hand and carries an open book in his left. On the left is a bookcase containing copies of the Gospels, a reference to the deacon's duty of keeping the Holy Scriptures. In the dome, the cross appears against a starry heaven, and in the spandrels, the symbols of the four Evangelists. In the lunettes immediately underneath stand four pairs of Apostles adoring the cross. The four remaining Apostles are in acanthus scrolls in the vaults of the east and west niches. In the lunettes of these niches are stags amid foliage, drinking from the fountain of life, and in the lunette over the entrance, Christ, as the Good Shepherd, is surrounded by his flock.

The spirit of these representations is still Hellenistic. In particular the portrayal of the Good Shepherd recalls Roman sepulchral art. Stylistically there are parallels with the mosaics in Sant'Aquilino, Milan, while the color pattern is reminiscent of the mosaics in Capua (Wilpert, *Mosaiken*, pl. 77) and Naples (Wilpert, *Mosaiken*, pls. 29–39). As for Roman mosaics, the apse of Santa Pudenziana [130] offers similarities that suggest a date before the middle of the 5th century for our mosaics. The illusionistic technique is close to the mosaics in the Baptistery of the Orthodox, especially the procession of the Apostles [142].

For the architecture: T. G. Jackson, *Byzantine and Romanesque Architecture*, Cambridge, 1920; C. Ricci, *Il Mausoleo di Galla Placidia in Ravenna*, Rome, 1914; G. Bovini, *Il cosidetto Mausoleo di Galla Placidia in Ravenna*, Vatican City, 1950.

For the decoration: Duetschke, *Studien*, p. 265; Venturi, *Storia*, I, p. 278, figs. 112–113; Wulff, *Altchristliche Kunst*, I, p. 348, fig. 310; R. Kömstedt, *Vormittelalterliche Malerei*, Augsburg, 1929, p. 19, figs. 50–53; Wilpert, *Mosaiken*, pls. 48–52; van Berchem and Clouzot, *Mosaïques*, p. 91, figs. 104–109; Grabar, *Martyrium*, II, p. 80; A. Grabar, *Byzantine Painting*, Geneva, 1953, pl. p. 53; Galassi, *Roma o Bisanzio*, I, 13, pls. 1–10; Lasareff, *History of Byzantine Painting*, p. 49, pls. 2, 3; Nordström, *Ravennastudien*, p. 12, pls. 1–4; P. Courcelle in *Cahiers archéologiques*, 1948, p. 29; Ammann, *Pittura*, p. 26.

**148**

ANGELS SUPPORTING THE MONOGRAM OF CHRIST AND SYMBOLS OF THE EVANGELISTS. Mosaics in the vault. About 494–519. Ravenna, Chapel of the Archiepiscopal Palace.

Under Ostrogothic rule, Archbishop Peter II (494–519) built this cruciform chapel with a small apse and a vestibule on the upper floor of his palace. The mosaic decoration of both chapel and vestibule is heavily restored (Ricci, *Tavole*, V, p. 47, pls. 34–45). The masonry is similar to that of Sant'Apollinare Nuovo, the walls faced with Proconnesian marble. Above the vestibule entrance appears the victorious Christ (only upper part original), shouldering the cross and holding an open book with the words: EGO SVM VIA VERITAS ET VITA. He treads on a lion and an adder (Psalm 91). On the side walls of the vestibule a metrical inscription: AVT LVX HIC NATA EST.... The vault is decorated with flowers and birds, the apse of the chapel with a cross. In the main vault the monogram of Christ is borne by four angels [148]; between them the symbols of the Evangelists. The iconographic scheme derives from the ceiling of the Oratory of the Holy Cross in the Lateran Baptistery (Wilpert, *Mosaiken*, II, p. 728). Inside the supporting arches medallions with portraits of Christ, flanked by SS. Peter and Paul, followed by other Apostles, and saints. In style the mosaics recall the decoration of the Arian period in Sant'Apollinare Nuovo. The medallion portraits of the saints are akin to the later ones in San Vitale [160, 161] which, in turn, look forward to the somewhat later, probably 7th-century medallions in Panagia Panakaria, in Cyprus (L. B. Ottolenghi in *Felix Ravenna*, 1957, p. 25, fig. 8; J. Bolten, *Die Imago Clipeata*, Paderborn, 1937).

Wulff, *Altchristliche Kunst*, I, p. 350, fig. 311; Wilpert, *Mosaiken*, I, p. 47, col. III, pls. 89–95; van Berchem and Clouzot, *Mosaïques*, p. 115, figs. 129–135; G. Gerola in *Felix Ravenna*, 1932, p. 71; Galassi, *Roma o Bisanzio*, I, p. 79, pls. 62, 67; Morey, *Early Christian Art*, p. 159, fig. 169; Cabrol and Leclercq, *Dictionnaire*, vol. XII, pt. 1, col. 194, fig. 8501; Nordström, *Ravennastudien*, p. 86, pl. 10; L. B. Ottolenghi in *Felix Ravenna*, 1957, p. 5, figs. 1–7; Ammann, *Pittura*, p. 33; H. Michaelis in *Forschungen und Fortschritte*, 1958, p. 87.

**149**

THE BAPTISM AND THE APOSTLES BEFORE THE APOCALYPTIC THRONE. Mosaics in the dome. About 500. Ravenna, Baptistery of the Arians (Santa Maria in Cosmedin).

The edifice, as Agnellus records, was built under Theodoric (493–526), probably in the early part of his reign, as a baptistery adjoining his church of Santo Spirito. Only the mosaic in the dome has been preserved. Following the scheme in the Baptistery of the Orthodox [141], the center is taken up by *The Baptism of Christ*. St. John the Baptist stands on a rock to the right of Christ, toward whom the dove of the Holy Ghost descends from above. On the left the personified river Jordan in an attitude of amazement. In the outer zone the procession of the Apostles, separated from each other by plant candelabra, converge on the throne. This stands in the axis of the dove and is surmounted by the cross. The most recent restoration (1955) revealed that the mosaics were made in two stages; three hands can be distinguished for the first stage, and probably two for the second (G. Bovini in *Felix Ravenna*, 1957, p. 5). The tesserae are of marble, whereas in the Baptistery of the Orthodox they are of glass paste.

G. Gerola, *Studien zur Kunst des Ostens*, Leipzig, 1923, p. 112; Wilpert, *Mosaiken*, pl. 101; C. Ricci in *Felix Ravenna*, 1929, p. 1; Ricci, *Tavole*, III, p. 28; Wulff, *Altchristliche Kunst*, I, p. 342, fig. 308; Galassi, *Roma o Bisanzio*, I, p. 69; Morey, *Early Christian Art*, p. 157, fig. 166; Nordström, *Ravennastudien*, p. 32, pl. 9; Ammann, *Pittura*, p. 32.

## 150–153

SANT'APOLLINARE NUOVO, RAVENNA.

[150] Mosaic panel in the nave. Early 6th century. *The Multiplication of Loaves and Fishes.*

[151] Mosaic panel in the nave. Early 6th century. *The Separation of Goats from Sheep.*

[152] Mosaic frieze in the nave; bottom zone. Above: Palace of Theodoric, early 6th century. Below: female saints and the Magi, second half of the 6th century; Virgin enthroned, with Angels, early 6th century.

[153] Mosaic frieze in the nave. Second half of the 6th century. Detail: the Magi.

Theodoric built this three-aisled basilica as his palace church and dedicated it, probably about 504, to the Saviour. After its conversion to the orthodox cult by Archbishop Agnellus (557–70) it bore the name of Sancti Martini in Coelo Aureo, and was dedicated to Apollinaris only in the 9th century when the saint's relics were transferred to it from Classis.

The apse was partly destroyed by earthquake and replaced.

The gilded ceiling *(in coelo aureo)* has disappeared. The plan is similar to that of Sant'Apollinare in Classe [173] and there are other basilicas of this type in Parenzo (Wulff, *Altchristliche Kunst*, II, fig. 346), Grado, and Pola. The capitals already recall Eastern models (Kautzsch, *Kapitellstudien*, p. 187, pl. 37; A. Colasanti, *L'arte bizantina in Italia*, Milan, 1923, pl. 49).

The walls of the nave carry mosaic decoration in three zones. Parts of it date from the time of Theodoric. In the top zone of the north side are rectangular fields with scenes from the early life of Christ: reading from west to east, *The Healing of the Paralytic, The Healing of the Demoniac, The Healing of the Sick, The Separation of Goats from Sheep* [151], *The Widow's Mite, The Pharisee and the Publican, The Raising of Lazarus, The Samaritan Woman at the Well, The Woman with the Issue of Blood, The Healing of the Blind, The Miraculous Draught, The Multiplication of Loaves and Fishes* [150], and *The Miracle at Cana* (?). In the top zone on the south side are Passion scenes: reading from east to west, *The Last Supper, Christ in Gethsemane, The Kiss of Judas, Christ Led to Caiaphas, Christ Before Caiaphas, Christ Foretelling the Denial of Peter, The Denial of Peter, The Repentance of Judas, Christ Before Pilate, The Road to Calvary, The Marys at the Sepulcher, The Road to Emmaus,* and *The Incredulity of Thomas.* On both walls panels, showing confronting birds surmounting large shells containing crowns, alternate with the scenes. Directly below these panels and between the windows are 32 Old Testament patriarchs and prophets, each holding a book or a scroll. In the bottom zone a number of representations of an Arian or political character were removed when the church was converted to Orthodoxy about 560. On the north

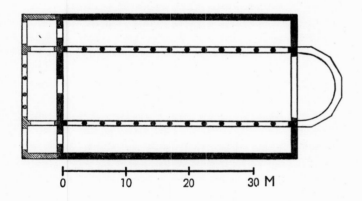

0   10   20   30 M

FIGURES 20 AND 21. Sant'Apollinare Nuovo, Ravenna. Plan and longitudinal section. After: G. Dehio and G. von Bezold, *Die kirchliche Baukunst des Abendlandes*, Stuttgart, 1887–1901.

341

side reading from west to east: the port and city of Classis with ships in the harbor; five figures originally standing in front of the walls have been removed. From the city gate issues a procession of 22 female martyrs carrying wreaths who are preceded by the Magi [152, 153]. Of the original composition of Theodoric's time only the Virgin enthroned between four angels has remained. In the section with the Magi, the upper part down to the gifts they bear [153] is a modern restoration. It is noteworthy that the portrayal of the Virgin enthroned as the Mother of God implies that the Arians accepted the dogma promulgated by the Orthodox Council of Ephesus (431); Archbishop Agnellus could thus keep this part. On the south side the opening scene shows the Palace of Theodoric [152 above], not directly depicted, but represented by its peristyle, the arcades on the sides being the lateral wings of the peristyle rendered in the flat. On the columns remain traces of the hands of court dignitaries who originally appeared under the arcades. In the central pediment the representation of Theodoric on horseback was also removed (G. Bovini in *Festschrift für R. Egger*, Klagenfurt, 1952, I, p. 206; E. Dyggve, *Ravennatum Palatium Sacrum*, Copenhagen, 1941). From the palace 26 male saints carrying wreaths in their hands, some veiled, move toward the enthroned Christ; at their head is St. Martin of Tours. This procession, too, replaced an earlier, unknown mosaic. The portrayal of Christ on an ornate throne between four angels holding golden staffs is a direct borrowing from Eastern court ceremonial.

The differentiation of the earlier from the later mosaics was clarified during the restorations after 1944, when the layers of stucco underneath were examined (G. Bovini in *Atti del I° Congresso nazionale di archeologia cristiana, Siracusa, 1950*, Rome, 1951, p. 101). For modern restorations, see especially C. Ricci (*Tavole*, IV, 1933, p. 121) and R. Bartoccini (in *Felix Ravenna*, 1932, p. 168). For the iconography of the scenes from the life and Passion of Christ, see A. Baumstark (in *Rassegna Gregoriana*, 1910, p. 33, and *Festbrevier und Kirchenjahr der syrischen Jakobiten*, Paderborn, 1910), who thinks they are illustrations of Gospel lessons in the local liturgy in which he discerns strong Syrian influences. C. O. Nordström (*Ravennastudien*, p. 63) has rejected this theory. He shows that the scenes with Christ are influenced by a North Italian Lectionary rather than one from outside Italy. The mosaics from Theodoric's time already approach the Byzantine style. Those put up by Archbishop Agnellus are very close to the mosaics in San Vitale and reflect a purely Byzantine trend which established itself in Rome as well as in Santi Cosma e Damiano (Toesca, *Storia*, I, fig. 135, p. 136) and San Lorenzo fuori le Mura [185]. Many scenes appear as a further development of the columnar sarcophagus. There are also connections with 5th-century ivories, such as the four panels of the Maskell casket [98], and, to an even greater degree, the five-part diptych in Milan [100, 101]. The scenes from the life of Christ on the Chair of Maximian [230-233] belong to the same group.

Venturi, *Storia*, I, p. 285, fig. 123-125; Wulff, *Altchristliche Kunst*, I, p. 438, figs. 371-373, pl. XXIV, Nachtrag, p. 55; Wilpert, *Mosaiken*, pls. 97-100; van Berchem and Clouzot, *Mosaïques*, p. 125, figs. 143-181; Cabrol and Leclercq, *Dictionnaire*, vol. XII, pt. 1, col. 206, figs. 8508-8511; P. Muratoff, *La peinture byzantine*, Paris, 1928, p. 50; Galassi, *Roma o Bisanzio*, I, p. 123, pls. 22-61; von Simson, *Fortress*, p. 69, pls. 30, 32, 44; Morey, *Early Christian Art*,

p. 159, figs. 170, 172-176; Nordström, *Ravennastudien*, p. 55, figs. 15-21; L. B. Ottolenghi in *Felix Ravenna*, 1955, p. 5; C. Cecchelli in *Felix Ravenna*, 1957, p. 66; G. Bovini in *Fede e arte*, 1958, p. 33; Ammann, *Pittura*, p. 29.

## 154

### MAUSOLEUM OF THEODORIC, RAVENNA.

The structure was never finished. The Anonymous Valesianus (ed. T. Mommsen, *Chronica minora*, I, p. 308) writing not long after Theodoric's death, and the chronicler, Agnellus, in his 9th-century *Liber pontificalis*, describe it as the king's sepulchral monument. Recently his porphyry sarcophagus was reinstalled in the mausoleum. The two-storied, domed structure is decagonal on the lower floor and on the lower part of the upper floor; the uppermost part is circular. The lower floor is articulated by ten deep semicircular arches; in one, on the west, is the entrance. The upper floor is set back and has a gallery, at present without a balustrade. Directly above the ground-floor entrance is a door into the interior of the upper level, on the opposite, eastern side is an apse with altar, on the other eight sides, eight pairs of niches surmounted by an equal number of semicircular arches. The top circular part is encompassed by a cornice with a barbaric ornament. The heavy domical monolith is decorated with twelve corbel stones carrying the names of the Apostles.

The earlier theory of the Germanic character of the monument (A. Haupt, *Die älteste Kunst, insbesondere die Baukunst der Germanen*, Berlin, 1923, p. 145, fig. 90; S. Fuchs, *Kunst der Ostgotenzeit*, Berlin, 1944, p. 39, figs. 24-26) has now been generally abandoned. According to Dyggve (in *Corsi di cultura*, 1957, p. 67) the architect based himself on Late-Antique monumental mausoleums, conceived as *heroa*, which would explain the two stories. The lower, which housed the sarcophagus, may also have been intended as a family tomb, like the Mausoleum of Galla Placidia [145], while the upper was a chapel for funerary services. The corbel stones on the dome with the names of the Apostles recall the Mausoleum of Constantine the Great in which the emperor had himself buried amid twelve cenotaphs bearing the names of the Apostles. It is known that Theodoric, like Charlemagne later, was in the habit of appearing surrounded by twelve friends, thus imitating the Byzantine emperor who likened himself to Christ. A technical innovation was the horizontal buttressing of the exceedingly heavy monolith of the dome. The upper floor was adequately lit through the small drum (E. Dyggve in *Corsi di cultura*, 1957, p. 67).

G. T. Rivoira, *Architettura romana*, 1921, p. 240; C. Diehl, *Ravenne*, Paris, 1928; Wulff, *Altchristliche Kunst*, I, p. 245, figs. 22, 23; A. M. Schneider in *Byzantinische Zeitschrift*, 1941; V. Guberti in *Felix Ravenna*, 1952, p. 5; S. Ferri in *Settimane di studio del centro italiano di studi sull'alto medioevo*, Spoleto, 1956, p. 57; C. Cecchelli in *Felix Ravenna*, 1956, p. 5; E. Dyggve, *Kong Theoderik og den nordiske runddysse*, Copenhagen, 1957; A. Gottsmich in *Universitas*, 1957, p. 1183.

## 155-167

### SAN VITALE, RAVENNA. 525/26-47.
[155] Exterior from the south.
[156] Ambulatory.
[157] Interior facing the apse.
[158] Mosaic in the apse. Christ Enthroned, flanked by St. Vitalis, the Archbishop Ecclesius, and two angels.

[159] Mosaics on the north side of the sanctuary. In the lunette: *The Sacrifice of Abraham.*

[160] Mosaics in the vault and on the south side of the sanctuary. In the lunette: *The Sacrifice of Abel* and *The Sacrifice of Melchizedek.*

[161] Mosaics in the vault of the sanctuary and the soffit of the entrance arch.

[162] Capitals and arcade. Above: gallery to the north of the sanctuary. Below: gallery to the south of the sanctuary.

[163] Columns and arcade on the south of the sanctuary.

[164] Mosaic in the apse. The Emperor Justinian accompanied by the Archbishop Maximian and by his suite.

[165] Mosaic in the apse. The Empress Theodora with her suite.

[166] Mosaic in the apse. Detail: the Emperor Justinian, the Archbishop Maximian, and other officials.

[167] Mosaic in the apse. Detail: the Empress Theodora and some of her attendants.

San Vitale was built on the site of a small church by Archbishop Ecclesius (522–32), after his return from Constantinople in 525, perhaps also after Theodoric's death (526); continued by his successors Ursicinus (533–36) and Victor (538–45), and dedicated in 547 by Maximian during Justinian's reign. The building was financed by Julianus Argentarius, a wealthy banker. As the monograms on the floor of the central octagon and in the gallery of the sanctuary are those of Archbishop Victor (F. W. Deichmann in *Arte del primo millennio, Atti del II° Convegno per lo studio dell'arte dell'alto medioevo,* Turin, 1953, p. 114), it is likely that most of the actual construction was done during his episcopate. This inference is indirectly supported by the date of the mosaics that were put up shortly before the dedication.

Ground plan and structure follow Byzantine models; observe the similarity with the Constantinopolitan churches of St. John in the Palace of the Hebdomon (destroyed), and of SS. Sergius and Bacchus [186, 187 and figs. 26, 27]. In individual features, on the other hand, the more Western character of Ravenna asserts itself. For this new type of structure, particularly the vaulting, see H. Glück (*Der Ursprung des römischen und abendländischen Wölbungsbaues,* Vienna, 1953, p. 140, fig. 81). Byzantine also are the capitals with impost blocks (Kautzsch, *Kapitellstudien,* p. 139 ff).

For the architecture: Wulff, *Altchristliche Kunst,* II, p. 369, fig. 318, Nachtrag, p. 50; C. Ricci in *Felix Ravenna,* 1915, p. 758; G. Gerola in *Felix Ravenna,* 1916, p. 879; A. Testi-Rasponi, *Codex pontificalis ecclesiae ravennatis,* Bologna, 1924, p. 165; R. Bartoccini in *Felix Ravenna,* 1931, p. 77, and 1932, p. 133; J. Ebersolt, *Monuments d'architecture byzantine,* Paris, 1934; von Simson, *Fortress,* p. 23; G. Bovini, *San Vitale di Ravenna,* Milan, 1955; for the stucco work in the western part of the church: J. Shapley in *Studien zur Kunst des Ostens,* 1923, p. 19.

The celebrated wall and ceiling mosaics are in the sanctuary and the apse. In the latter, Christ as World Ruler tenders the martyr's crown to the church patron, St. Vitalis, whom an angel introduces; on His left, the founder of the church, Ecclesius, presents a model of the church. In the vault of the sanctuary the Lamb of God, against the starry heaven, is set within a wreath held by four angels. The segments of the vault are filled with acanthus scrolls and paradisical animals. In the soffit of the arch between the apse and sanctuary the monogram of Christ is the center between two series of cornucopias and eagles. In each lunette of the sanctuary are two sacrificial scenes from the Old Testament: *The Sacrifice of Abel* and *The Sacrifice of Melchizedek* on the south side, and *The Sacrifice of Abraham* combined with *The Visit of the Three Angels* on the north. In the spandrels scenes from the life of Moses, *The Call on Mount Horeb* and *Moses Receiving the Law,* are shown.

On the side walls of the apse are the two imperial mosaics [164, 165]. To the left of the altar Justinian and his retinue, including Archbishop Maximian who carries a cross. Between the emperor and his bodyguard stand two patricians wearing chlamydes with broad purple stripes, between the Emperor and the Archbishop a senator, sometimes identified as the banker Julianus. Further to the right two deacons with Gospel Book and censer. On the opposite wall, the Empress Theodora with her ladies-in-waiting is being led into the church by an official. Models for the portraits of the imperial couple and of their retinue were, no doubt, supplied from Constantinople. The apsidal mosaics exemplify ceremonial court art, while those in the sanctuary show a more popular, narrative style. The medallions in the soffit of the triumphal arch are akin to the mosaics in the Archiepiscopal Chapel, and, in their style, related also to the (heavily restored) mosaic from San Michele in Affricisco,

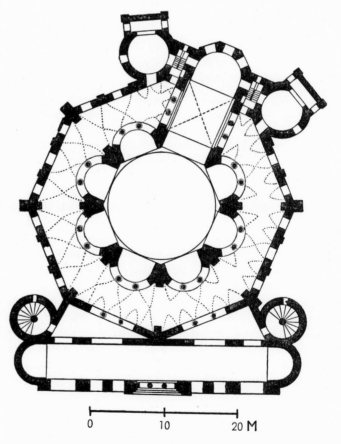

FIGURE 22. San Vitale, Ravenna. Plan. The narthex in front of the church on the west. Observe the deflection of the presbytery and apse from the east-west axis. After: G. Dehio and G. von Bezold, *Die kirchliche Baukunst des Abendlandes,* Stuttgart, 1887–1901.

now in Berlin, Staatliche Museen (K. Wessel, *Das Ravenna-tische Mosaik in den Staatlichen Museen zu Berlin und seine Wiederherstellung*, Berlin, 1953), donated in 545 by Julianus Argentarius and his son-in-law Bacauda. The chief figure here is Christ Immanuel standing between two angels in the semi-dome of the apse while in the zone above, flanked by angels blowing trumpets, He sits in judgment over the living and the dead. Unfortunately in Constantinople no monument has survived that documents as unmistakably as the mosaics in San Vitale the penetration of court ceremonial into church ritual (von Simson, *Fortress*, p. 23 ff.).

Wulff, *Altchristliche Kunst*, II, p. 369, figs. 318–320; van Berchem and Clouzot, *Mosaïques*, p. 145, figs. 183–198; Cabrol and Leclercq, *Dictionnaire*, vol. VII, pt. 1, col. 212, figs. 8512–8519; Galassi, *Roma o Bisanzio*, I, p. 81, pls. 71–93; Colasanti, *Arte bizantina*, pls. 9–19; Grabar, *L'Empereur*, p. 106; Grabar, *Peinture byzantine*, p. 62, pl. pp. 58–72; Lasareff, *Byzantine Painting*, p. 58, pls. 28–33; G. Rodenwaldt in *Jahrbuch des deutschen archäologischen Institutes*, 1944–45, p. 88; C. Cecchelli in *Felix Ravenna*, 1950, p. 5; R. Delbrueck in *Antike Denkmäler*, IV, pl. p. 11; P. Toesca, *S. Vitale in Ravenna*, Milan, 1952; G. Bovini, *San Vitale di Ravenna*, 1955; Nordström, *Ravennastudien*, p. 88, pl. 22–26; Ammann, *Pittura*, p. 45, fig. 5; A. W. Byvanck in *Corsi di cultura*, 1958, p. 49.

#### 168–173

SANT'APOLLINARE IN CLASSE, RAVENNA. About 533–49.

[168] Exterior from the east.
[169] Exterior from the west.
[170] Interior, left aisle.
[171] Interior facing east.
[172] Mosaic in the apse. Detail: the Archbishop Ursus.
[173] Apse and triumphal arch.

The church was begun by Archbishop Ursicinus (533–36) and dedicated in 549; it, too, was financed by Julianus Argentarius. Up to the 9th century the church enshrined the body of St. Apollinaris who had suffered martyrdom in Classis. It is a three-aisled basilica of the type of Sant'Apollinare Nuovo, with the apse raised above a crypt [171]; on either side of the apse is a sacristy. The capitals with their acanthus ornament may be Byzantine imports (Kautzsch, *Kapitellstudien*, p. 148). The exterior is very simple, with blind arcades and a dentil frieze, articulated in the Byzantine fashion. The round campanile is later (M. Mazzotti in *Corsi di cultura*, 1958, I, p. 85).

The mosaic decoration is confined to the apse and the triumphal arch. The central mosaic in the apse is probably contemporary with the dedication, while the representations on the triumphal arch and on the side walls of the apse, the donor scene on the north, and the sacrificial scene on the south are 7th century. The representation of the Emperor Constantine IV handing the scroll of privileges to Bishop Reparatus dates them about 675. In the central mosaic [173] the titular saint, Apollinaris, is portrayed transfigured, as the shepherd interceding for his flock at the Last Judgment. Above him the cross against the starry heavens, within a medallion flanked by Moses and Elijah, symbolizes the Last Judgment. The three lambs lower down represent SS. Peter, John, and James, thus alluding to the Transfiguration. Between the windows are figures of the most distinguished archbishops of Ravenna—Ecclesius, Severus, Ursus [172], and Ursicinus. In the apex of the triumphal arch is Christ

flanked by the symbols of the Evangelists; below, on the side panels that are level with the windows, the Archangels Michael and Gabriel stand guard over the entrance to the sanctuary.

The style of the mosaic in the semidome of the apse is close to San Vitale but of an inferior quality.

Wulff, *Altchristliche Kunst*, II, pp. 396, 441, figs. 343–345, 374–375, Nachtrag, p. 55; van Berchem and Clouzot, *Mosaïques*, p. 159, figs. 201–215; Ricci, *Tavole*, VII, p. 36, pls. 46–70; Colasanti, *Arte bisantina*, pls. 25–27; Galassi, *Roma o Bisanzio*, I, p. 187, pls. 94–99, 116–117; Grabar, *Martyrium*, I, p. 467, fig. 118; G. Mesini, *Basilica di S. Apollinare in Classe*, Ravenna, 1949; von Simson, *Fortress*, p. 8, pls. 21–23; Nordström, *Ravennastudien*, p. 120, pls. 29–30; M. Mazzotti, *La Basilica di S. Apollinare in Classe*, Vatican City, 1954; M. Mazzotti in *Rivista di Archeologia Cristiana*, 1956, p. 201; Ammann, *Pittura*, p. 48.

#### 174–179

The literature on RAVENNA SARCOPHAGI has, in recent times, grown considerably. Many of the pieces are treated in works on Early Christian sarcophagi (see 4–6) but the general

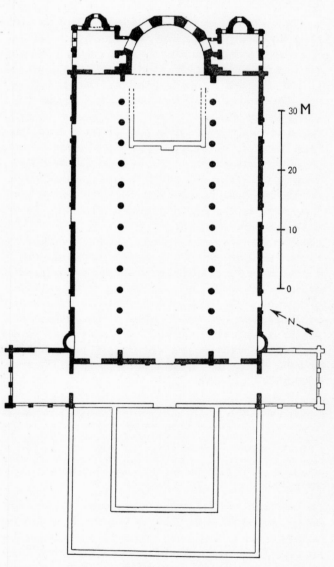

FIGURE 23. Sant'Apollinare in Classe, Ravenna. Plan. In front of the basilica on the west the narthex (preserved) and the atrium (destroyed). After: M. Mazzotti in *Rivista di Archeologia Cristiana*, 1954.

344

handbooks—Venturi, Wulff, Toesca, Dalton, and Morey—also offer material on the subject.

Among specialized works: Goldmann, *Sarkophage*; Duetschke, *Studien*; G. Rodenwaldt in *Römische Mitteilungen*, 1922–23, p. 58; Haseloff, *Vorromanische Plastik*; Lawrence, *Sarcophagi*; G. Bovini in *Felix Ravenna*, 1950, p. 31, 1952, p. 25, 1954, p. 22; G. Bovini, *Sarcofagi*; Kollwitz, *Sarkophage*; J. Kollwitz in *Corsi di cultura*, 1956, pp. 55, 61; K. Wessel in *Corsi di cultura*, 1957, p. 73; G. de Francovich in *Corsi di cultura*, 1957, p. 17.

## 174

SARCOPHAGUS WITH CHRIST GIVING THE LAW TO SS. PETER AND PAUL. Height 29½ in. (0.75 m.), length 6 ft., 9½ in. (2.07 m.). About 400. From San Severo. Ravenna, San Francesco.

It is almost identical with the so-called sarcophagus of Bishop Liberius III [175] who died in 378, which would make our sarcophagus late 4th century, as well. G. de Francovich (in *Corsi di cultura*, 1957, p. 31) suggests about 390, but the beginning of the 5th century is more likely. On the front, five niches; in the middle one the youthful Christ gives the Scroll of the Law to St. Paul, who is in the niche on His right. Other Apostles, wearing tunic and pallium, stand under the remaining niches. The rooflike lid (original?) has lions' heads decorations. The armorial bearings on the acroteria are 17th-century additions. This type of sarcophagus derives from the earlier columnar sarcophagi. There is not only a stylistic kinship with Eastern monuments [65], but also with early 5th-century Roman works [64], as well as with the marble vase showing Christ among the Apostles, now at the Museo Nazionale Romano in Rome (Wulff, *Altchristliche Kunst*, I, fig. 89; Toesca, *Storia*, I, fig. 38).

Venturi, *Storia*, I, p. 210, fig. 197; Goldmann, *Sarkophage*, p. 2 ff.; Duetschke, *Studien*, no. 56, fig. 23; L. von Sybel, *Christliche Antike*, Marburg, 1909, II, fig. 47; Lawrence, *Sarcophagi*, p. 15, fig. 26; Bovini, *Sarcofagi di Ravenna*, p. 27, figs. 18–20; Gerke, *Christus*, fig. 76; J. Kollwitz in *Corsi di cultura*, 1956, p. 57; Kollwitz, *Sarkophage*, p. 13, pls. 4–7.

## 175

SARCOPHAGUS OF BISHOP LIBERIUS. Marble. Lid missing. Height 31 in. (0.79 m.), length 7 ft. (2.13 m.). Late 4th century. Ravenna, San Francesco.

Detail: *Christ Giving the Law to St. Paul.*

According to Lawrence (*Sarcophagi*, p. 13) the entombed bishop is Liberius III. J. Kollwitz (in *Corsi di cultura*, 1956, p. 61) thinks, however, that the sarcophagus is a later replica of a sarcophagus of the same type as the other one in San Francesco [174]. The treatment of the stone seems to support Kollwitz's thesis. Almost all other scholars have, so far, dated the piece to the time of Liberius (Bovini, *Sarcofagi di Ravenna*, p. 32, figs. 21, 22; de Francovich in *Corsi di cultura*, 1957, p. 21). According to Bovini, it was retouched. On the base the inscription: HIC IACET CORPVS D. LIBERII ARCHIEP.

The front is divided into five niches by six columns. In the central one sits the youthful Christ who gives the Scroll of the Law to St. Paul. In the remaining niches stand three other Apostles. The representation on the back is similar except that the Apostle next to Christ does not reach out for the Scroll. On the sides, as on the other sarcophagus in San Francesco [174], are pairs of Apostles.

G. de Francovich (in *Corsi di Cultura*, 1957, p. 17) dates it

about 378–80. He compares it with the Sarcophagus of a Prince in Istanbul [75] and with other sarcophagi in Ravenna, the one in San Francesco [174] and that of Pietro Onesti (*il Peccatore*) in Santa Maria in Porto Fuori [178]. For iconographic affinities with Eastern types of sarcophagi, see Wulff, *Altchristliche Kunst*, I, Nachtrag, p. 21; O. Wulff in *Byzantinisch-Neugriechisches Jahrbuch*, 1921–22, p. 362.

Garrucci, *Storia*, V, pl. 348, 2–5; Venturi, *Storia*, I, p. 438, fig. 198; Goldmann, *Sarkophage*, p. 1, pls. 1, 2; Duetschke, *Studien*, no. 54; Haseloff, *Vorromanische Plastik*, pl. 29; Lawrence, *Sarcophagi*, p. 13, fig. 25; Morey, *Early Christian Art*, p. 104, fig. 110.

## 176

SARCOPHAGUS. Marble. Height 40 in. (1.02 m.), length 6 ft., 11 in. (2.11 m.). Early 5th century. Ravenna, Museo Nazionale.

Above: front, *Christ Giving the Law to St. Peter*. Below: detail of the left side, a bird in a tree.

At one time it was in front of San Giovanni Battista, then, still complete, it was moved to the sacristy of San Vitale (Garrucci, *Storia*, V, pl. 332); today only three sides are preserved. On the front, Christ gives the Scroll of the Law to St. Peter, who receives it with veiled hands. The two persons at the ends, standing beside palms, may be the deceased husband and wife. On the left side is *The Raising of Lazarus*; the tree with a bird behind Christ is noteworthy. On the right side is *Daniel in the Lions' Den*.

Stylistically the sarcophagus belongs to the earliest 5th-century works in Ravenna and is also reminiscent of the Passion panels of the Maskell casket [98]. The treatment of folds is still somewhat more Hellenistic than on the Rinaldo sarcophagus in the Cathedral [177] and the Pignatta sarcophagus, in the Braccioforte Chapel, adjoining San Francesco (Lawrence, *Sarcophagi*, fig. 31).

Wulff, *Altchristliche Kunst*, I, p. 178, fig. 176; Wilpert, *Sarcofagi*, I, p. 187, pl. 141, 6; Goldmann, *Sarkophage*, p. 10; Duetschke, *Studien*, p. 181; Gerke, *Christus*, pls. 78, 79; Lawrence, *Sarcophagi*, p. 20, figs. 35–37; Bovini, *Sarcofagi*, p. 18, figs. 10–13; *Catalogue*, Paris, no. 6, pl. 3; Kollwitz, *Sarkophage*, pl. 8; J. Kollwitz in *Corsi di cultura*, 1956, p. 58; K. Wessel in *Corsi di cultura*, 1957, I, p. 75; G. de Francovich in *Corsi di cultura*, 1957, p. 27.

## 177

SARCOPHAGUS WITH CHRIST BETWEEN SS. PETER AND PAUL. Early 5th century. Ravenna, Cathedral.

The sarcophagus contains the remains of Archbishop Rinaldo Concoreggio (died 1321; S. Muratori in *Bolletino d'arte*, 1908, p. 324). It has a lid in the form of a barrel vault. On the front the enthroned Christ, holding an open book, is hurriedly approached from the sides by SS. Peter and Paul who carry wreaths in veiled hands. On the back the monogram of Christ appears between confronting peacocks; on the left side the monogram is in a wreath; the right side has a vase with scrolls, and a monogrammatic cross between confronting lambs on the pediment.

It is closest to the Sarcophagus of the Twelve Apostles in Sant'Apollinare in Classe (Lawrence, *Sarcophagi*, fig. 2). The relief on the back recalls the richer execution of the same motif on that sarcophagus (Lawrence, *ibid.*, fig. 5) and on the

Theodore sarcophagus also in Sant'Apollinare in Classe (Lawrence, *ibid.*, fig. 6). Stylistically our piece is a further development of the sarcophagus in the Museo Nazionale [176], and belongs with the similar but somewhat coarser Sarcophagus of Barbatianus, also in the Cathedral (Lawrence, *ibid*, fig. 39).

Venturi, *Storia*, I, p. 438; Goldmann, *Sarkophage*, p. 7, pl. 5; Duetschke, *Studien*, no. 13, fig. 4; Wulff, *Altchristliche Kunst*, I, p. 177, pl. 13, 2; Toesca, *Storia*, I, p. 253, fig. 150; Lawrence, *Sarcophagi*, p. 4, figs. 1, 4, 7, 8; Bovini, *Sarcofagi*, p. 45, fig. 34; G. de Francovich in *Corsi di cultura*, 1957, p. 28.

## 178

SARCOPHAGUS WITH CHRIST GIVING THE LAW TO ST. PAUL. Height 23½ in. (0.60 m.), length 7 ft., ¾ in. (2.16 m.). 5th century. Ravenna, Santa Maria in Porto Fuori.

In 1119 the sarcophagus was reused for Pietro Onesti, called *il Peccatore*. The decoration of the lid imitates tiles. On the front, Christ, enthroned in the center, gives the Scroll of the Law to St. Paul; another Apostle stands on each side. On each lateral face are two Apostles holding crowns in veiled hands; on the back, a cross in a shield with two doves flying toward it. The *traditio legis* is very close to the corresponding scene on the sarcophagus in San Francesco [174].

Venturi, *Storia*, I, p. 437, fig. 196; Goldmann, *Sarkophage*, p. 4, pl. 31; Duetschke, *Studien*, no. 72, fig. 28; Cabrol and Leclercq, *Dictionnaire*, vol. XIV, pt. 2, col. 2122; Wulff, *Altchristliche Kunst*, I, p. 177, pl. 13, 1; Wilpert, *Sarcofagi*, II, p. 326, pl. 253, 1, 2, 4; Lawrence, *Sarcophagi*, p. 12, figs. 20, 23; Bovini, *Sarcofagi*, p. 33, figs. 23–25; G. de Francovich in *Corsi di cultura*, 1957, p. 23.

## 179

SARCOPHAGUS. Height 27⅛ in. (0.69 m.), width 28¼ in. (0.72 m.), length 7 ft., ¾ in. (2.16 m.). Early 5th century. Ravenna, San Vitale.

Above: *The Adoration of the Magi*. Below: detail, *Madonna and Child*.

The lid, which is not original, carries an inscription in Latin and Greek, recording the burial, before 650, of the Exarch Isaac. On the front: *The Adoration of the Magi*. On the back: the monogram of Christ between confronting peacocks. On the left side, *The Raising of Lazarus;* on the right side, *Daniel in the Lions' Den*. Though somewhat inferior in quality, it is stylistically akin to the Rinaldo sarcophagus in the Cathedral [177]. The narrow sides are similar to those of the sarcophagus in the Museo Nazionale [176]. The back is comparable to that of the Rinaldo sarcophagus, the Sarcophagus of the Twelve Apostles in Sant'Apollinare in Classe (Lawrence, *Sarcophagi*, fig. 5), and a sarcophagus in the Cathedral of Ferrara (Lawrence, *ibid.*, fig. 11). Our piece could thus be dated to the beginning of the 5th century, like the Pignatta sarcophagus in the Braccioforte Chapel near Dante's tomb (Kollwitz, *Sarkophage*, p. 7, pls. 2–4; Toesca, *Storia*, I, 255, fig. 152) which, however, represents in Ravenna a pronouncedly Eastern trend, much as does the relief with Peter from Ajatzam, now in Berlin (Wulff, *Altchristliche Kunst*, I, fig. 178).

Goldmann, *Sarkophage*, p. 12; Duetschke, *Studien*, no. 12, fig. 3; Smith, *Iconography*, p. 43; Wulff, *Altchristliche Kunst*, I, p. 178, fig. 175; Cabrol and Leclercq, *Dictionnaire*, vol. XIV, pt. 2, col. 2116; Lawrence, *Sarcophagi*, p. 9, figs. 12, 13, 16, 17; Bovini, *Sarcofagi*, p. 51, figs. 36–40; G. de Francovich in *Corsi di cultura*, 1957, II, p. 26.

## 180

HERCULES WITH THE HIND. Marble relief. Height 3 ft., 7⅞ in. (1.12 m.), width 2 ft., 7½ in. (0.80 m.). 5th or 6th century. Ravenna, Museo Nazionale.

Hercules, his knee on the hind's back, presses her down to the ground. Quiver and bow are behind him, his mace is under the animal. No doubt 5th- or 6th-century Byzantine work, akin to 6th-century silver pieces [250–253], it imitates a classical model of the 4th century B.C. The hind recalls the animals on the back of the Pignatta sarcophagus (Lawrence, *Sarcophagi*, fig. 32). A later example of a similar animal is in Berlin (Wulff, *Beschreibung*, p. 36, no. 8).

G. Galassi in *L'arte*, 1915, p. 50; G. Gerola, *I monumenti di Ravenna bizantina*, Milan, 1930, pl. 42; Peirce and Tyler, *L'Art byzantin*, I, pl. 10; *Catalogue*, Paris, no. 7, pl. 2.

## 181

CLOSURE SLABS. 6th century. Ravenna, Sant'Apollinare Nuovo.

The two above are in openwork. The one on the left is decorated with a fret pattern forming crosses and crosses inscribed in circles. The one on the right has vine scrolls growing out of a vase and encircling a frame with an ornate cross between confronting peacocks.

Dalton, *Byzantine Art*, fig. 442; Colasanti, *Arte bisantina*, pl. 67; Haseloff, *Vorromanische Plastik*, p. 36, pl. 36; Wulff, *Altchristliche Kunst*, II, p. 441, fig. 354.

Below: screen panel or altar frontal. A monogrammatic cross between confronting peacocks perched on the stem of a vine scroll growing out of a vase. The ornament is akin to the capitals and the moldings in San Vitale and in Sant'Apollinare Nuovo and follows Byzantine models [182, 209–211].

Venturi, *Storia*, I, p. 210; Colasanti, *Arte bisantina*, pl. 67; Toesca, *Storia*, I, p. 263, fig. 161, 1; H. Glück, *Die christliche Kunst des Ostens*, Berlin, 1923, p. 7, fig. 22; Cabrol and Leclercq, *Dictionnaire*, vol. XIII, pt. 1, col. 1083, fig. 9606.

## 182

CLOSURE SLABS. Marble openwork. Mid-6th century. From San Vitale. Ravenna, Museo Nazionale.

Above: trellislike pattern of interlaced ribbon with acanthus leaves, a small cross at the top center. A companion piece is still in San Vitale (Wulff, *Altchristliche Kunst*, II, p. 408, fig. 353). Similar slabs in Sant'Apollinare Nuovo (Colasanti, *Arte bisantina*, pl. 68) are dated by the building to the 6th century. There are also similar Byzantine pieces [211].

Cabrol and Leclercq, *Dictionnaire*, vol. II, pt. 2, col. 1830, fig. 2007; Colasanti, *Arte bisantina*, pl. 66.

Below: height 2 ft., 8¼ in. (0.82 m.), length 5 ft. (1.52 m.). A cross in the center of a pattern of interlaced rosettes interspersed with birds. Similar pieces are in San Vitale (Colasanti, *Arte bisantina*, pl. 66). They are approximately dated by the building (536–47). The same acanthus decoration appears on contemporary Byzantine capitals [209] and wall decoration [198].

Venturi, *Storia*, I, p. 151, fig. 77; G. Galassi in *L'arte*, 1915, p. 45; Toesca, *Storia*, I, p. 263; Colasanti, *Arte bisantina*, pl. 66; Peirce and Tyler, *L'Art bizantin*, II, pl. 99; Haseloff, *Vorromanische Plastik*, p. 35, pl. 35; R. Kautzsch in *Römisches Jahrbuch für Kunstgeschichte*, 1939, p. 59, fig. 91; Bovini, *Guida del Museo*, p. 33; *Catalogue*, Paris, no. 9, pl. 15.

**183**

AMBO. Marble. Height 9 ft., 10 in. (3 m.), original length 21 ft., 4 in. (6.50 m.). Mid-6th century. Ravenna, Cathedral.

The steps and the upper parapet have been missing since the 18th century. At present the ambo is divided into two parts. The donor's inscription along the upper border, SERVVS XPI AGNELLVS EPISC. HVNC PYRGVM FECIT, dates it in the episcopate of Archbishop Agnellus (557-70). On the convex, middle front, on the sides, and formerly also on the stair supports, symbolic lambs, peacocks, stags, doves, and fish are set in square frames.

The marked decline in quality and tendency toward flatness, as compared with reliefs from the middle of the century, continues on the pulpit in Santi Giovanni e Paolo, dated 597 (R. Cattaneo, *L'architettura in Italia dal secolo VI al mille circa*, Venice, 1888, p. 19), and reaches its final phase in Ravenna in the Sarcophagus of Archbishop Felix (died 723) in Sant'Apollinare in Classe (Toesca, *Storia*, I, p. 261, fig. 159), and that of Archbishop Gratiosus (died 788) also there (Bovini, *Sarcofagi*, p. 74, fig. 63).

Tura in *Felix Ravenna*, I, p. 365; Cabrol and Leclercq, *Dictionnaire*, vol. I, pt. 1, col. 1341, fig. 313; Colasanti, *Arte bisantina*, pl. 69; R. Cattaneo, *Architettura in Italia*, Venice, 1840, figs. 1, 2; Haseloff, *Vorromanische Plastik*, p. 37, pl. 39; Peirce and Tyler, *L'Art bizantin*, vol. II, p. 132, pl. 188; Lawrence, *Sarcophagi*, p. 23, fig. 80; Toesca, *Storia*, I, p. 260, fig. 158; C. Cecchelli in *Atti del IV° Congresso internazionale di archeologia cristiana*, II, p. 122.

**184, 185**

SAN LORENZO FUORI LE MURA, ROME.
[184] Interior, the east basilica. Late 6th century.
[185] Interior, the east basilica in the foreground. Mosaics on the triumphal arch. Late 6th century.

The present structure consists of two basilicas that have been joined. Plate 184 shows the view from the later basilica, built by Pope Honorius III (1216-27), into the earlier one erected by Pope Pelagius II (579-90). This three-aisled basilica with gallery was erected over the tomb of St. Lawrence. When it was enlarged by Honorius in the early 13th century, the apse was taken down and the nave raised to serve as the sanctuary for the new double church. The columns with their capitals and the architrave are taken from antique monuments. Honorius' structure [185 far end] is a simple three-aisled basilica without gallery. Its front part, entrance wall, and vestibule (Toesca, *Storia*, I, 369) were heavily damaged by bombs in 1944; the modern paintings in the nave were removed during the subsequent reconstruction.

For the architecture: C. Hülsen, *Le chiese di Roma nel medioevo*, Florence, 1927, p. 285; Wulff, *Altchristliche Kunst*, I, p. 240, fig. 235; A. Muñoz, *San Lorenzo fuori le mura*, Rome, 1944; Deichmann, *Kirchen*, p. 86, figs. 65-66; W. Frankl, E. Josi, and R. Krautheimer in *Rivista di Archeologia Cristiana*, 1950, p. 9; G. da Ba, *San Lorenzo fuori le mura*, Rome, 1952.

The 6th-century mosaic decoration on the triumphal arch of Pelagius' basilica is heavily restored. In the middle, Christ is enthroned on the globe between SS. Peter and Paul. On the right beside Paul, SS. Stephen and Hippolytus. On the other side the titular saint, Lawrence, introduces the papal founder,

Pelagius, who carries a model of the church. In the spandrels the holy cities of Jerusalem and Bethlehem. The closest stylistic parallel in Rome is offered by the mosaics in Sant'Agnese (635-38) (Wulff, *Altchristliche Kunst*, II, fig. 377) but the triumphal arch in Sant'Apollinare in Classe [173] is also similar.

Wulff, *Altchristliche Kunst*, II, p. 444; Toesca, *Storia*, I, p. 221, fig. 137; van Berchem and Clouzot, *Mosaïques*, p. 189, figs. 241-243; Morey, *Early Christian Art*, p. 179, fig. 193; P. Baldass in *Gazette des Beaux-Arts*, 1957, p. 1.

**186-190**

CHURCH OF SAINTS SERGIUS AND BACCHUS, ISTANBUL. 527-36.
[186] Interior, facing northwest.
[187] Interior, facing east.
[188] Above: melon-shaped capitals and soffit of the architrave. Below: impost capitals in the gallery.
[189] Architrave and columns with melon-shaped capitals.
[190] Exterior, with the vestibule and minaret added by the Turks.

Justinian and Theodora had the church built between 527 and 536, perhaps employing Anthemius of Tralles, the architect of Hagia Sophia [191-205]. It adjoined the Palace of Hormisdas and the Church of SS. Peter and Paul, and a monastery may have been attached. When the church was transformed into a mosque soon after 1453 and called Kücük Aya Sophia, the atrium was pulled down and replaced by a vestibule with five cupolas [190].

It is a central plan building with an interior octagon whose eight piers carry the dome. The plan and the size of the corner niches are exceptionally irregular, as the architect had to take into account the adjacent buildings. The external walls, and the vaulting of the ambulatory and the galleries were executed together with the rest of the building (N. Erounoff in *Revue des études grecques*, 1926, p. 26). The interior is lit by windows in the dome and particularly through the three large windows in the apse [187]. On the architrave supporting the gallery is the foundation inscription of Justinian and his wife. The friezes, melon-shaped capitals, and imposts decorated with thorny acanthus [188, 189] are already in the mature Justinian style. The Ionic impost capitals find their nearest antecedents in the Church of Hagios Dimitrios in Salonika [214], and those in Hagia Sophia in Salonika are also in this line of descent (Kautzsch, *Kapitellstudien*, p. 185). For the development of this type of capital from the form current in Theodosian art, see Wulff, *Altchristliche Kunst*, II, p. 409ff.; J. Ebersolt, *Mélanges d'histoire et d'archéologie byzantine*, Paris, 1907, p. 119; E. Weigand in *Jahrbuch des deutschen archäologischen Institutes*, 1914, p. 37; and especially Kautzsch, *Kapitellstudien*, p. 182ff. with further literature.

G. Dehio and G. von Bezold, *Die kirchliche Baukunst des Abendlandes*, Stuttgart, 1887-1901, I, pl. 4, nos. 5-6; A. van Millingen, *Byzantine Churches in Constantinople*, London, 1912, p. 62, pls. 11-14; D. Pulgher, *Les anciennes églises de Constantinople*, Vienna, 1878-80, pls. 2-3; J. Ebersolt and A. Thiers, *Les églises de Constantinople*, Paris, 1913, p. 21, pls. 5-11; Wulff, *Altchristliche Kunst*, II, p. 373, figs. 321-322, Nachtrag, p. 50; C. Gurlitt, *Die Baukunst Konstantinopels*, Berlin, 1907-13, p. 18, pl. 7a-c; Dalton, *East Christian Art*, p. 96; Schneider, *Byzanz*, p. 71, fig. 33; Swift, *Roman Sources*, p. 38, pls. 44-47.

Justinian's first structure was dedicated December 27, 537; the present one, restored after the collapse of the dome, dedicated December 24, 562. After the conquest of Constantinople by the Turks, it became the chief mosque of the city but is now a museum, so that it has been possible to uncover a number of mosaics from the Middle Byzantine period (T. Whittemore, *The Mosaics of St. Sophia at Istanbul*, Oxford, 2nd ed., 1936). The original church that preceded Justinian's had probably already been intended by Constantine the Great as the cathedral of his new capital, but was built only by Constantius and dedicated by him February 15, 360. After the fire of June 20, 404, the church was rededicated October 10, 415 but burned down again January 15, 532. Two minarets [191–193] were erected

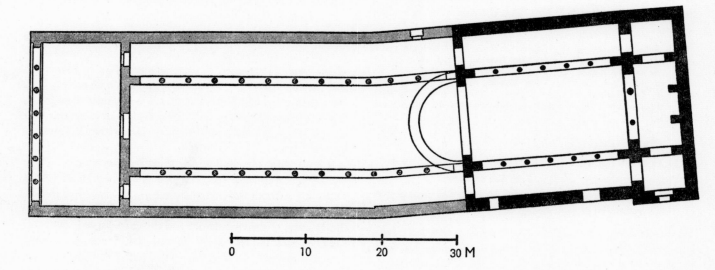

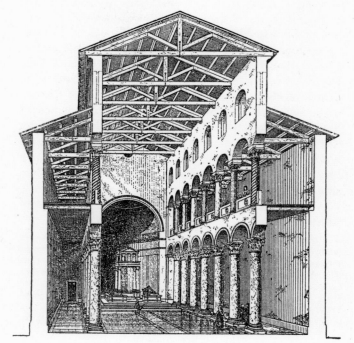

FIGURE 24. San Lorenzo fuori le Mura, Rome. Plan. In black the earlier, eastern basilica from the time of Pope Pelagius II (579–90); in gray the western, more recent basilica from the time of Pope Honorius III (1216–27).

FIGURE 25. Sant'Agnese fuori le Mura, Rome. Cross section in perspective. Built by Constantina, probably after Constantine's death (337), and restored by Pope Honorius I (625–38). The drawing shows the articulation of the aisles with their galleries *(matronea)* that are similar to San Lorenzo fuori le Mura [184, 185], but partly obscured in the latter church by subsequent alterations. After: G. Dehio and G. von Bezold, *Die kirchliche Baukunst des Abendlandes*, Stuttgart, 1887–1901.

near the entrance to the seraglio under Bayazid, and two others, as well as the powerful buttresses, by Sinan under Selim II (1572). At the same time several small annexes to the building were pulled down. The atrium was also destroyed. The excavations of 1935 revealed the remains of a large entrance, probably from the time of Theodosius II.

The interior is divided into a nave and two aisles by piers and columns. The dome is on pendentives, and there are galleries over aisles and narthex. The architects of Justinian's edifice were probably Anthemius of Tralles and Isidorus of Miletus. The admiration of contemporaries is recorded by various writers, including Agathias of Myrina, and Procopius, in his

work on Justinian's buildings (ed. E. Haury, Leipzig, 1913, *Opera*, II, p. 8; see also Pauly-Wissowa, *Realenzyclopädie der klassischen Altertumswissenschaft*, XIV, p. 572 ff). Particularly informative is the panegyric of Paulus Silentiarius composed for the dedication of 562, that gives a poetical description of the splendid edifice (P. Friedländer, *Johannes von Gaza und Paulus Silentiarius*, Leipzig, 1912).

The most recent excavations and research (A. Schneider, *Die Hagia Sophia zu Konstantinopel*, Berlin, 1939; Swift, *Roman Sources*, p. 123 ff.) have shed light not only on the connection of Hagia Sophia with Roman architecture, the Baths of Diocletian and the Basilica of Maxentius, but also with Eastern

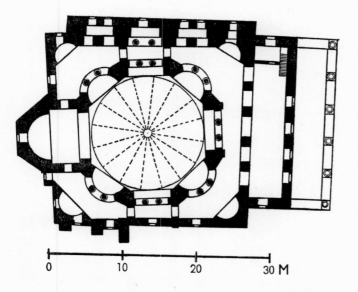

0      10      20      30 M

FIGURES 26 AND 27. Mosque of Küçük Aya Sophia, formerly Church of SS. Sergius and Bacchus, Istanbul. Plan and longitudinal section. Although actually octagonal, the central space approximates a square because the terminal niches on the sides corresponding to the diagonals of the exterior square are fully developed, while those on its main axes, except on the choir side, are closed off by straight colonnades. The columns between the piers carry architraves on the ground floor and arcades in the gallery. This—in contrast to San Vitale in Ravenna—serves to reduce the height of the octagon and thus optically increases its area. The dome has 16 ribs; its 16 segments are alternately flat and concave, the former rising from the sides of the octagon, the latter springing from the corners. The vestibule in front of the narthex, shown in outline on the plan, is a Turkish addition. After: G. Dehio and G. von Bezold, *Die kirchliche Baukunst des Abendlandes*, Stuttgart, 1887–1901.

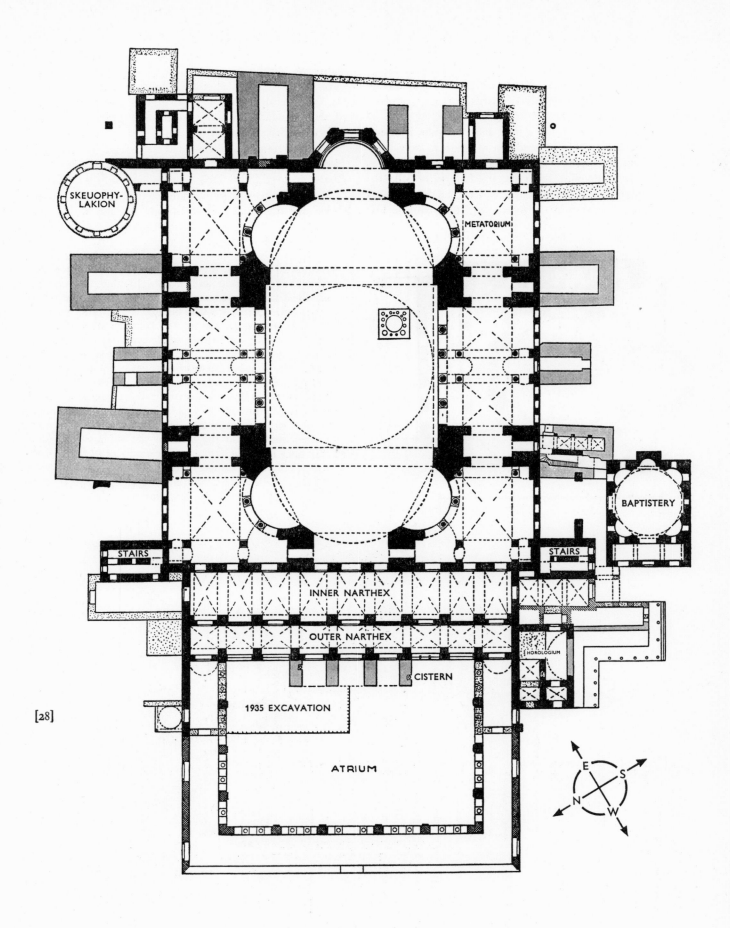

SKEUOPHY-LAKION

METATORIUM

BAPTISTERY

STAIRS

STAIRS

INNER NARTHEX

OUTER NARTHEX

HOROLOGIUM

CISTERN

1935 EXCAVATION

ATRIUM

E
S
N
W

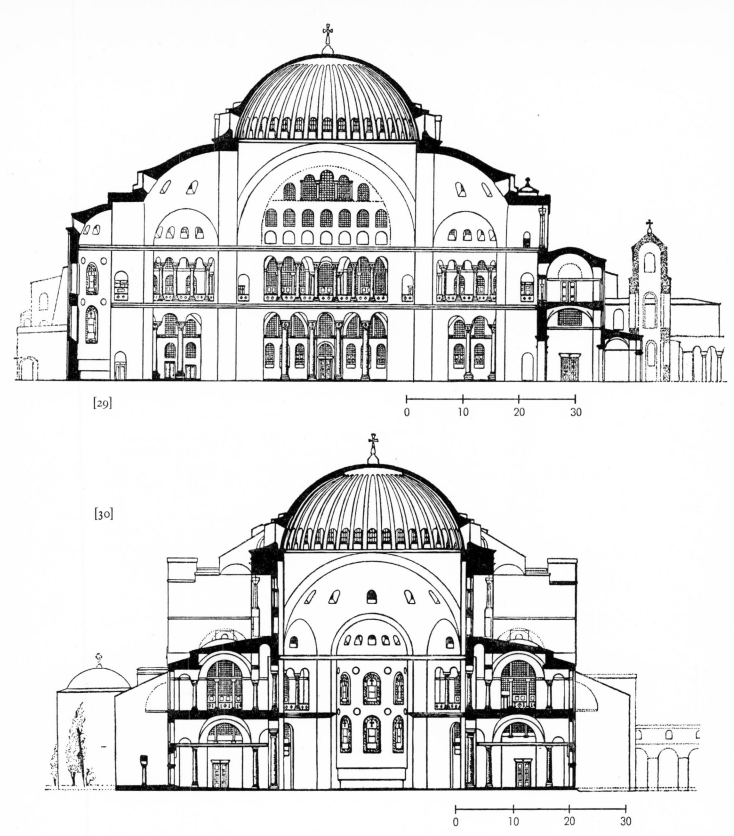

[29]

0   10   20   30

[30]

0   10   20   30

FIGURES 28–30. Hagia Sophia, Istanbul. Dimensions: length from the center entrance door behind the narthex to the farthest point of the apse on the southeast 80.9 m. (265 ft., 5 in.); excluding the apse, 74.8 m. (245 ft., 5 in.). Total width, 69.7 m. (228 ft., 9 in.). Dome: diameter 33 m. (108 ft., 3 in.); from floor to crown of dome, 55.6 m. (182 ft., 6 in.); from pendentives to crown, 13.8 m. (45 ft., 3 in.). Span of the arches carried by the main piers, 31 m. (101 ft., 8 in.) in the transversal axis and 24 m. (78 ft., 8 in.) in the vertical axis. [28] Plan, showing the original atrium which is no longer extant. [29] Longitudinal section (southeast—northwest); on the right, narthex and outer narthex, and the southeast end of the atrium. [30] Cross section (southwest—northeast) facing the apse in the southeast. After: A. M. Schneider, *Die Hagia Sophia zu Konstantinopel*, Berlin, 1939.

351

edifices, particularly in Asia Minor, such as Meriamlik (S. Guyer and E. Herzfeld, *Monumenta Asia Minoris Antiqua*, Manchester, 1930, p. 46; J. Haury in *Byzantinische Zeitschrift*, 1935, p. 294) and SS. Sergius and Bacchus [186], establishing the fundamental importance of the latter (Wulff, *Altchristliche Kunst*, II, p. 372, Nachtrag, p. 50; O. Wulff in *Byzantinische Zeitschrift*, 1930, p. 531). For the purely Byzantine ornament on the walls, friezes, and capitals that almost completely masks the structure, see Wulff (*Altchristliche Kunst*, II, p. 411, Nachtrag, p. 55), Kautzsch (*Kapitellstudien*, p. 163 ff.), and Dalton (*East Christian Art*, p. 359 ff.).

Because the nave is open on its main axis and screened by arcades on the sides, a pronouncedly longitudinal emphasis is given to the central portion of the interior, although in its totality it is almost square (245 ft., 5 in. [74.8 m.] by 229 ft., [69.7 m.]). The dome dominates it completely. It rests on four mighty piers which, in spite of numerous piercings, present a unified system of resistance, and are besides so powerfully reinforced that the span of the supporting arches over the side openings on the southwest and northeast is only 79 ft. (24 m.) as compared to 102 ft. (31 m.) in the case of the two supporting arches on the southeast and the northwest. The southeast and the northwest arches are backed by half-domes each buttressed by a barrel vault in the middle and half-domes at the sides which, in turn, are secured on both levels by broad abutting vaults. On the southwest and the northeast the buttressing system is different because there the portions of the interior adjacent to the nave function as separate and secondary units and are two-storied, thus ruling out the abutment of semi-domes. The space between the buttressing piers on these two sides is spanned by supporting arches about 16 ft. (5 m.) deep and again buttressed by the aisle vaults. Despite these structural precautions, the points lying on the diagonal axes of the central square, to which the pendentives transmit the thrust of the dome, are precisely the weakest. The thrust acts on the buttressing piers not along their vertical axis but at an oblique angle for which there is no proper abutment. As a result there are continual shifts in the whole structure and the danger of collapse is always present.

G. Fossati, *Aya Sophia*, London, 1852; W. Salzenberg, *Altchristliche Baudenkmäler von Constantinopel vom V. bis XII. Jahrhundert*, Berlin, 1854; W. R. Lethaby and H. Swainson, *The Church of St. Sophia, Constantinople*, New York, 1894; E. M. Antoniadi, *Hagia Sophia*, Athens, 1907–9; G. Gurlitt, *Die Baukunst Konstantinopels*, Berlin, 1907–13, p. 19; W. R. Zaloziecky, *Die Sophienkirche in Konstantinopel und ihre Stellung in der Geschichte der abendländischen Architektur*, Vatican City, 1936; Schneider, *Byzanz*; A. M. Schneider, *Die Hagia Sophia zu Constantinopel*, Berlin, 1939; E. H. Swift, *Hagia Sophia*, New York, 1940; Swift, *Roman Sources*, p. 38 ff., pls. 44–45; P. Schweinfurth, *Die Byzantinische Form*, 2nd ed., Mainz, 1954, p. 142, figs. 1–2; S. Eyice, *Istanbul*, Istanbul, 1955, p. 13.

## 206, 207

CISTERN OF YEREBATAN SERAY, ISTANBUL. 6th century.

The 336 columns are disposed in 12 rows of 28 columns each, that create the impression of a basilica. Length 459 ft. (140 m.), width 230 ft. (70 m.).

But its nickname "Basilica" derives from the old basilica above it, which up to 425 housed the university and thereafter was used as a court of law (Schneider, *Byzanz*, p. 23, fig. 6).

Some such building is mentioned in the *Notitia urbis* for the *IV regio* (O. Seeck, *Notitia dignitatum...*, Berlin, 1846, p. 232). The large cistern under it was excavated by Justinian. The columns with rich capitals carry domes on pendentives.

Underground water reservoirs of this type seem to have been built from the time of Constantine onward. The earliest preserved example is the Cistern of Pulcheria. One of the largest, with 224 columns, was constructed about 528 and became popularly known as Binbirdirect (the cistern with 1001 columns). The shafts of its columns are remarkably high, each consisting of two shafts placed on top of one another. For cisterns still in existence, see P. Forchheimer and S. Strzygowski (*Die Wasserbehälter von Konstantinopel*, Vienna, 1893); for the capitals, see R. Kautzsch (*Kapitellstudien*, p. 63 ff.). Kautzsch considers the capitals with their delicate, thorny acanthus [206] the forerunners of those in SS. Sergius and Bacchus [188] and in Hagia Sophia [203].

F. Unger, in E. Mamboury and T. Wiegand, *Die Kaiserpaläste von Konstantinopel zwischen Hippodrom und Marmarameer*, Berlin, 1934, p. 54; Dalton, *East Christian Art*, p. 115; K. Lehmann-Hartleben in *Byzantinische Zeitschrift*, 1935, p. 252; Schneider, *Byzanz*, p. 23; Swift, *Roman Sources*, p. 83.

## 208

PILLAR FROM ACRE. Late 6th century. Venice, San Marco, in front of the southwest corner.

The square pillar is one of a pair brought from Acre in 1258. The lower faces are either left plain or have a large, flat cross in a simple frame; the upper halves are decorated with vine scrolls rising out of a vase or vine scroll trellises, the capital with palmettes.

Since the type of scrolls suggests a possible influence of Sassanian silk fabrics and anticipates the ornamentation in the Taq-i-Bostan (K. Erdmann, *Die Kunst Irans*, Berlin, n.d., fig. 9) and Mshatta (Dalton, *Byzantine Art*, fig. 447), it may be a late 6th-century work by Syrian artists.

J. Strzygowski in *Oriens Christianus*, 1902, p. 421; Dalton, *Byzantine Art*, p. 704, fig. 449; Diehl, *Manuel*, II, p. 48; Cabrol and Leclercq, *Dictionnaire*, vol. XIV, pt. 1, col. 1041, fig. 10281; Wulff, *Altchristliche Kunst*, I, p. 269, fig. 254.

## 209 ABOVE

CAPITALS. 7th century. Venice, San Marco, façade.

The two outside ones both have pine cones in the corners and large vine leaves in the middle. The flat relief suggests the 7th century. Both seem to have been imported. The impost capital in the center with acanthus decoration enveloping a cross is, no doubt, also from this late period. Compare similar pieces in Cairo (Kautzsch, *Kapitellstudien*, fig. 686) and in Berlin (Wulff, *Beschreibung*, I, no. 170).

Colasanti, *Arte bisantina*, pl. 58; Wulff, *Altchristliche Kunst*, II, p. 411, fig. 356.

## 209 BELOW, LEFT

IMPOST-CAPITAL. 6th century. Istanbul, Archaeological Museum.

No doubt it is a Constantinopolitan product of Justinian's time, though similar foliage is seen in Parenzo and Ravenna [209 below right].

IMPOST-CAPITAL. Marble. Height 29½ in. (75 cm.), width 23½ in. (60 cm.). Second quarter of the 6th century. From San Michele in Africisco. Ravenna, Museo Nazionale.

In every way this capital resembles others in Constantinople.

G. Galassi in *L'arte*, 1915, p. 47; Colasanti, *Arte bisantina*, pl. 49; Bovini, *Guida del Museo*, p. 34; *Catalogue*, Paris, no. 11, pl. 14.

## 210

TWO IMPOST-CAPITALS WITH ENTABLATURE. 6th century. Venice, San Marco, on the north side.

No doubt both are from Constantinople. The one on the left has a melon-shaped composition of acanthus leaves. For dating, compare related pieces in San Vitale, Ravenna (Wulff, *Altchristliche Kunst*, II, p. 412, fig. 358) and in the Dome of the Chain in Jerusalem (Kautzsch, *Kapitellstudien*, p.189, fig. 597) and other parallels. The basket-shaped capital on the right receives its name from the trellis work that enclosed the trapezoid field containing a lotus palmette.

Capitals of this type are frequent and seem to be of Constantinopolitan origin. Compare the pieces in Berlin (W. F. Volbach in *Felix Ravenna*, 1934, p. 125), in San Vitale, Ravenna (Colasanti, *Arte bisantina*, pl. 49), in the Cathedral of Parenzo (Colasanti, *ibid.*, pl. 52), in Cairo (Kautzsch, *Kapitellstudien*, figs. 630, 632), and elsewhere.

Colasanti, *Arte bisantina*, pl. 53.

## 211

TWO ORNAMENTAL PANELS. 6th century. Venice, San Marco, set into the north wall.

Byzantine work, the pieces were no doubt imported from the East. The panel above has double borders of acanthus leaves and a late version of the Lesbian cyma, and, in the central field, a symmetrically arranged double pattern of wide-toothed acanthus spirals. The acanthus recalls the ornament on the ambo from Salonika [78, 79] and on the entablature in the Church of St. John Studion (Wulff, *Altchristliche Kunst*, I, fig. 257).

Colasanti, *Arte bisantina*, pl. 87; Wulff, *Altchristliche Kunst*, I, p. 273, fig. 256.

The panel below has the same border ornament and was, no doubt, originally intended as a companion piece. Here the central field is occupied by a double series of wide-lobed acanthus leaves. This type of leaf recalls Byzantine capitals from the first half of the 6th century, for instance those outside San Marco [209 above], from the Church of St. John Studion, now in Berlin (Wulff, *Beschreibung*, I, no. 162), from Nicaea (Wulff, *ibid.*, no. 163), also in Berlin, and in Hagios Dimitrios [214 below]. For the development of this type of ornament, see E. Weigand (in *Jahrbuch des deutschen archäologischen Institutes*, 1914, p. 38) and K. Ginhart (*Das christliche Kapitell zwischen Antike und Spätgotik*, Vienna, 1923, p. 102).

## 212

THE SO-CALLED PALACE OF THEODORIC, RAVENNA. Next to Sant'Apollinare Nuovo.

The most recent excavations, in 1955 (G. Mazzotti in *Corsi di cultura*, 1956, I, 81) and in 1956 (G. Mazzotti in *Corso di cultura*,

1957, I, 63), have confirmed what the excavations of 1907 had already suggested; the remains of this palace stand over various earlier structures, in particular over a palatial complex earlier than Theodoric's time, which, it seems, Theodoric used, indeed enlarged and embellished. The buildings, of which the western part stands to this day on the Via di Roma, were erected after Theodoric—according to G. Mazzotti after the fall of the exarchate—and underwent constant subsequent alterations. Here too are the remains of the Basilica of San Salvatore, built after Theodoric's time, perhaps later than the 9th century and destroyed in the 16th century. G. Gerola (*L'architettura religiosa dell'alto medioevo nell'Italia settentrionale*, Milan, 1942) dates it to the time of the exarchate, as does E. Dyggve (*Ravennatum Palatium Sacrum*, Copenhagen, 1941).

C. Ricci, *Guida di Ravenna*, Bologna, 1897; Wulff, *Altchristliche Kunst*, II, p. 407, fig. 352, Nachtrag, p. 55; Galassi, *Roma o Bisanzio*, I, p. 227, fig. 116, mosaics, figs. 51–52; G. Galassi in *Felix Ravenna*, 1928, p. 95; A. Testi-Rasponi, *Note al Liber pontificalis di Agnello*, II, 3, p. 128; A. Testi-Rasponi in *Palladio*, 1938.

## 213–217

HAGIOS DIMITRIOS, SALONIKA.

[213] Exterior, from the west.
[214] Left: capital and impost, north transept. Right: capital, pier on the west wall. Late 5th century.
[215] Interior, facing east.
[216] Mosaics. 7th century. Left: St. Demetrius as patron of children. Right: St. Sergius.
[217] Mosaic. 7th century. St. Demetrius between the founders, Leontius and the Bishop John.

This five-aisled cruciform Byzantine basilica has a gallery, a narthex, and open roof timbers. The crypt, below the raised choir, contains the alleged tomb of the titular saint; the atrium has been destroyed; the rest of the church was completely rebuilt after the fire of 1917 (width 108 ft. [33 m.], length 141 ft., 9 in. [43 m.], with 60 columns). In the opinion of most scholars the church was built in the 5th century to serve the numerous pilgrims (A. Xyngopoulos, *The Basilica of St. Demetrius in Salonika*, Salonika, 1946 [in Greek]). Though it was founded by Leontius, prefect of Illyricum, about 412–13, such architectural features as have been preserved [214] suggest the end of the 5th century. The church was burned down some time between 629 and 634 (O. Tafrali in *Revue archéologique*, 1909, pp. 83, 380) and soon rebuilt with alterations, the most important of which concerned the transept (Cabrol and Leclercq, *Dictionnaire*, vol. XV, pt. 1, col. 655, figs. 10742–10749).

Most of the capitals from the original edifice have been preserved. In the nave some are composite, as in Eski Djuma (the former Hagia Paraskevi), others are leaf capitals with wind-blown acanthus (Kautzsch, *Kapitellstudien*, p. 73 ff., fig. 5). There are similar capitals in Constantinople dating from the period 475–510 and in other Byzantine churches of about 500, such as the church in Stobi (R. Egger in *Jahreshefte des österreichischen archäologischen Institutes*, 1929, p. 42), and Sant'Apollinare Nuovo in Ravenna (Dalton, *Byzantine Art*, fig. 101). The capital [214 above] on the west wall, decorated with peacocks (Kautzsch, *Kapitellstudien*, p. 159), has a parallel in Stobi. The ornamentation of the door frame, now in Athens

(Peirce and Tyler, *L'Art byzantin*, I, pl. 83), suggests the same period. Also see K. Ginhart (*Das christliche Kapittel zwischen Antike und Spätgotik*, Vienna, 1923, p. 14, pl. 1 ff.). The mosaics of the church suffered considerably in the fire of 1917 and those that survived lost much of their force. Above the arcades separating the main aisle from the side aisles on the north side there are various representations donated by pious visitors, no doubt in gratitude for healing. The most typical scenes are parents bringing their daughters to the saint, St. Demetrius with three of the faithful, medallions with the Mother of God and saints, and St. Demetrius as *orans* with three small figures of worshipers. The best preserved are the mosaics on the piers flanking the entrance to the transept. In these votive representations as well, the miracle-working saint is the main figure. Thus we see him in his chlamys with wide stripes as the protector of two children [216]. On the pier to the right appears St. Sergius [216] wearing a tunic and chlamys with red clavus, and around his neck a golden collar. Most important for dating is the mosaic on the other face of this pier, showing St. Demetrius between the two founders, the original one, no doubt Leontius, and the restorer, Bishop John. The dedicatory inscription below mentions the miraculous rescue of the city from the Slavs in 617 (or 619). The pier mosaics are thus datable to the first half of the 7th century, and are connected with the restoration of the church after the fire between 629 and 634. They are executed in the advanced style of the period of Heraclius, in contrast to the mosaics in the aisle and on the west wall which recall San Vitale, and are probably 6th century (C. Diehl and M. Le Tourneau in *Monuments Piot*, 1911, p. 225, pls. 16–19; Lasareff, *Byzantine Painting*, pls. 22–23). That the decorative mosaics with leaf scrolls also belong to the original church can be seen from their similarities with the blossom wreaths and palmettes surrounding a cross inscribed in a circle under the arcades of Eski Djuma in Salonika (P. Muratoff, *La peinture byzantine*, Paris, 1928, p. 67, pl. 24; S. Pelekanidis, *Early Christian Memories of Salonika*, Salonika, 1939, pls. 7–10).

For the architecture: Wulff, *Altchristliche Kunst*, I, p. 231, fig. 229, II, p. 29, fig. 535; C. Diehl, M. Le Tourneau, and H. Saladin, *Les Monuments chrétiens de Salonique*, Paris, 1918; Grabar, *Martyrium*, I, p. 299 ff., III, pl. 10; Dalton, *East Christian Art*, p. 143, pl. 11; Cabrol and Leclercq, *Dictionnaire*, XV, pt. 1, col. 655, figs. 10742–10749; G. Sotiriou, *The Christian Churches of Greece*, Athens, 1931, p. 211, fig. 41 [in Greek]; G. Sotiriou in *Atti del IV° Congresso internazionale di archeologia cristiana.*, I, 367; G. Sotiriou, *St. Demetrius in Salonika*, Athens, 1952 [in Greek]; P. Lemerle, *Philippes*, Paris, 1945, p. 312; P. Lemerle in *Bulletin de Correspondance Hellénique*, 1953, p. 660; J. Ebersolt, *Monuments d'architecture byzantine*, Paris, 1934, p. 16, pl. 6; A. Xyngopoulos, *The Basilica of St. Demetrius in Salonika*, Salonika, 1946 [in Greek].

For the mosaics: van Berchem and Clouzot, *Mosaïques*, p. 73, figs. 80–85; N. Kondakov, *Ikonografia Bogomateri*, St. Petersburg, 1914, p. 345; Wulff, *Altchristliche Kunst*, II, p. 446, fig. 380, Nachtrag, p. 57; Grabar, *Martyrium*, II, p. 25 ff.; Grabar, *Byzantine Painting*, pls. pp. 48, 50; Galassi, *Roma o Bisanzio*, I, p. 161, figs. 76–79; J. Kollwitz in *Römische Quartalschriften*, 1953, p. 3.

## 218–237

For 6th-century IVORY WORK, see also the notes to plates 84–101.

## 218

ARIADNE (?) High relief in ivory. Height 16½ in. (42 cm.), width 5⅜ in. (13.8 cm.). Early 6th century. Paris, Musée Cluny.

Apparently found in the neighborhood of Trier together with two lions' heads of rock crystal, no doubt decorations for a chair, now in the Louvre (Volbach, Salles, and Dutuit, *Art byzantin*, pl. 41 c). Two putti hold a Corona Borealis over Ariadne's head. She leans on a thyrsus staff. The piece is akin to the six panels of the pulpit in Aachen (Volbach, *Elfenbeinarbeiten*, nos. 72-77) and its technique recalls the imperial diptych in the Louvre [219]. Similar mannerisms are known from Egyptian bone carving (H. Stern in *Ars orientalis*, 1954, p. 119). Like the imperial diptych, it dates in the first half of the 6th century.

J. Strzygowski, *Hellenistische und koptische Kunst in Alexandria*, Vienna, 1902, p. 52; Peirce and Tyler, *L'Art byzantin*, II, p. 75, pl. 35 b; A. Prosdocimi in *Rivista d'arte*, 1941, p. 222, fig. 3; Volbach, *Elfenbeinarbeiten*, no. 78, pl. 22; G. Dutuit, *Le Musée inimaginable*, Paris, 1956, pl. 141 a; K. Wessel in *Wissenschaftliche Zeitschrift der Universität Greifswald*, 1952–53, p. 79, fig. 19.

## 219

THE EMPEROR ANASTASIUS (?). Ivory diptych. High relief. Height 13 7/16 in. (34.1 cm.), width 10½ in. (26.6 cm.). Early 6th century. From the Barberini Collection, Rome. Paris, Louvre.

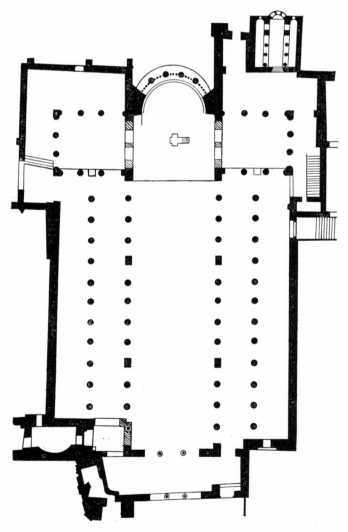

FIGURE 31. Hagios Dimitrios, Salonika. Plan. After: A. Xyngopoulos, *The Basilica of St. Demetrius in Salonika*, Salonika, 1946.

The panel on the right is missing. On the back the episcopal list of Trier up to 675; in the center piece, the emperor, wearing armor, and on horseback. A Scythian(?) touches his lance. Under the horse, a personification of the Earth holding fruit.

The emperor has not, so far, been securely identified. R. Delbrueck's first hypothesis (*Konsulardiptychen*, no. 48), the Emperor Anastasius, soon after 500, seems the most likely. There are similarities with the horseman on the pulpit in Aachen (Volbach, *Elfenbeinarbeiten*, no. 77, pl. 25) and the Ariadne in the Musée Cluny [218]. In date it is close to the consular diptych of Areobindus of 506, now in Zurich (Delbrueck, *Konsulardiptychen*, no. 9, pl. 9).

Ebersolt, *Arts somptuaires*, p. 34, fig. 6; E. Capps, Jr. in *Art Bulletin*, 1927, p. 63; Delbrueck, *Konsulardiptychen*, no. 48; R. Delbrueck in *Felix Ravenna*, 1952, p. 5; Volbach, *Elfenbeinarbeiten*, no. 48, pl. 12; E. Weigand in *Kritische Berichte zur kunstwissenschaftlichen Litteratur*, 1930–31, p. 41; Grabar, *L'Empereur*, pl. 4; A. Grabar in *Cahiers Archéologiques*, 1948, p. 61, fig. 2; K. Wessel in *Jahrbuch des deutschen archäologischen Institutes*, 1948–49, p. 112, fig. 2.

## 220

DIPTYCH OF THE CONSUL ANASTASIUS. Ivory. Constantinople, 517. Height 14⅛ in. (36 cm.), width 5⅛ in. (13 cm.). Formerly in Bourges. Paris, Cabinet des Médailles.

Inscription: FL(avius) ANASTASIVS PAVLVS PROBVS SABINIAN(us) POMPEIVS ANASTASIVS VIR INL(ustris) COM(es) DOMESTIC(orum) EQUIT(um) ET CONS(ul) ORDIN(arius). In the bottom zone, circus scenes.

Cabrol and Leclercq, *Dictionnaire*, vol. IV, pt. 1, col. 1116, fig. 3761; Delbrueck, *Konsulardiptychen*, no. 21, pl. 21; E. Capps, Jr. in *Art Bulletin*, 1927, p. 72, fig. 7; Volbach, *Elfenbeinarbeiten*, no. 21, pl. 5.

## 221

POET (SENECA?) AND MUSE. Ivory diptych. Height 13⅜ in. (34 cm.), width 4⅞ in. (12.5 cm.). 6th century. Monza, Cathedral Treasury.

The Muse, wearing a diadem, strikes a lyre. The poet wears a himation that leaves the chest partly exposed. Various contemporary identifications have been suggested for the poet—Ausonius, Claudius Claudianus, Boethius—and a historical one, Seneca (Rumpf, *Stilphasen*, p. 29, fig. 94). Dates in the 5th and the 6th century have been proposed though the mannerist treatment of the folds already approaches the Ariadne in the Musée Cluny, Paris [218].

R. Delbrueck in *Antike Denkmäler*, IV, pl. 7; E. Weigand in *Kritische Berichte zur kunstwissenschaftlichen Litteratur*, 1930–31, p. 51; K. Weitzmann and S. Schultz in *Jahrbuch des deutschen archäologischen Institutes*, 1934, p. 128, pl. 185; E. Capps, Jr. in *Art Bulletin*, 1949, p. 236; P. de Loos-Dietz, *Vroeg-christelijke Ivoren*, Assen, 1947, p. 141, fig. 28; W. Weisbach, *Manierismus in der mittelalterlichen Kunst*, Basel, 1942, fig. 2; Volbach, *Elfenbeinarbeiten*, no. 68, pl. 22; J. Kollwitz in *Germania*, 1952, p. 226; G. Belloni, *Avori tardo-classici e alto-medioevali*, Milan, pl. 9.

## 222

ADORATION OF THE MAGI. Ivory plaque. Height 8⅜ in. (21.5 cm.), width 3⅜ in. (8.5 cm.). 6th century. London, British Museum.

The Mother of God enthroned, facing front, is flanked by the Magi bearing gifts and an angel with a cross staff. *The*

*Nativity* appears in the narrow register below. Perhaps this piece was originally the center of a five-part diptych like the one from Murano [223], the central panel of which, now in Manchester (Volbach, *Elfenbeinarbeiten*, no. 127, pl. 39) is close to our relief, as is also the panel with Christ in a private collection in Paris (Volbach, *ibid.*, no. 133, pl. 41). The shapes of the heads recall the diptych of Anastasius of 517 [220].

Dalton, *Catalogue Ivories*, no. 14, pl. 9; Dalton, *East Christian Art*, p. 205, pl. 26; E. Capps, Jr. in *Art Bulletin*, 1927, p. 74, fig. 9; Volbach, *Elfenbeinarbeiten*, no. 131, pl. 41; K. Wessel in *Wissenschaftliche Zeitschrift der Universität Greifswald*, 1952–53, pl. 4; Kitzinger, *Early Mediaeval Art*, p. 27, pl. 9.

## 223

FIVE-PART LEAF OF A DIPTYCH. Ivory. Early 6th century. From Murano. Ravenna, Museo Nazionale.

In the lower zone of the center panel, beneath the main representation of *Christ Among the Apostles*, *The Three Hebrews in the Fiery Furnace*. Left side panel, *The Healing of the Blind* and *The Healing of the Demoniac;* right side panel, *The Raising of Lazarus* and *The Healing of the Paralytic.* Lower panel, scenes from the story of Jonah; upper panel, two angels supporting a wreath with the monogram of Christ.

The companion piece, with the Virgin, has been taken apart, and the individual panels are now dispersed in different collections: the center piece in Manchester (Volbach, *Elfenbeinarbeiten*, no. 127, pl. 39), the top panel in Berlin (O. Wulff and W. F. Volbach, *Die altchristlichen und mittelalterlichen Bildwerke, Ergänzungsband*, Berlin, 1923, no. 2978, pl. III), the bottom panel in Paris, Collection de Gandy (Volbach, *Elfenbeinarbeiten*, no. 128, pl. 45), and the left side panel in Leningrad (Volbach, *ibid.*, no. 129, pl. 40). Because of stylistic similarities with the diptych of Anastasius [220] it may be dated in the beginning of the 6th century. In spite of its kinship with metropolitan work, the relief could well be the product of a provincial center, for instance in Asia Minor.

Venturi, *Storia*, I, p. 511, fig. 394; J. Strzygowski, *Hellenistische und koptische Kunst in Alexandria*, Vienna, 1902, p. 85, figs. 63–66; Wulff, *Altchristliche Kunst*, I, p. 189, fig. 186, Nachtrag, p. 22; Dalton, *East Christian Art*, p. 205; Smith, *Iconography*, p. 89, fig. 85; K. Wessel in *Archäologischer Anzeiger*, 1948–49, p. 238; K. Wessel in *Corsi di cultura*, 1958, I, p. 111; Volbach, *Elfenbeinarbeiten*, no. 125, pl. 39; Bovini, *Guida del Museo*, p. 63; G. Bovini in *Felix Ravenna*, 1956, p. 53, fig. 2; Bovini, *Avori*, no. 47, fig. 63; J. Natanson, *Early Christian Ivories*, London, 1953, p. 32, no. 45.

## 224, 225

DIPTYCH. Ivory. Height 11⅜ in. (29 cm.), width 5⅛ in. (13 cm.) and 5 in. (12.7 cm.) respectively. The lower border (roughly 2⅛ in. [5.5 cm.]) cut off. Mid-6th century. Berlin, Staatliche Museen.

[224] Left panel: the bearded Christ, holding a book in His left hand and blessing with His right, is flanked by SS. Peter and Paul.

[225] Right panel: the Madonna enthroned is flanked by two angels wearing the diadem, fillet, and chlamys.

The letter C, partly cut off, at the bottom of each panel is no doubt the remainder of Archbishop Maximian's monogram, similar to the one on the episcopal chair [226]. The figures in our diptych recall those on the front of that piece [227–229], hence the similar dating in the middle of the 6th century. The sharp rendering of folds suggests a Byzantine artist. The five-part diptychs in Paris (Volbach, *Elfenbeinarbeiten*, no. 145, pl. 47) and in Etschmiadzin (Volbach, *ibid.*, no. 142, pl. 44) should also be compared to the central panels.

Wulff, *Altchristliche Kunst*, I, p. 195, fig. 198; W. F. Volbach, *Die Elfenbein-bildwerke* (Die Bildwerke der deutschen Museums), Berlin, 1923, p. 5, pl. 6; Volbach, *Elfenbeinarbeiten*, no. 137, pl. 42; E. Capps, Jr. in *Art Bulletin*, 1927, p. 79, fig. 15; Morey, *Early Christian Art*, p. 95; Bovini, *Avori*, no. 66.

## 226–235

EPISCOPAL CHAIR OF ARCHBISHOP MAXIMIAN. 546-56. Ivory. Height 4 ft., 11 $\frac{1}{16}$ in. (1.50 m.), width 23 $\frac{5}{8}$ in. (0.605 m.). Ravenna, Museo Arcivescovile.

[226] The chair from the front.
[227] St. John the Baptist.
[228] Two Evangelists.
[229] Two Evangelists.
[230] *Joseph's Dream* and *The Journey to Bethlehem.*
[231] *The Annunciation.*
[232] *The Baptism;* ornamental bands.
[233] *The Multiplication of Loaves and Fishes;* ornamental bands.
[234] Above: *Joseph Interrogating His Brothers.* Below: *The Filling of the Sacks with Corn.*
[235] Above: *Joseph's Brothers Announce His Death.* Center: *Joseph in the Well* and *The Slaying of the Kid.* Below: *Joseph Sold to the Ishmaelites.*

The episcopal throne has undergone numerous restorations and a few panels are missing (G. de Jerphanion in *Rendiconti della Pontificia Accademia Romana di archeologia*, 1939, p. 29). On the front, below the seat, is the Archbishop's monogram, usually read: MAXIMIANVS EPISCOPVS. Below, in niches with conches, St. John the Baptist, holding the Lamb of God [227], is flanked by the Evangelists [228, 229]. Above and below these figures are broad ornamental panels. On the sides of the chair are scenes from the story of Joseph [234, 235]: *Joseph's Brothers Announce His Death, Joseph in the Well, Joseph Sold to the Ishmaelites, Joseph Sold to Potiphar, Joseph's Seduction and Imprisonment, Judah's Entreaty to Jacob, Joseph Interrogating His Brothers, The Filling of the Sacks with Corn, Joseph Interprets Pharaoh's Dream, The Meeting with Jacob, Pharaoh's Dream.* On both faces of the back, scenes from the life of Christ [230–233]: *The Nativity, The Adoration of the Magi, The Journey to Bethlehem, The Proof of the Virgin, The Annunciation, The Baptism, The Entry into Jerusalem, The Multiplication of Loaves and Fishes, The Marriage at Cana, The Samaritan Woman at the Well,* and *The Healing of the Blind.*

Several artists worked on the chair: the most distinguished is the one responsible for the front; the master of the scenes from the life of Christ is stylistically weaker and the master of the story of Joseph differs from both in that his scenes are more plastically and spatially conceived. The place of origin is in dispute. The variants of the Byzantine style seem to be those of Ravenna, but O. Wulff (*Altchristliche Kunst*, p. 191, fig. 191) and K. Wessel (in *Corsi di cultura*, 1958, p. 145) suggest Egypt, while G. W. Morath (in *Freiburger Theol. Studien*, Freiburg i.B., 1940) prefers Constantinople. On the basis of parallels with the Barberini diptych [219], some scholars (Delbrueck,

*Konsulardiptychen*, p. 195) have dated the chair a generation earlier than Maximian but it is now generally held to be contemporary with him.

D. V. Ainalov in *Byzantion*, 1924, p. 59; Ricci, *Tavole*, p. 39; J. Strzygowski, *Byzantinische Denkmäler*, I, Vienna, 1891; C. Diehl, *Ravenne*, Paris, 1928, p. 92; Dalton, *Byzantine Art*, p. 203; Smith, *Iconography*, p. 24; Toesca, *Storia*, I, p. 316, fig. 189; J. Baum in *Pantheon*, 1929, p. 378; E. Weigand in *Kritische Berichte zur Kunstwissenschaftlichen Litteratur*, 1930–31, p. 33; Bréhier, *Sculpture*, p. 27; C. Cecchelli, *La cattedra di Massimiano*, Rome, 1936; E. Capps, Jr. in *Art Bulletin*, 1942, p. 99; Volbach, *Elfenbeinarbeiten*, no. 140, pl. 43; M. Schapiro in *Gazette des Beaux-Arts*, 1952, p. 27; K. Wessel in *Wissenschaftliche Zeitschrift der Universität Greifswald*, 1953–54, p. 1; K. Wessel in *Corsi di cultura*, 1958. p. 145; M. Mazzotti in *Studi romagnoli*, 1954, p. 483; Bovini, *Avori*, no. 65, figs. 85–91; G. Bovini, *La cattedra eburnea del vescovo Massimiano di Ravenna*, Faenza, 1957.

## 236 ABOVE

IVORY PYXIS. Height 3 $\frac{1}{2}$ in. (9 cm.), diameter 4 in. (10.2 cm.). 6th century. From Moggio (Udine). Washington, D.C., Dumbarton Oaks Collection.

Left: *Daniel in the Lions' Den.* Right: *Moses Receiving the Law.*

The lid has metal fixtures. On the pyxis: *Moses Receiving the Law, The Brazen Serpent,* and *Daniel in the Lions' Den.* The pyxis belongs to a group of ivory boxes of which there are examples in London (Volbach, *Elfenbeinarbeiten*, no. 167), Rome (Volbach, *ibid.*, no. 164), and Leningrad (Volbach, *ibid.*, no. 179). On this group and its place in the development of ivory carving, see K. Wessel (in *Wissenschaftliche Zeitschrift der Universität Greifswald*, 1953–54, p. 11 ff). Iconographically these pieces already belong to the 6th century.

A. Venturi in *L'arte*, 1911, p. 469; C. R. Morey in *Dumbarton Oaks Papers*, 1940, p. 43, figs. 1–2; *Handbook of the Dumbarton Oaks Collection*, Washington, 1955, p. 104, no. 227; Volbach, *Elfenbeinarbeiten*, no. 168, pl. 54.

## 236 BELOW

IVORY PYXIS. Height 3 $\frac{1}{8}$ in. (8 cm.), diameter 4 $\frac{1}{4}$ in. (10.7 cm.). 6th century. Found in Rome, in a sanctuary of St. Menas near San Paolo fuori le Mura. London, British Museum.
Left: *The Execution of St. Menas.* Right: St. Menas as *orans.*

The trial and execution of the saint are carved on one side and on the other the saint as *orans* with four worshipers. On the strength of the pyxis' relation to the Joseph scenes on the Chair of Maximian [234, 235] and to the pyxis with Isis in Wiesbaden (Volbach, *Elfenbeinarbeiten*, no. 105, pl. 30), most scholars assign it to Egypt (K. Wessel in *Wissenschaftliche Zeitschrift der Universität Greifswald*, 1953–54, p. 2, pl. 5); J. Kollwitz (in *Germania*, 1952, p. 227) is doubtful. Certainly already 6th century.

Dalton, *Catalogue Ivories*, no. 12, pl. 7; Dalton, *Catalogue Antiquities*, no. 297, pl. 9; Wulff, *Altchristliche Kunst*, I, p. 192; S. Poglayen-Neuwall in *Münchner Jahrbuch*, 1923, p. 58, fig. 6; Grabar, *Martyrium*, II, p. 76, III, pls. 67–68; Volbach, *Elfenbeinarbeiten*, no. 182, pl. 56; Morey, *Early Christian Art*, p. 94, fig. 87.

## 237

IVORY PLAQUE WITH ST. PAUL. Originally, no doubt, part of a revetment (perhaps of an episcopal throne). Height 9 in. (22.9 cm.), width 4 $\frac{1}{4}$ in. (10.7 cm.). 6th or 7th century. From the Abbey of Mettlach (Saar). New York, The Metropolitan Museum of Art.

The Apostle, wearing a tunic and holding a book, stands within an open curtain. The piece exemplifies the final evolution of portraits of Evangelists and Apostles as they appear on the Chair of Maximian [228]. Other pieces in this group, all found in the neighborhood of Trier, suggest a Merovingian (6th–7th century) workshop in northeast Gaul that used Eastern models. This group includes the Apostles in Tongres (Volbach, *Elfenbeinarbeiten*, no. 153, pl. 50), Brussels (Volbach, *ibid.*, no. 154, pl. 50), and Cambridge (Volbach, *ibid.*, no. 152, pl. 51). On this so-called Gallic school, see W. F. Volbach (in *Festschrift des römisch-germanischen Zentralmuseums*, Mainz, 1952, p. 44).

M. Laurent, *Les Ivoires prégotiques en Belgique*, Brussels, 1912, p. 15; J. Baum in *Pantheon*, 1929, p. 377, fig. p. 376; Volbach, *Elfenbeinarbeiten*, no. 155, pl. 49; *Catalogue*, Baltimore, no. 102, pl. 14.

For the history of BYZANTINE MINIATURE PAINTING of the 6th and 7th centuries, see also the notes to plates 122–173, as well as J. Ebersolt, *La Miniature byzantine*, Paris, 1926, and A. Grabar, *Miniatures byzantines*, Paris, 1939.

## 238–241

GOSPEL BOOK (CODEX PURPUREUS ROSSANENSIS). Greek uncials written in silver on parchment. Height 12⅛ in. (30.7 cm.), width 10¼ in. (26 cm.), 188 leaves. 6th century. Rossano, Museo dell'Arcivescovado.

[238] Folio 3, recto: *The Last Supper* and *The Washing of Feet*.
[239] Folio 8, verso: *Pilate with Christ and Barabbas*.
[240] Folio 3, verso: *The Communion of the Apostles*.
[241] Folio 2, verso: *The Wise and the Foolish Virgins*.

Pages with miniatures: fol. 1r, *The Raising of Lazarus;* fol. 1v, *The Entry into Jerusalem;* fol. 2r, *The Money-Changers Driven out of the Temple;* fol. 2v, *The Wise and the Foolish Virgins* [241]; fol. 3r, *The Last Supper* and *The Washing of Feet* [238]; fol. 3v, *The Communion of the Apostles with Wine;* fol. 4v, *Christ in Gethsemane;* fol. 7v, *The Healing of the Blind;* fol. 8r, *Christ Before Pilate, The Death of Judas;* fol. 8v, *Pilate with Christ and Barabbas* [239]; fol. 121r, the Evangelist Mark and Holy Wisdom; fols. 5r and 6r have decorative ornament.

The Codex contains the Gospels according to Matthew and Mark. The miniatures are no longer in the original sequence. They follow older models, perhaps from Syria or Asia Minor (A. Baumstark in *Ehrengabe deutscher Wissenschaft . . . dem Prinzen Johann Georg Herzog zu Sachsen zum 50. Geburtstag gewidmet*, Freiburg i.B., 1920, p. 233), such as the two stylistically related purple codices, the Sinope Gospels in Paris (H. Omont, *Les Miniatures des plus anciens mss. grecs de la Bibliothèque Nationale*, Paris, 1929; A. Grabar, *Les Peintures de l'Évangéliaire de Sinope*, Paris, 1948), and the Vienna Genesis (H. Gerstinger, *Die Wiener Genesis*, Vienna, 1931). These manuscripts are, no doubt, still 6th century. Their exact provenance has not, so far, been established but the connection with undoubtedly metropolitan manuscripts, like the Vienna Dioscurides (A. von Premerstein, K. Wessely, and J. Mantuani, *De Codicis Dioscuridei, Aniciae Iulianae*, Leipzig, 1906), is obvious. However, stylistically it could be attributed to a provincial school, perhaps one in Asia Minor.

O. von Gebhardt and A. von Harnack, *Evangeliorum Codex Purpureus Rossanensis*, Leipzig, 1880; A. Muñoz, *Il codice purpureo di Rossano e il frammento Sinopense*, Rome, 1907; Wulff, *Altchristliche Kunst*, I, p. 299, fig. 282, pl.

18, 2, Nachtrag, p. 41; H. Glück, *Die christliche Kunst des Ostens*, Berlin, 1923, p. 6, pls. 8–10; J. Ebersolt, *La Miniature byzantine*, Paris, 1926, p. 78, pls. 6–7; A. M. Friend in *Art Studies*, 1927, p. 139; R. Kömstedt, *Vormittelalterliche Malerei*, Augsburg, 1929, p. 31, figs. 84–96; Cabrol and Leclercq, *Dictionnaire*, vol. XV, pt. 1, col. 15; Peirce and Tyler, *L'Art byzantin*, II, p. 115, pls. 145–151; E. Weigand in *Kritische Berichte zur kunstwissenschaftlichen Litteratur*, 1930–31, p. 51; G. de Francovich in *Commentari*, 1951, p. 16, fig. 26; K. Weitzmann, *Illustrations in Roll and Codex*, Princeton, 1947, p. 93; Morey, *Early Christian Art*, p. 108, fig. 112; G. Guerrieri, *Il codice purpureo di Rossano Calabro*, Naples, 1950; Ammann, *Pittura*, p. 55.

## 242, 243

SANTA MARIA DI CASTELSEPRIO. Cycle of frescoes in two zones with scenes from the life of the Virgin and the infancy of Christ.
[242] *The Nativity* and *The Annunciation to the Shepherds*.
[243] *The Presentation in the Temple*.

The heavily damaged frescoes were discovered in 1944 in the choir of a tiny single-aisled church near Milan that dates from Lombard times. A chronological indication is supplied by a graffito in the apse made before 945. The cycle begins with *The Annunciation;* then come *The Visitation, Trial by Water, The Dream of Joseph, The Journey to Bethlehem, The Nativity* and *The Annunciation to the Shepherds* [242], *The Adoration of the Magi*, and *The Presentation in the Temple* [243]; the scenes that follow have been destroyed. The upper sequence is interrupted by a medallion with a bust of Christ above the middle window. On the inner face of the triumphal arch is the Apocalyptic Throne *(etimasia)* with two worshiping angels. Since its discovery and publication (G. P. Bognetti, G. Chierici, and A. de Capitani d'Arzago, *Santa Maria di Castelseprio*, Milan, 1948), the fresco cycle has been the subject of much controversy. So far no consensus has been reached on its date or on the origins of its master. The style of the paintings is to be found in no other Lombard work but has certain affinities with the Byzantinizing frescoes in Santa Maria Antiqua in Rome (Wilpert, *Mosaiken*, II, p. 678, IV, pls. 143, 144, 163; M. Avery in *Art Bulletin*, 1925, p. 149). Both the iconography and color scheme leave no doubt of the artist's Eastern origins though no comparative Eastern material from the pre-Iconoclastic period has survived; but it is impossible to consider our frescoes post-Iconoclastic on both iconographic or stylistic grounds as, among others, V. Lasareff (in *Sibrium*, 1956–57, p. 87) has shown. A date in the Macedonian period (10th century) is put forward by K. Weitzmann (*The Fresco Cycle of S. Maria di Castelseprio*, Princeton, 1951), while A. Grabar (in *Frühmittelalterliche Kunst in den Alpenländern*, Olten, 1954, p. 85) and M. Schapiro (in *Art Bulletin*, 1952, p. 147, 1957, p. 292) have adopted an intermediate view, dating the cycle in the 8th or 9th century; Grabar points out affinities with the school of Reims and the Utrecht Psalter.

J. Hubert in *Bulletin de la Société des Antiquaires de France*, 1948–49, p. 191; C. Nordenfalk in *Dagens Nyheter*, 1950; P. Toesca in *L'Arte*, 1951, p. 3; C. R. Morey in *Art Bulletin*, 1952, p. 173; Morey, *Early Christian Art*, p. 194, figs. 211–215; C. Cecchelli in *Byzantinische Zeitschrift*, 1952, p. 97; P. Lemerle in *Byzantion*, 1952, p. 184; Galassi, *Roma o Bisanzio*, p. 331; V. Lasareff in *Vizantiiskii Vremennik*, 1953, p. 359; G. P. Bognetti in *Sibrium*, 1953–54, p. 111; G. P. Bognetti, *Cahiers Archéologiques*, 1954, p. 139; W. Arslan in *Storia di Milano*, 1954, p. 631, figs. pp. 632–642; Grabar, *Byzantine Painting*, p. 83, pl. pp. 84, 85; G. de Francovich in *Settimane di studio*, p. 455; D. Tselos in *Art Bulletin*, 1956, p. 26.

**244**

MEDALLION OF JUSTINIAN I (527–65). Cast of a gold medallion equivalent in weight to 36 solidi (160.2 gr., i.e., half a Byzantine pound). Diameter 3⅜ in. (8.5 cm.). Original struck in 535. London, British Museum.

Justinian struck the original medallion in 535 to celebrate the victory of his general Belisarius over the Vandals. It was found in 1751 at Kayseri in Cappadocia, and came into the possession of Louis XV as a gift from Count Desalleurs, but was stolen in 1831 and has not reappeared. Fortunately impressions had been made of it before the theft occurred, and these found their way to the British Museum.

Obverse: bust of the Emperor Justinian I facing frontally, with plain nimbus. He wears the diadem over a richly decorated helmet with crest of peacock feathers. Cuirass, covered by a *paludamentum*, is fastened on the right shoulder with an ornate fibula. A spear is in his right hand, a shield behind his left shoulder.

Reverse: Justinian, on a richly caparisoned horse, is preceded by a winged Nike who carries on her left shoulder a palm branch and a trophy of arms. The Emperor has the same plain nimbus, crested helmet, and diadem as on the obverse, and wears the short military tunic with cuirass, *pteryges*, and *paludamentum*.

British Museum Catalogue: Justinian I, p. 25; R. Delbrueck in *Römische Mitteilungen*, 1914, p. 80, fig. 4; M. Pinder and J. Friedländer, *Münzen des Justinianus*, Berlin, 1843; Rice, *Byzantine Art*, 1958, p. 91.

**245–255**

LATE ANTIQUE SILVERWORK of the 6th and early 7th centuries.

A relatively large number of single pieces and treasures have survived. A chronological framework for the 4th and 5th centuries is supplied by the dated votive platter [109]; the same function is performed for the 6th and 7th centuries by the large number of plates and vessels carrying imperial stamps that not only date them with the ruler's monogram but almost certainly also permit an attribution to the workshop of the imperial court (Matzulewitsch, *Byzantinische Antike;* Rosenberg, *Merkzeichen*, IV; A. Alföldi and E. Cruikshank in *Dumbarton Oaks Papers*, 1957, p. 237). Furthermore, some pieces can be dated from coins that either are part of the ornament [255] or else belong to the same find. A large number of imperial stamps is known for the period from Anastasius I (491–518) to Heraclius (610–41). They can be considered as actual datings because they were impressed into the silver before embossing and not added subsequently as hallmarks (L. Matzulewitsch, *L'Art byzantin chez les Slaves*, 2 vols., Paris, 1932, p. 300). Occasionally pieces, like the Cross of Justin II (565–78) at St. Peter's in Rome, are dated by the identity of the donor (Dalton, *Byzantine Art*, fig. 337). Most of this Byzantine silver comes from isolated finds in the region of the Black Sea [245, 252, 253], and is today in the Hermitage in Leningrad (Matzulewitsch, *Byzantinische Antike*).

Several treasures containing precious pieces have also been discovered elsewhere. The best known of these are, no doubt, the two found in Cyprus in 1899 and 1902 [248–250]. The first, including two plates [249], a censer, and 24 spoons, has found

its way to the British Museum (Dalton, *Catalogue Antiquities*, nos. 397–424, and in *Archaeologia*, 1900, p. 159). The second, consisting of a series of plates embossed with scenes from the life of David [250], five flasks, jewelry, a medallion [248], and coins with effigies of Mauricius, Justin, Justinian, and Theodosius, has been dispersed. Only a few of the plates, the jewelry, and the flasks have remained in the Museum in Nicosia; most of the other pieces are in the Metropolitan Museum of Art in New York; one plate in the Walters Art Gallery in Baltimore, another in the Fagan Collection in San Francisco *(Byzantinische Zeitschrift*, 1906, p. 615), and a Christian medallion [248] in the collection at Dumbarton Oaks (O. M. Dalton in *Burlington Magazine*, 1906, p. 355; M. C. Ross in *Dumbarton Oaks Papers*, 1957, p. 247). Of these plates, the nielloed one in the British Museum carries five control marks of Mauricius (582–602); most of those in the United States carry those of Heraclius of about 610 (Rosenberg, *Merkzeichen*, IV, nos. 9647 ff.). Other interesting treasures were found in Carthage, now in the British Museum (Dalton, *Catalogue Antiquities*, nos. 356–375), in Lampsacus, today divided between Istanbul [247] and the British Museum (Dalton, *Catalogue Antiquities*, nos. 376–396), in Canossio (E. Giovagnoli in *Rivista di Archeologia Cristiana*, 1935, p. 1), in Canicattini Bagni (G. Agnello in *Pepragmena tou 9 diethnous byzantinologikou Synedriou* [*Thessalonike 1953*], Athens, 1955, p. 110), and in Lesbos (A. Vavritsas in *Praktika*, 1957, p. 317). These securely identified pieces make it possible to classify isolated finds (G. de Francovich in *Commentari*, 1951, p. 13). Thus the fine plate with the personification of India in Istanbul (Volbach, Salles, and Dutuit, *Art byzantin*, pl. 52) belongs to the early part of the period in its style and technique and in its understanding of the Hellenistic model. Other reliefs, like the plate with Hercules in Paris [251], or the one with Meleager in Munich (H. Kähler in *Die Kunst*, 1952, p. 321), should be placed later, with pieces from the end of the 6th century.

A series of objects found in Syria are distinct from those produced in the imperial workshop: those found in Riha and Antioch, now in the Metropolitan Museum (Volbach, *Metallarbeiten*, p. 17), the Hamah find (C. Diehl in *Syria*, 1926, p. 105), and the Rusafa find, now in Cleveland (L. Bréhier in *Syria*, 1951, p. 256). They look more provincial, and are, no doubt, of local origin, although the distinction is not clear-cut in every case. The medallion from the second Cyprus treasure [248], for instance, is closer to the contour style of Syria. This group also contains the iconographically important ampullae in Monza [254] and Bobbio. We know from the plates from Valdonne bearing imitated control marks, now at the Louvre, that there were workshops in Gaul. There are plates from the flourishing towns of North Africa, and it can be assumed that there were workshops in other countries as well.

**245**

SILVER PLATE. Embossed and touched up with the engraver's tool. Diameter 7⅛ in. (18 cm.). Late 6th century. Found in the Berezovo Islands in Siberia. Leningrad, Hermitage.

Two winged angels, each with his right hand raised and a staff in his left, stand on either side of a jeweled cross planted on the Mountain of Paradise.

Since the agitated drapery recalls ivories like the Ariadne in Paris [218], it is possible to date it earlier than the plates with scenes from the life of David [250].

N. Kondakov, J. Tostoy, and S. Reinach, *Antiquités de la Russie méridionale*, Paris, 1891; J. Smirnov, *Argenterie orientale*, St. Petersburg, 1909, no. 37, pl. 15; Dalton, *Byzantine Art*, p. 571; Dalton, *East Christian Art*, p. 325, pl. 59, 1; Gabrol and Leclercq, *Dictionnaire*, vol. I, pt. 2, col. 2096, fig. 616; Wulff, *Altchristliche Kunst*, I, p. 199, fig. 201; Diehl, *Manuel*, I, p. 317, fig. 160.

## 246

VASE. Silver repoussé. Height 17¾ in. (44 cm.), diameter 11⅜ in. (29 cm.). Late 6th century. Found near Emesa (Homs), Syria. Paris, Louvre.

Rope ornament encircles the base and neck and a narrow middle zone containing eight medallions with the bust of Christ between the Apostles Peter and Paul (see plate), SS. John the Baptist and John the Evangelist, as well as the Virgin between two archangels. Palmettes decorate the spaces between the medallions.

The ornament and the style of the reliefs point to the 6th century. Similar medallions already occur on 5th-century pieces, like the ewer in the Vatican [121] and the reliquary in Grado (A. Morassi, *Antica orificeria italiana*, Milan, 1936, fig. 19). For Byzantine parallels compare the busts on the censer from Cyprus in the British Museum (Dalton, *Catalogue Antiquities*, no. 399, ill.) with stamps of about 600, on a reliquary from the Chersonese (Rosenberg, *Merkzeichen*, IV, fig. no. 9965), and on the oval pyxis at the Vatican (Rosenberg, *ibid.*, no. 9971). On the strength of its similarity to these works the vase is to be attributed to a Byzantine rather than a Syrian workshop.

C. Diehl in *Syria*, 1921, p. 86, pls. 12–13, 1926, p. 119; Bréhier, *Sculpture*, p. 85, pl. 53; Coche de la Ferté, *Antiquité*, p. 107, no. 49, fig. p. 51; Rice, *Byzantine Art*, 1958, no. 44.

## 247

THE COMMUNION OF THE APOSTLES. Silver repoussé paten. Diameter 14½ in. (37 cm.). On the back, stamp of the Emperor Justin II (565–78). Found in Stuma. Istanbul, Archaeological Museum.

The find also included two other plates and two flabella. Christ appears twice behind a canopied altar and administers the sacrament to Apostles gathered on both sides. Near the rim palmettes alternate with circular depressions; on the rim a Greek inscription: HYPER EUCHES KAI SOTERIAS SERGIOV TOV ARGYROPRATOV KAI TON AVTON GOMEON. The script is that current in Syria in the second half of the 6th century and the beginning of the 7th. Although the imperial stamps suggest a metropolitan origin, the style of the relief is closer to Syrian pieces, such as the dish with *The Communion of the Apostles* in the Dumbarton Oaks Collection (G. de Francovich in *Commentari*, 1951, p. 14, fig. 7), the book covers from Antioch in the Metropolitan Museum (*Catalogue*, Baltimore, nos. 390–391, pl. 54), and the chalices in Cleveland (L. Bréhier in *Syria*, 1951, p. 256, figs. 1–2, pls. 18–20). The types of heads recall the vase from Emesa [246] and the Cross of Justin II in the Vatican (Cecchelli, *Vita*, I, p. 4).

J. Ebersolt in *Revue archéologique*, 1911, p. 407, pl. 8; L. Bréhier in *Gazette des Beaux-Arts*, 1920, p. 174; Volbach, *Metallarbeiten*, p. 18, no. 5; Peirce

and Tyler, *L'Art byzantin*, II, p. 114, pl. 140; G. de Francovich in *Commentari*, 1951, p. 14, fig. 24; E. Cruikshank in *Dumbarton Oaks Papers*, 1957, p. 244, note 30; Rice, *Byzantine Art*, 1958, p. 13, no. 8.

## 248

GOLD MEDALLION. Diameter 2½ in. (6.5 cm.). Early 7th century. Washington, D.C., Dumbarton Oaks Collection. Obverse: *Madonna and Child with Angels;* below, *The Nativity* and *The Adoration of the Magi*. Reverse: *The Baptism*.

The medallion was found near Lamboussa, Cyprus, together with two pieces of gold chain, part of a gold neckband, a pair of earrings, a girdle set with eighteen gold medallions, two gold crosses, and two bracelets. The medallion was for some time in the collection of J. Strzygowski. The David plates [250] from the same find, now in the Metropolitan Museum, New York, the Walters Art Gallery in Baltimore, and the Fagan Collection in San Francisco, carry stamps of Heraclius (ca. 610). Coins on the girdle date as early as Mauricius (582–602).

The medallions can be assumed to have originated in an imperial workshop between 600 and 610. On the obverse, the Madonna enthroned between two angels, above smaller reliefs of *The Nativity* and *The Adoration of the Magi*. On the reverse, *The Baptism of Christ* with two attendant angels; underneath the personification of the river Jordan and two Nereids. Both style and technique are similar to the four gold consular medallions of Mauricius found with it, now in the Metropolitan Museum. Iconographically it is close to the ampullae of Monza [254]. For Christian amulets compare pieces found mainly in South Italy, now in Berlin, Naples, Catanzaro, etc. (Volbach in *Archivio storico per la Calabria e la Lucania*, XIII, p. 65). Stylistically different are the two medallions from Adana, now in Istanbul (Cabrol and Leclerq, *Dictionnaire*, vol. I, pt. 2, col. 1818, fig. 485).

J. Strzygowski in *Oriens christianus*, 1915, p. 96; Smith, *Iconography*, p. 80; Volbach, *Metallarbeiten*, p. 17, no. III, 3; M. C. Ross in *Dumbarton Oaks Papers*, 1957, p. 247, figs. 1–3.

## 249

ST. SERGIUS. Plate, silver repoussé with niello. Diameter 9 7/16 in. (24 cm.). Early 7th century. Found near the Monastery of Acheropitos, Kyrenia, Cyprus. London, British Museum.

This first of the two important finds in Cyprus comprises another silver plate, a censer, and 24 spoons (Dalton, *Catalogue Antiquities*, nos. 397–424, pls. 24–25). Around the raised edge, a classicizing leaf ornament. In the central medallion, a beardless, nimbed saint (no doubt Sergius), wearing a chlamys with *tablion*, fastened on the right shoulder by a fibula, and a collar with medallions. In his right hand he holds a staff terminating in a cross. The medallion is surrounded by a nielloed trellis ornament. On the back of the bottom, five control marks, most likely of the Emperor Phocas (602–10). The other plate in this find, with a nielloed cross, carries the stamp of Emperor Mauricius (582–602).

The stamps date the plate in the beginning of the 7th century, to about 600, and classify it as a metropolitan work. The date is confirmed by stylistic comparisons with the Meleager plate in Munich (H. Kähler in *Die Kunst*, 1952, p. 321) and the David plates from the second Cyprus find [250]. Nielloed ornament is also a common feature in this later metropolitan group; compare for example the bottom of a plate in Berlin (Wulff, *Beschreibung*, I, no. 1107, pl. 57) and in Canoscio (E. Giovagnoli in *Rivista di Archeologia Cristiana*, 1935, p. 7, fig. 5). For the technique, see M. Rosenberg (*Niello*, II, p. 68), and for the medallions on the neck bands, see M. Rosenberg (*Niello*, II, p. 255).

Dalton, *Catalogue Antiquities*, no. 398, pl. 24; Dalton, *Byzantine Art*, p. 572, fig. 360; A. Sambon in *Le Musée*, 1906, p. 123; Kitzinger, *Early Mediaeval Art*, p. 25, pl. 11.

## 250

DAVID KILLING THE LION. Plate, silver repoussé. Diameter 5½ in. (14 cm.). On the back, five control marks with the name of the Emperor Heraclius (610–41). New York, The Metropolitan Museum of Art.

The plate is part of the second Cyprus treasure, found at Karavas in 1902, which includes ten other plates, five flasks, jewelry, and a Christian medallion [248]. The edge is raised. *David Killing the Lion* (I Samuel 17:34–36) is shown in relief.

The model was no doubt an illustration of an earlier psalter. Stylistically it is similar to the other plates in the find as well as to secular pieces of the time of Heraclius [253]. The rendering of the lion, with intensive punctation, recalls the Paris plate with Hercules [251].

O. M. Dalton in *Burlington Magazine*, 1906–7, p. 355; O. M. Dalton in *Archaeologia*, 1906, p. 1; Dalton, *Byzantine Art*, p. 572, fig. 360; Dalton, *East Christian Art*, p. 328; Wulff, *Altchristliche Kunst*, I, p. 198, fig. 201; Volbach, *Metallarbeiten*, p. 16, no. 3; Matzulewitsch, *Byzantinische Antike*, p. 22; J. Strzygowski in *Art Bulletin*, 1928, p. 375; Rosenberg, *Merkzeichen*, IV, no. 9656; C. R. Morey in *Art Bulletin*, 1924, p. 23; Morey, *Early Christian Art*, p. 97; *Catalogue*, Baltimore, no. 413, pl. 53; G. de Francovich in *Commentari*, 1951, p. 14.

## 251

HERCULES STRANGLING THE NEMAEAN LION. Plate, silver. Embossed and finished with the engraver's tool. Diameter 23⅝ in. (60 cm.). Foot-rim without stamps. 6th century. From the Trivulzio Collection, Milan. Paris, Cabinet des Médailles.

Below the combatants lie Hercules' mace, bow, and quiver; the edge is ornamented. Although the scene derives from an earlier model (compare the 4th-century plate with Artemis in Berlin [106]), the stylized treatment seems to point to the 6th century, as may be seen in a comparison with the technique of silver plates of that period [250].

Venturi, *Storia*, I, p. 547, fig. 435; Cabrol and Leclercq, *Dictionnaire*, vol. IV, pt. 1, col. 1176, fig. 3775; E. Babelon, *Le Cabinet des Médailles*, Paris, 1924, no. 2875.

## 252

PUTTI MARKING A NILOMETER. Silver dish. Diameter 9⅝ in. (24.5 cm.), length of handle 4⅞ in. (12.3 cm.). On the back of the handle, four stamps (Rosenberg, *Merkzeichen*, IV, nos. 9625–9631) with the bust of Anastasius I (491–518). Bought in Perm in 1859. Leningrad, Hermitage.

The flat rim of the deep bowl is decorated with a landscape that includes crocodiles, birds, and water roses. On the handle, Neptune with trident steps on a dolphin. The central medallion shows a Nilometer on a hill surrounded by fish and plants.

To the left a naked putto on the back of another is carving a figure into the wall to indicate the level of the Nile. Further to the left, two birds in a flower cup. The representation, derived from a Hellenistic Alexandrian model, is close to the somewhat later basin from Cherchell in the Louvre (Matzulewitsch, *Byzantinische Antike*, p. 9, figs. 7–8), carrying stamps of Justinian I (527–65). Two related dishes from South Russia with later Byzantine stamps are at the Hermitage (Matzulewitsch, *ibid.*, pls. 12, 17; Rosenberg, *Merkzeichen*, IV, nos. 10028, 9899). One, formerly in the Obolenskij Collection (Matzulewitsch, *op. cit.*, pl. 12), has a Neptune on its handle and similar Nilotic scenes on the bowl. The elegant decoration of the edge of the other, the dish of Bishop Paternus of Tomi (ca. 518), also with the stamps of Anastasius (Matzulewitsch, *op. cit.*, pl. 26), is in a similar Hellenistic style.

A. Odobesco, *Trésor de Petrossa*, Leipzig, 1889–1900, I, p. 149; F. Drexel in *Bonner Jahrbuch*, 1909, p. 229; R. Zahn in *Berliner Museen, Amtliche Berichte*, 1917, p. 286; Matzulewitsch, *Byzantinische Antike*, p. 6ff., figs 9–11, pl. 16; Rosenberg, *Merkzeichen*, IV, no. 9631, fig. 631.

## 253

NEREID RIDING A SEA MONSTER. Silver flask. Lid and handle missing. Several leaves soldered together. First half of the 7th century. Height 9 15/16 in. (25.2 cm.), diameter 5 5/16 in. (13.5 cm.). Leningrad, Hermitage.

On the bottom are four stamps with the effigy of the Emperor Heraclius (610–45) as it appears on coins of the 2nd and 3rd decades of the 7th century (Rosenberg, *Merkzeichen*, IV, no. 10036). No doubt from the region of Perm.

On both sides of the flask, in a round central field, a Nereid on a sea monster; on one side she faces forward and holds a mirror, on the other, seen from behind, she examines a sea shell. A classical, no doubt Alexandrian, model was used. The treatment of the animals recalls the David plate [250]. Stylistically it is similar to the dish from the Obolenskij Collection, now at the Hermitage (Matzulewitsch, *Byzantinische Antike*, pls. 12–15). For stamps with Heraclius and examples in the Dumbarton Oaks Collection, see E. Cruikshank (in *Dumbarton Oaks Papers*, 1957, p. 241).

Matzulewitsch, *Byzantinische Antike*, no. 8, p. 89, pls. 19–21.

## 254

AMPULLA. Silver repoussé, two halves soldered together. Height 7½ in. (19 cm.), diameter 5⅞ in. (15 cm.). Early 7th century. Monza, Cathedral Treasury.

Upper right: reverse, *The Ascension*. Lower left: obverse, *The Adoration of the Magi* and *The Annunciation to the Shepherds*.

Probably one of fifteen similar ampullae in the Cathedral Treasury presented about 600 by Pope Gregory the Great to Queen Theodelinda. Other pieces, not so well preserved, are in San Colombano, Bobbio.

On the obverse: the Mother of God enthroned, to the left the adoring Magi, to the right *The Annunciation to the Shepherds*. Above, two flying angels. Underneath the scene, a Greek inscription: *Immanuel* (God with us); below the inscription, the shepherds' sheep. Inscription around the edge: "Oil from the wood of life, from the holy places of Christ." On the reverse: *The Ascension*. In the center, the Virgin as *orans* wearing the *maphorion;* on either side, six Apostles; above, Christ in a mandorla borne by four angels.

As the inscription around the edge shows, the ampulla is a souvenir from a pilgrimage to the Holy Land. Similar pieces found in various places are now in Berlin (Wulff, *Beschreibung*, I, no. 1097, pl. 55; O. Wulff and W. F. Volbach, *Die altchristlichen und mittelalterlichen Bildwerke, Ergänzungsband*, Berlin, 1923, no. 6697, p. 26) and London (Dalton, *Byzantine Art*, p. 624, 399). These ampullae, in which pilgrims from every land brought back with them consecrated oil from the holy places, must have helped to spread the iconography of monumental art in the Holy Land. Similar ampullae made of earthenware were doubtlessly used for preserving particles of soil from Palestine. Stylistically the scenes on the ampullae recall representations on reliquaries and medallions, in particular on those from Cyprus [248] and Assiut [255].

A. Heisenberg, *Grabeskirche und Apostelkirche*, Leipzig, 1908, p. 173 ff.; Dalton, *Byzantine Art*, p. 623; Wulff, *Altchristliche Kunst*, I, p. 340; Cabrol and Leclercq, *Dictionnaire*, vol. I, pt. 2, col. 1737, fig. 460; C. Cecchelli in *Rivista di Archeologia Cristiana*, 1927, p. 115; G. de Jerphanion, *La voix des monuments*, Paris, 1930, p. 44 ff.; *Storia di Milano*, p. 145, fig.; Grabar, *Martyrium*, II, p. 82 ff.; A. Grabar, *Les Ampoules de Terre Sainte*, Paris, 1958.

## 255

NECK AND BREAST ORNAMENT WITH THE ANNUNCIATION. Gold, with coins. Diameter 9 $\frac{5}{16}$ in. (23.6 cm.). Early 7th century. Berlin, Staatliche Museen.

This piece is part of a large treasure from Egypt (Assiut or Antinoopolis) now divided among Berlin, the Metropolitan Museum in New York, and the Freer Collection, Washington D.C. (W. Dennison and C. R. Morey, *Studies in East Christian Art*, New York, 1918). On the collar, coins of Justinian (527–65), Justin II (565–78), Tiberius II (578–82), and Mauricius (582–602) surround the large medallion in the center that bears an imitation of an imperial bust, with the Greek legend, "Lord, help the wearer"; on the reverse, Constantinopolis. In the small fields, *Phōs-Zōe* (light and life). The medallion is set in a wide openwork ornamental band. On the obverse, *The Annunciation;* on the reverse, *The Marriage at Cana*.

Large collars like this were often used as marks of distinction for the military (*draconarii*), as in plate 249. For this type of ornament, see the notes to plate 248 and A. Grabar (in *Dumbarton Oaks Papers*, 1951, p. 34) on the *encolpion* from the Mersine Treasure, now in the Hermitage. Stylistically our piece recalls the medallion from the second Cyprus find in the Dumbarton Oaks Collection [248]. The two are probably roughly contemporary.

R. Zahn in *Berliner Museen, Amtliche Berichte*, 1916, p. 42, fig. 12, 1917, p. 304; Peirce and Tyler, *L'Art byzantin*, II, pl. 205; Volbach, in Bossert, *Geschichte*, V, p. 66, pl. 3; W. F. Volbach in *Corsi di cultura*, 1958, I, p. 96.

## 256–258

The SILK INDUSTRY in Constantinople reached its highest development under Justinian, according to the sources. Already Constantine had granted privileges to the industry by special edict; now a state monopoly was created for certain types of material, such as purple twills and gold lace (Ebersolt, *Arts somptuaires*, p. 20). In spite of the comparatively large quantity of fabrics that have survived, a clear differentiation between metropolitan products and those of other manufactories has not so far been established. In the past, many fabrics with figured decoration, such as the one with Samson [256], and that with *The Annunciation* [257] and *The Nativity*, were assigned to Alexandria and dated in the 6th century (L. D. Longman in *Art Bulletin*, 1930, p. 115); the role of Constantinople is now better recognized, without prejudice to the importance, in this late period, of Syrian manufactories. Fabrics with purely ornamental designs, flowers, and scattered foliage are certainly to be assigned in part to the imperial workshops, since their affinity with patterns on materials shown in mosaics [166, 167] is obvious. In various church treasuries, Sens, Aachen, and Trier, fragments of fabrics in a Hellenistic manner have been preserved (von Falke, *Seidenweberei*).

Numerous fragments of silk fabrics with figured decoration, found in Egyptian tombs, are now in various collections, such as Lyons, London, and Berlin (O. Wulff and W. F. Volbach, *Spätantike und koptische Stoffe*, Berlin, 1926). Many of them are now known to be imitations of precious silks of Syrian or Sassanian origin. The latter are of superior quality and are characterized by the presence of three inner warps between every binding warp. There are clear subdivisions: pieces like the fabric with pheasants at the Vatican (Volbach, *Tessuti*, no. T 108) are of secure Sassanian origin; others are clearly a Byzantine adaptation of the Sassanian type, like the famous textile of Jesdegerd III in Berlin (H. J. Schmidt, *Alte Seidenstoffe*, Brunswick, 1958, p. 61, fig. 45); then there are fabrics with a red ground in which the influence of Hellenistic models is still clearly recognizable [256]. The second and the third category may very well be of Syrian origin. Related fabrics, like the one with *The Annunciation* in the Vatican [257], are stylistically so reminiscent of Byzantine miniatures that they are perhaps the products of metropolitan workshops. Their origin is later than the 6th century. In the first half of the 7th century an ever-growing Islamic influence establishes itself in Constantinople and the piece with the monogram of Heraclius (610–41) in a lozenge pattern, now in Liége (Ebersolt, *Arts somptuaires*, fig. 17), already leads to such fabrics as the fine fragment in the Cooper Union Museum in New York [258] that would be inconceivable without Islamic models. For the use of color, see R. Pfister in *Seminarium Kondakovianum*, 1935, p. 1; R. Pfister, *Textiles de Palmyre*, Paris, 1934–40; for the technique, see N. Reath and E. Sachs, *Persian Textiles*, New Haven, 1937; Weibel, *Textiles;* W. F. Volbach in *Kunstchronik*, 1955, p. 322; J. Beckwith in *Kunstchronik*, 1955, p. 324.

## 256

SAMSON KILLING THE LION (?). Silk fabric in white, green, brown, yellow, and blue on red ground. Compound twill. Length 3 ft., 1 $\frac{13}{16}$ in. (96 cm.), width 15 $\frac{15}{16}$ in. (40.5 cm.). About 8th century. Formerly from the church treasury in Chur. Washington, D.C., Dumbarton Oaks Collection.

Other fragments of the same silk have survived and are in various collections: Ottobeuren (*Sakrale Gewänder des Mittelalters*, catalogue, Munich, 1955, no. 2), Nuremberg, Chur,

London (T. D. Kendrick, *Catalogue of Early Mediaeval Woven Fabrics*, London, n.d., no. 1001, pl. 11), Vatican (Volbach, *Tessuti*, no. T 103), Berlin, Lyons, Paris, Florence, Maastricht, and Vienna.

Samson (?) kneels with one leg on the back of the lion and wrenches open its jaws. This group is repeated in rows of confronted pairs; bands with a pattern of heart-shaped blossoms separate the rows.

*Exposition internationale d'art byzantin*, Paris, 1931, no. 214, pl. 9; O. von Falke in *Pantheon*, 1932, p. 63; W. F. Volbach, *Spätantike und frühmittelalterliche Stoffe*, Mainz, 1932, no. 61; Volbach, *Tessuti*, p. 38, fig. 15; *Catalogue*, Baltimore, pl. 120c; Weibel, *Textiles*, no. 44; *Handbook of the Dumbarton Oaks Collection*, no. 308, fig. 164; Rice, *Byzantine Art*, 1958, p. 30.

## 257

THE ANNUNCIATION. The companion piece has *The Nativity*. Silk twill in purple, brown, and green on red ground. The red ground dyed in kermes, the Virgin's dress in true purple. Length 27⅛ in. (69 cm.), width 13¼ in. (33.6 cm.); height of the circle 12⅝ in. (32 cm.). 7th century (?). From the Sancta Sanctorum. Rome, Musei del Vaticano.

The scene is isolated in a roundel with heart-shaped blossoms. The winged angel approaches from the right and raises his right hand. The Virgin sits on a bejeweled throne and spins. According to K. Pfister (in *Atti del XIX Congresso internazionale degli orientalisti*, Rome, 1938, p. 661) the colors of this silk are different from those of the silk with *The Nativity*, but the two pieces nonetheless go together. Our silk is one of a large group

of twills on red ground [256], like the Amazons in Säckingen, the rider in Maastricht, and the quadriga in Brussels (von Falke, *Seidenweberei*, figs. 45, 48, 49). Von Falke assigned the silk to the Alexandrian school and dated it to the 6th century; he was followed by L. D. Longman (in *Art Bulletin*, 1930, p. 127). But the iconography is more Syrian in type and the style has affinities with Byzantine work, so that it should be dated after 600.

H. Grisar, *Il Sancta Sanctorum e il suo tesoro sacro*, Rome, 1907, p. 177, fig. 60; C. Cecchelli in *Dedalo*, 1926–27; p. 469, fig. 471; von Falke, *Seidenweberei*, p. 8, pl. III; Dalton, *Byzantine Art*, p. 598; Dalton, *East Christian Art*, p. 354, pl. 64; Wulff, *Altchristliche Kunst*, I, p. 359, fig. 313; W. R. Lethaby in *Burlington Magazine*, 1913–14, p. 145, fig. 4; Volbach, *Tessuti*, no. T 104, pls. 29, 31, 35.

## 258

COCKS AND PALMETTES. Silk twill in blue and yellow. Byzantine. Length 9⅞ in. (25 cm.), width 7⅛ in. (18 cm.). 8th century. New York, Cooper Union Museum for the Arts of Decoration.

The cruciform network pattern alternates with circles occupied alternately by a cock and a spread palmette. The markedly stylized cocks (peacocks?) and the palmette motif are borrowings from early Islamic art. For dating compare the Byzantine fabric with a similar lozenge pattern and the monogram of the Emperor Heraclius in Liége (Ebersolt, *Arts somptuaires*, p. 50, fig. 17) as well as the piece in Berlin (von Falke, *Seidenweberei*, II, fig. 226; Weibel, *Textiles*, p. 95, no. 61, pl. 61).

ACKNOWLEDGMENTS

The photographs made especially for this book have been supplemented by the following: Berlin, Staatliche Museen, Abt. Frühchristliche und Byzantinische Kunst: 73, 106, 119 below right, 255. Cesena, Biblioteca Malatestiana: 108. Hartford, Conn., Wadsworth Atheneum: 13. Leningrad, Hermitage: 245, 252, 253. London, Victoria and Albert Museum: 91. Milan, Soprintendenza alle Belle Arti: 132. Munich, Bayerisches Nationalmuseum: 93, 224, 225. New York, Cooper Union Museum for the Arts of Decoration: 258. New York, Metropolitan Museum of Art: 237, 250. Washington, D.C., Dumbarton Oaks Collection: 236 above, 248, 256. Rome, Foto Anderson: 131, 148, 149, 168. Rome, Banco Santo Spirito: 128, 129. Rome, Dr. Enzo Crea, Studio di Consulenza grafica editoriale: 146, 147, 242, 243. Rome, Deutsches Archäologisches Institut: 14, 15. After R. Delbrueck, *Spätantike Kaiserporträts*: 53. After N. Pevsner, *European Architecture*: Plates A and B.

# INDEX OF PLATES AND FIGURES BY LOCATION

## Date Due

| MAR 2 7? | | | | |
|---|---|---|---|---|
| DEC 15 7? | | | | |
| NOV 2 2 1988 | | | | |
| OCT 2 4 1989 | | | | |
| FACULTY | | | | |
| | | | | |
| | | | | |
| | | | | |
| | | | | |

PRINTED IN U.S.A.    CAT. NO. 23 231